Approximative Justice and Cross-Border Evidence in the EU

This book confronts the difficulties raised by cross-border evidence in order to propose a new understanding of justice as approximative.

Can there be any common sense of justice across the European Union (EU)? This book takes up this question which is raised directly in cases where the understanding of cross-border evidence encounters national and linguistic differences. The interpretive challenges this introduces impact the possibility of justice in a way that, the book argues, cannot be resolved with recourse to some ideal of harmonization that would simply flatten these differences. Rather, these cases – taken here from Sweden and France – raise a practical, but also a theoretical, question about how justice can be done. In response, the book draws on contemporary theorizations of justice to argue against a common sense of justice in the sense of what would be a correct legal judgment. In its place, the book elaborates an idea of justice that maintains, rather than collapsing, the differences presented in cases of cross-border evidence; and which therefore aims to be 'approximative,' or 'good enough,' rather than simply correct.

This book will be of interest to readers in legal theory, socio-legal studies, comparative law and European Union law.

Anna G. Waldenström is Senior Lecturer in Law at the University of Gothenburg, Sweden.

Approximative Justice and Cross-Border Evidence in the EU

Anna G. Waldenström

Routledge
Taylor & Francis Group
a GlassHouse Book

First published 2025
by Routledge
4 Park Square, Milton Park, Abingdon, Oxon OX14 4RN

and by Routledge
605 Third Avenue, New York, NY 10158

Routledge is an imprint of the Taylor & Francis Group, an informa business

A GlassHouse book

British Library Cataloguing-in-Publication Data
A catalogue record for this book is available from the British Library

Library of Congress Cataloging-in-Publication Data
Names: Waldenström, Anna G., author.
Title: Approximative justice and cross-border evidence in the EU / Anna G. Waldenström.
Description: Abingdon, Oxon [UK] ; New York, NY : Routledge, 2025. | Includes bibliographical references and index.
Identifiers: LCCN 2024049912 (print) | LCCN 2024049913 (ebook) | ISBN 9781032800912 (hardback) | ISBN 9781032800929 (paperback) | ISBN 9781003495383 (ebook)
Subjects: LCSH: Evidence (Law)—European Union countries. | Evidence (Law)—European Union countries—Philosophy. | Justice, Administration of—European Union countries.
Classification: LCC KJE3926 .W35 2025 (print) | LCC KJE3926 (ebook) | DDC 347.24/06—dc23/eng/20241023
LC record available at https://lccn.loc.gov/2024049912
LC ebook record available at https://lccn.loc.gov/2024049913

ISBN: 978-1-032-80091-2 (hbk)
ISBN: 978-1-032-80092-9 (pbk)
ISBN: 978-1-003-49538-3 (ebk)

DOI: 10.4324/9781003495383

Typeset in Sabon
by Apex CoVantage, LLC

Contents

Grace, Gratitude and the Importance of Pompoms

European culture has underestimated the role of pompoms – or at least the role of joyous encouragement for the sake of gay science. Not before Maria Grahn-Farley took on the role as my supervisor and my subsequent joining Birkbeck have I experienced and so deeply understood the blissful effectiveness of positive support and clarity. At Birkbeck College, University of London, Michelle Everson and Adam Gearey showed me what true trust in the stranger looks like. They offered the indispensable validation and mercifully took on to nudge me forward in my wish to explore and put into words a sense of something missing in the theories of evidence and justice in European jurisprudence. They gave clear and inspiring guidance and something which is more than job satisfaction – they gave me job joy. I have done my best to learn the lessons they have taught. If I am not understood, it is not for not having been given the possibility to be heard. For this, I live with the luxury of gratitude.

A more remote sense of gratitude is directed to the late Me Roland Rappaport who let me shadow him at work at his law firm one autumn in Paris in 1995 and who also put me in contact with the law firm in Barcelona. Without the experiences I made there, this book would not have come about.

Brian, Leonard, Trinity and Lauryn, thank you for being so patient. I didn't even ask for it, you just had to be anyway. You are all rock solid and free as the wind. You're simply the best. Bibbi, thank you for reading – you can do anything. Grace.

Chapter 1

Introduction

Approximative Justice

This book is about approximative justice. Approximative justice is a response to the *differend* which occurs when what is expressed by the addressor cannot be perceived in the idiom of the addressee.[1] This happens when evidence is taken from one jurisdiction to another, because a jurisdiction is a regimentation of a local commonality, here referred to as a 'spatio-temporal commonality.'[2]

Approximative justice appears in the tension between a judgment which considers the parties and the singular case on the one hand and the possibility for the person in the street to accept the judgment as just[3] on the other. In that sense the judgment is found to be just when the parties perceive it as subjectively just – they have been heard and treated fairly – and at the end of the process, the public perceives it as objectively correct. This distinguishes between justice as procedure and justice as result but seeks justice as a legal symphonic arrangement[4] of the constitutive parts of the case.[5] Approximative justice is suggested as a descriptive expression of what the conscientious judgment may be.[6]

1 Lyotard, Jean-François. *The Differend – Phrases in Dispute.* Translated by Georges Van Den Abbeele, University of Minnesota Press, 1988. Both the original French version (Lyotard, Jean-François. *Le Différend.* Minuit, 1983) and the English translation have been studied.

2 Chapter 3.

3 Teubner, Günther. "Self-Subversive Justice: Contingency or Transcendence Formula of Law?" *The Modern Law Review*, vol. 72, no. 1, 2009, pp. 1–23; Ekelöf, P. O. et al. *Rättegång I*. 9th ed., Norstedts Juridik, 2016, §1.

4 The wording here refers to the perception of an entity despite the many sounds, a perception which is partly due to the impossibility to decipher each sound of which the symphony is composed. It therefore focusses on the receiver (the listener) rather than the composer. Walter, Bruno. "Bruckner and Mahler." *Chord and Discord*, vol. 2, no. 9, 1948, p. 41.

5 Gearey, Adam. *Law and Aesthetics*. Bloomsbury Publishing Plc, 2001.

6 Cf. 35:1 CJP, https://www.riksdagen.se/sv/dokument-och-lagar/dokument/svensk-forfattningssamling/rattegangsbalk-1942740_sfs-1942-740/. Accessed 30 Nov. 2024. *Also,* 353 Code de procédure pénale (which code does fall outside of this study) explicitly requires the judges in criminal cases to ask themselves, after 'conscientiously' considering the evidence, whether they have

DOI: 10.4324/9781003495383-1

This book argues that an understanding of justice as approximative is not only a possible, but also a sensible approach to judicial justice particularly in proceedings with cross-border aspects. As such, approximative justice may be seen as a proposal for what a common sense of justice within the EU may be. From the EU point of view, for the cooperation between the judiciaries of the Member States to be seen to render justice, to offer access to justice, and for the national courts to be seen to render just judgments that put EU law into effect, the EU may just be forced to accept that there is no justice in the sense of the correct application of the law[7] but that an approximative justice may simply have to be good enough. It is argued in this book therefore, that with an understanding of approximative justice as good enough, there may be a common sense of justice and there may be access to good enough justice. Good enough justice may not just be good enough, it may be the most just sense of concrete[8] justice for the commonality of the EU – for its citizens.

Approximative justice mediates between the parties' sense of being heard and a sense of objective correctness of the judgment which may also be recognized[9] by the general public.[10] Such an objectivity relies on what is perceived as commonplace, such as commonplace generalizations,[11] common sense and common knowledge[12] – a muddle of knowledge[13] and pre-conceptions of which one is mostly unaware.[14] This makes the cross-border evidence a particularly unreliable source of information for the judge. From the perspective of the parties, it is an equally unreliable means of conveying an argument and being heard.

Approximative justice is an understanding of justice where the calculation of probability is irrelevant – because the interpretation of facts is

reached a *conviction intime*, https://www.legifrance.gouv.fr/codes/texte_lc/LEGITEXT000006071154. Accessed 30 Nov. 2024. *See also*, Tournier, Clara. *L'intime conviction du juge de jugement*. ANRT, 2003. Lille thèses; Normand, Jacques. *Le juge et le litige*. L.G.D.J., 1965, pp. 305, 327, 353 ff; Blanc, Emmanuel. *La Preuve judiciaire. Commentaire du Décret du 17 décembre 1973*, Librairie du Journal des notaires et des avocats, 1974, p. 19.

7 Bentham, Jeremy. *Rationale of Judicial Evidence*. Edited by J. S. Mill, Vol. I, Hunt and Clarke, 1827; Anderson, Terence et al. *Analysis of Evidence*. 2nd ed., CUP, 2010; Ekelöf, P. O. *Rättegång II*. 8th ed., Norstedts Juridik, 2010, p. 20.

8 Perelman, Chaïm. *Justice et raison*. Editions de l'Université de Bruxelles, 1972, p. 41.

9 Lyotard, pt. 78; Derrida, Jacques. "Force de loi: le Fondement mystique de l'autorité." *Cardozo Law Review*, vol. 11, nos. 5–6, Jul/Aug. 1990, pp. 949–1046.

10 With 'public' is here meant the local community, the persons in the street, who share the same spatio-temporal commonality, as developed in Chapter 3.

11 Schum, David. "Inference Networks and their Many Subtle Properties." *Information and Decision Technologies*, vol. 16, 1990, pp. 69–98 as quoted in Goodwin, Jean. "Wigmore's Chart Method." *Informal Logic*, vol. 20, no. 3, 2000, pp. 223–243.

12 Chapter 3.

13 Cf. Günther, Gotthard. "Life as Polycontexturality." *Wirklichkeit und Reflexion*, (first published in) edited by H. Fahrenbach (Hrsg.), Festschrift für Walter Schulz, 1973, pp. 187–210, http://vordenker.de/ggphilosophy/gg_life_as_polycontexturality.pdf, 2014, p. 4.

14 Chapter 3.

indeterminate. This puts the conscientious judge in a position of anxiety.[15] Whereas this book wishes to cater for the problem of the indeterminacy of facts, it does not attempt to release the judge of their duty to adjudicate, to be the judge who determines the case and decides a solution – on the contrary.[16] The idea of an approximative justice does however seek a more hopeful as well as realistic understanding of justice in law and specifically the formation of a just judgment than anxiety and resignation. An approximative justice reminds more of watercolor depiction than digital pixels, more of a symphony than a solo.

The Machete and Little Sweetheart

As a young intern first at a law firm in Paris and then in Barcelona, I was mostly shadowing the lawyers in their meetings with clients, at negotiations between parties or the oral debates at the courts – as the young and innocent Swedish woman who could do no harm. At the few occasions when my being a young Swedish woman was not sufficient to be ignored (for example, if I had chosen an outfit "as if directly from a film by Ingmar Bergman") and I could therefore not appear without appearing, I was referred to the firm's archives to read old case files. This was unexpectedly enlightening. French and Spanish civil procedure was mainly written, with evidence being included in written form in the case file. Reading a case file was therefore to some – comparatively larger – extent, to read the case as such. The oral debates may have cast new light on the written evidence, but they did not contribute new evidentiary facts specific to the case.

One case in Barcelona was particularly bewildering. It concerned a fight at a nightclub. The defendant was accused of having cut a man with a knife. As I recall it, both the defendant and the victim were at the nightclub with their wives, children as well as parents. I knew the night life of Barcelona, and the club was one of those that opened around midnight and closed at 6 o'clock in the morning; I was however, not familiar with the custom of bringing both children and elderly parents along to the nightclub – or otherwise expressed, the custom of clubbing as a family activity. The reading of the case confused me. And as I carried on reading the confusion grew. The father/defendant had run into the victim, a person with whom he had a long-lasting conflict, and the two had carried on the argument until one of them had taken a knife out of his jacket pocket. Not good, I thought. This person obviously was prepared for a fight at all times, and so he must regularly end up in one. I then read that the other man also pulled out a knife from his jacket and concluded that perhaps it was a kind of club I wasn't familiar with after all.

15 Derrida, pp. 952–956; Poché, Fred. *Penser avec Derrida: Comprendre la déconstruction*. Chronique sociale, 2007, pp. 102–103.
16 Kennedy, Duncan. *A Critique of Adjudication: Fin de Siècle*. Harvard UP, 1997.

I pictured the knives to be of the same size as the common Swedish knife with the particularly Swedish name *morakniv*. It is a knife with an approximately 10 cm long edge, and the same size handle. Its name is particularly Swedish because it refers to a town in Dalecarlia, a region often seen as the most Swedish of all regions. Despite these very Swedish cultural connotations to the knife, I perceived it as a "normal knife" and so it was the kind of knife I imagined the two men to have pulled out. I was therefore surprised as I understood that the first knife to have been pulled out was maybe three times that size! And it was even more surprising to read that the other antagonist also had that same size knife in his pocket as he went to the nightclub with his family. I subsequently learnt that the knives were what in British English are referred to as machetes, and that such knives are as common to the South American family man as the *morakniv* is to the Swedish. The machete and the *morakniv* don't serve the same purpose; they serve the needs of the particular landscape of each place – in the case of the machete, to cut down bush outside one's house or to behead a snake hanging in a tree in one's back yard. Although downtown Barcelona is not the environment South Americans (and Caribbeans) have developed a custom to carry a machete (in Caribbean English referred to, simply, as a knife), the custom is taken along by some as they relocate from one continent to another.

Evidence of accidental occurrences often come in the form of witness testimonials. Sometimes investigators take pictures, or nowadays, with cameras in mobile phones, witnesses to such events may have also photographed the event and may contribute with the photos to the investigation. But witness testimonials and the hearing of the parties constitute the warp of the texture, into which the forensic evidence is woven. Had the case been tried in Sweden, the judge may have fallen into the same trap: namely, first, to visualize the witnessed and related knife as a type of knife one thinks one understands the use and value of; second, to understand the machete – once that penny had dropped – as a sword rather than an everyday tool; and third, to understand the carrying of that tool as a sign – evidence – of a particularly brutal and consequently criminal personality, and even more importantly, as a sign of a criminal intent for that particular evening. The fact that the prosecuted person had carried such a knife involved a long chain of links of misunderstandings based on the wrong, inadequate and culturally charged prejudices. In this case, the occurrences do not seem to have been misunderstood by the judge; I was the person whose prejudices led to the chain of links of misunderstandings, and I was just a young Swedish intern, perhaps dressed in a Bergmanian outfit, at a law firm studying the case after it had been adjudicated.

A similar problematic arose in a different context and caused tumultuous debate in the daily press, as well as a report for hate speech. In 2012 a children's cartoon was released in Sweden. It portrayed a number of beings, most of whom were unidentifiable in the sense that it was not clear if they were animals, children or cuddly toys. It was clear, however, that such identification was irrelevant. Many, if not most, of them carried details which are either neither boyish nor girlish or both; neither sex nor gender were issues. These beings were just supposed to be cute in the way that toddlers *are* cute, and they looked as if they were meant to invite such small children to identify with them on their own premises. Beings on a discovery trip into the world they have just been born into and in which they wonder how to belong, how to make friends and deal with the complex conflict between the I and the Other – with whom the I also wants to belong.

One of the characters was black in color, and had five plaits standing up and out from the character's head. At the end of each plait was an orange heart. The character's mouth was a wide white circle with an orange middle. This character caused the lively debate.[17] Some readers found the character delightful.[18] Its name, Little Sweetheart,[19] was a clear message to these readers that this was a character whose function in the book was to cause anti-racist opinion already in the youngest of us. Many saw in the character the creator's good will and appreciated it.[20] Perhaps some also saw her references to the African, Caribbean and Asian figurative language.[21] Little Sweetheart filled their hearts with warmth. And perhaps also hope for a warmer future with less confrontation between people and a world with fewer persons who consider it relevant to define themselves and each other as belonging to different groups, races, sexes etc.

Other readers, however, reacted differently. Some found the character to be an outrageous mockery – or, at the very best, a sign of a dreadful lack

17 Jonsson, Sherlot. *Dagens Nyheter*, 12 Nov. 2012, http://www.dn.se/kultur-noje/kulturdebatt/vagra-se-varlden-vit-och-svart/; Dalén, Karl. *Dagens Nyheter*, 22 Nov. 2012, http://www.dn.se/dnbok/forlaget-det-ar-sa-otroligt-sorgligt/; Helmersson, Erik. *Svenska Dagbladet*, 23 Sep. 2012, http://www.dn.se/ledare/signerat/filmdebatt-den-mest-krankta-har-inte-alltid-ratt/ are just a few examples of the debate taking place in the Swedish newspapers in the Autumn of 2012.

18 The following are reviews of the film in which the character was part, and which was released 21 September 2012: Juggas, Bodil. *Arbetarbladet*, 28 Sep. 2012, http://www.arbetarbladet.se/noje/film/fantastisk-film-for-de-allra-minsta; Eklund, Bernt. 26 Sep. 2012, http://allavibarn.blogspot.se/2012/09/stina-wirsen-och-lilla-hjartat.html; Pousette Blomé, Lisa. 4 Sep. 2012, http://kulturbloggen.com/?p=59937; Janson, Malena. *Helsingfors Dagblad*, 21 Sep. 2012, http://hd.se/kultur/film/2012/09/21/oemotstandligt/?from=rss; Sigroth-Lambe, Susanne. *Uppsala Nya Tidning*, 21 Sep. 2012, http://www.unt.se/kultur/film/film-liten-skar-och-alla-sma-brokiga-1863697.aspx.

19 The character's Swedish name is Lilla Hjärtat, the translation is my own. The creator's name is Stina Wirsén.

20 Eklund, Bernt. *Expressen*, 20 Sep. 2012, http://www.expressen.se/noje/recensioner/film/liten-skar-och-alla-sma-brokiga/, *Svenska Dagbladet*, 25 Jul. 2013, http://www.svd.se/kultur/wirsen-talar-ut-om-lilla-hjartat_8373942.svd.

21 Wirsén, Stina. *Dagens Nyheter*, 23 Oct. 2012, http://www.dn.se/kultur-noje/kulturdebatt/mina-kritiker-har-begransad-utblick/.

of insight into the history of racism.[22] In the picture of Little Sweetheart they did not see a delightful little being on a discovery trip into the world, but a reminder of slavery.[23] Of men and women in chains attached to their necks, hands and feet. Men and women who were robbed of their freedom, culture and context, ripped up from their soil and exported as goods to another land where they were forced to work or tortured to death – or to life, whipped and raped and forced to give birth to the rapist's child, as a creation of more manpower, more workforce.[24] Hundreds of years of slavery followed by decades of police brutality and police shootings more based on skin color than behavior, by unemployment and poverty and a general suspicion against the Other, between the mutual Others. The image was reported to the police as a hate crime, but what kind of assessment was needed to judge this case?

The assessment is clearly not purely legal. Neither could it rely on any other scientific field of knowledge to say what the image "was," as the assessment varied from expertise to expertise (art, toddler pedagogics, art history, race theory). The establishment of the case was not an answer to the question of "what happened?" nor "are the allegations true?"[25] Nor could the question "is this legal?" be answered with reference to what had already been considered legal.[26] Nor could one refer to some general consensual sense of justice, because it was quite clear that no consensual sense of justice existed.[27] The legal instance with the responsibility to bring legal action in freedom of speech cases declared that this was not a case of hate speech, but a matter of artistic expression (with antiracist intent).[28] Period. The law had spoken. The preconceptions that had seen centuries of slavery were disregarded. Artistic freedom and good intent won.[29]

22 The following conclude that the picture is racist or a carrier of a racist tradition: *Sveriges Television*, 11 Sep. 2012, http://www.svt.se/kultur/film/barnfilm-anklagas-for-rasistisk-stereotyp; Fredrik Söderling interviews Associate Professor John Jennings at University at Buffalo, The State University of New York in Swedish newspaper *Dagens Nyheter*, 22 Nov. 2012, http://www.dn.se/dnbok/lilla-hjartat-uppenbart-rasistisk-enligt-forskare/, *Sveriges Radio*, 22 Nov. 2012, http://sverigesradio.se/sida/artikel.aspx?programid=478&artikel=5354382; Karlsson, Elise. *Svenska Dagbladet*, 15 Sep. 2012, http://www.svd.se/kultur/gulligt-kan-ocksa-vara-stereotypt_7500338.svd.

23 Polite, Oivvio. *Expressen*, 15 Oct. 2012, http://www.expressen.se/kultur/det-ar-ju-ratt-ruttet/.

24 Sörenson, Margareta. *Expressen*, 22 Oct. 2012, http://www.expressen.se/kultur/fargade-historier/; Polite, Oivvio. *Expressen*, 26 Oct. 2012, http://www.expressen.se/kultur/brokiga-ar-business/, *Sveriges Radio*, 7 Sep. 2012, http://sverigesradio.se/sida/artikel.aspx?programid=1646&artikel=5262162.

25 35:1 CJP; 6 and 9 CPC; Lévy-Bruhl, Henri. *La Preuve judiciaire*. Essai de sociologie juridique, Marcel Rivière et Cie, 1963, p. 21.

26 Luhmann, Niklas. *Law as a Social System*. OUP, 2004.

27 Lyotard, Jean-François. *The Postmodern Condition: A Report on Knowledge*. Translated by Geoff Bennington and Brian Massumi, Manchester University Press, 1984, p. 60.

28 Decision of the Chancellor of Justice of 2013.01.18, Dnr 8473-12-32.

29 Lyotard, pt. 234.

The Unavoidable Differend

The preceding anecdotes are examples of experiences many of us have. They are illustrations of situations where we apply our own understandings of the world, our preconceptions of what is normal behavior, of what words and other expressions normally convey. It is not astonishing that we should also think that this is the correct understanding ontologically as well as ethically. Nevertheless, these anecdotes illustrate both unsolvable conflicts of interpretations and plain misunderstandings that may hide behind our preconceptions – that is our understandings of the world, our making sense of the world. They illustrate what injustice it leads to when different people attribute different senses, meanings and significations to events, facts and behavior, words, pictures and other means of communication. They indicate what injustice it leads to when we take evidence from one idiom to another.[30]

Approximative justice deals with the conflicts of senses, what may be argued to be the literal meaning in Swedish *meningsskiljaktigheter*, same as German *Meinungsverschiedenheiten*, translated into 'differences of opinion' in English (but perhaps better expressed, in the context of this book as difference of view, meaning, sense) similar to *différences d'opinion* in French, synonymous to *différends*, the word used, and concept explored by Jean-François Lyotard in *The Differend*. Lyotard develops this thought through the distinction between *litige* and *différend*.[31] *Litige* is a dispute between parties that can be solved because it exists in a neutral space, where a universal rule makes it possible to cut[32] through the dilemma and so distinguish between what is and what is not (legal, healthy, right . . .[33]). The *différend* is a dispute which takes place outside of this neutral space, and where there is no universal rule to apply. In a *litige*, the parties to the dispute submit to the same rule, they both themselves acknowledge that rule. Lyotard argues that this is not a real possibility, but as will be discussed in this book, he describes how what is here referred to as a 'spatio-temporal commonality' works as though it were.

And the EU Said: "Let There Be Justice"

Through the Treaty of Amsterdam[34] the Member States of the EU in 1997 unanimously stipulated the constituting of an Area of Freedom, Security and Justice within the Union.[35] It was perceived that the multitude of legal cultures and judicial orders in the EU constitute hinderances in ordinary people's

30 Lyotard, pt. 37.
31 Lyotard, p. xi.
32 Derrida, p. 963.
33 Teubner.
34 Treaty of Amsterdam amending the Treaty on European Union, the Treaties establishing the European Communities and certain related acts, OJ C 340, 10.11.1997, p. 1.
35 Articles 29 and 40.1 (b) Treaty of Amsterdam.

lives; differences between Member States' legal and judicial[36] cultures were perceived as a real problem for ordinary citizens.[37] The Council thus established the aim "to give the citizens a common sense of justice throughout the Union."[38] Paradoxically, the Council simultaneously held that a common sense of justice is at the very foundation of the union itself.[39] The Tampere Conclusions[40] declared the freedom of the citizens as dependent on security and justice. Justice must therefore be equally accessible through the national courts and authorities.[41] With the Stockholm Programme[42] the EU expressed the need that EU citizenship[43] become a tangible reality.[44] For this, the "current fragmentation" of the judiciaries in the EU must be left behind and the area of justice "consolidated" for easier access to justice.[45] Since the Stockholm Programme, the EU has seemingly lowered its ambitions in terms of unification, and the plan is to build "bridges between different justice systems

36 Regarding the wording 'legal' and 'judicial' respectively, *see* Storskrubb, Eva. *Civil Procedure and EU Law, A Policy Area Uncovered.* OUP, 2008, pp. 9–12.

37 Report on the initiative of the Federal Republic of Germany with a view to adopting a Council Regulation on cooperation between the courts of the Member States in the taking of evidence in civil or commercial matters, A5 73/2001, 27.2.2001 (not published in OJ), as in Storskrubb, Civil Procedure, p. 116.

38 Towards an Area of Freedom, Security and Justice, Brussels, COM(1998) 459 final of 14 July 1998, p. 8; Action Plan of the Council and the Commission on how best to implement the provisions of the Treaty of Amsterdam on an area of freedom, security and justice – Text adopted by the Justice and Home Affairs Council of 3 December 1998, OJ C, C/19, 23.01.1999, p. 1; Communication from the Commission to the Council and the European Parliament – Scoreboard to review progress on the creation of an area of "Freedom, security and justice" in the European Union, COM(2000) 167 final/2 of 13 April 2000.

39 Article 8 Treaty of Amsterdam, now in articles 2 and 6 Treaty on European Union, OJ C 202, 7.06.2016 (Consolidated). (TEU).

40 European Union: Council of the European Union. *Presidency Conclusions, Tampere European Council, 15–16 October 1999*, 16 Oct. 1999, pts. 1–2, https://www.europarl.europa.eu/summits/tam_en.htm. Accessed 30 Nov. 2024.

41 Tampere Conclusions, Title VI.

42 The Stockholm Programme – An open and secure Europe serving and protecting citizens, OJ C 115, 4.5.2010, p. 1. The Stockholm Programme was not succeeded by any equivalent program for the development of the Area of Freedom, Security and Justice, but merely by "strategic guidelines." (Léonard, Sarah and Christian Kaunert. "Beyond Stockholm: In Search of a Strategy for the European Union's Area of Freedom, Security, and Justice." *European Politics and Society*, vol. 17, no. 2, 2016, p. 144.) It was succeeded by European Council, Conclusions 26–27 June 2014, EUCO 79/14, 27 June 2014.

43 The EU citizenship was an idea from the Maastricht Treaty (Treaty on European Union, OJ C 191, 29.7.1992, p. 1). *Re* the further development of a European citizenship, see Everson, Michelle. "A Citizenship in Movement." *German Law Journal*, vol. 15, no. 5, August 2014, pp. 965–984.

44 The Stockholm Programme, p. 4. *See also* EU Citizenship Report 2010 – Dismantling the obstacles to EU citizens' rights, Brussels, COM(2010) 603 final of 27 October 2010.

45 The Stockholm Programme, p. 4.

and traditions."[46] The ambition to increase citizens' access to justice throughout the Union is nevertheless unaltered.[47]

In its aiming for an ever-closer union,[48] with increased integration through harmonization of law,[49] the EU has undertaken to increase access to justice among other means, through that of simplified procedures for cross-border taking of evidence. To overcome the obstacle of accessing evidence found on the territory of another jurisdiction than that of the court trying a specific case, in 2001[50] the EU Evidence Regulation[51] was adopted.

This instrument follows the international private law tradition of *forum regit processum* and the EU law sibling of national procedural autonomy and

46 European Council, Conclusions 26–27 June 2014, EUCO 79/14, 27 June 2014, p. 19.

47 Regulation (EU) No 1382/2013 of the European Parliament and of the Council of 17 December 2013 establishing a Justice Programme for the period 2014 to 2020, OJ L 354, 28.12.2013, p. 73.

48 *Déterminés à établir les fondements d'une union sans cesse plus étroite entre les peuples européens.* Treaty Establishing the European Community, 25 Mar. 1957 (Treaty of Rome) p. 11; Preamble and article 1 TEU.

49 Cappelletti, Mauro et al., editor. *Integration Through Law: Europe and the American Federal Experience.* de Gruyter, 1985; Augenstein, Daniel, editor. *"Integration through Law" Revisited: The Making of the European Polity.* Ashgate Pub., 2012. *Re* harmonization of civil procedure, see for example Stürner, Rolf. "Principles of European Civil Procedure or a European Model Code? Some Considerations on the Joint ELI-UNIDROIT Project." *Uniform Law Review*, vol. 19, no. 2, Jun. 2014, pp. 322–328; Kramer, Xandra E. "The Structure of Civil Proceedings and Why It Matters: Exploratory Observations on Future ELI-UNIDROIT European Rules of Civil Procedure." *Uniform Law Review*, vol. 19, no. 2, Jun. 2014, pp. 218–238; Nylund, Anna, and Magne Strandberg, editors. *Civil Procedure and Harmonisation of Law: The Dynamics of EU and International Treaties.* Intersentia, 2019.

50 Council Regulation (EC) No 1206/2001 of 28 May 2001 on cooperation between the courts of the Member States in the taking of evidence in civil or commercial matters, OJ L 174, 27.6.2001, p. 1.

51 Regulation (EU) 2020/1783 of the European Parliament and of the Council of 25 November 2020 on cooperation between the courts of the Member States in the taking of evidence in civil or commercial matters (taking of evidence) (recast), OJ L 405, 2.12.2020, p. 1. Until August 2024, four cases at the Court of Justice directly concern the interpretation and application of the Evidence Regulation: Order of 27 September 2007, *Tedesco*, C-175/06, EU:C:2007:552; judgment of 17 February 2011, *Werynski*, C-283/09, EU:C:2011:85; judgment of 6 September 2012, *Lippens*, C-170/11, EU:C:2012:540; judgment of 21 February 2013, *ProRail*, C-332/11, EU:C:2013:87. Judgment of 28 April 2005, *St Paul Dairy*, C-104/03, EU:C:2005:255, only indirectly concerns the Evidence Regulation. It is the same with case C491/10 (judgment of 22 December 2010, *Aguirre Zarraga*, C491/10, EU:C:2010:828) which concerns child abduction, and the Court declares that the rules regarding the administration of evidence as part of fundamental rights (in particular, the hearing of the child according to 24(1) CFR) are found within the national legislation of the court of origin. In case C-412/10 (judgment of 17 November 2011, *Homawoo*, C-412/10, EU:C:2011:747) the Evidence Regulation is only referred as a point of comparison in a question regarding the entry into force of a regulation. In case C-226/13 (judgment of 11 June 2015, *Fahrenbrock & Others*, EU:C:2015:383) the AG considers in their opinion the *Werynski* case in discussing the jurisdiction of the Court of Justice.

leaves it to national legal orders to regulate the proceedings for the taking of evidence.[52] The Evidence Regulation is a technical solution to the problem of access to cross-border justice. This book questions whether such a technical view on evidence and law does in fact benefit access to justice. The ambition of an ever-closer union, where justice is to be increased and perhaps somehow also harmonized, requires a deeper understanding of what may be involved for parties to civil proceedings. As evidence is seen as a means to justice it is relevant to seek an understanding of how evidence operates in the legal judgment. In this book, the EU's ambitions to integrate the different senses of justice in Europe through law, specifically through the Evidence Regulation, will be studied from the perspective of the differends. Based on a comparative study of Swedish and French civil procedural fact-finding, I question whether the Evidence Regulation does in fact contribute to the ambition to increase access to justice in the EU and argue that an understanding of evidence which does not take into account the many possibilities to interpret and misinterpret evidence and evidentiary facts risks thwarting justice. It will be held that although evidence is a *sine qua non* for legal justice in concrete[53] evidence's weakness as conveyer of truth renders justice as the correct application of law to the case unreliable – in particular in cross-border cases.

The Gap of Justice

Two problems may be noted with the EU's analysis of the problem and its suggested solutions. The first is the obvious lack of a common sense of justice in the EU that the radical denying of justice as a legal matter in the legal traditions of some of the Member States reveals. From a Swedish point of view the aims to harmonize the senses of justice in the union might seem particularly confusing. Since the era of Scandinavian legal realism,[54] the term justice is scarcely used in relation to law. The attitude towards the concept of justice

52 Under the principle of effectiveness national procedural rules may not be shaped in such a way that EU law is discriminated against. (Judgment of 16 December 1976, *Rewe-Zentralfinanz*, 33–76, EU:C:1976:188, pt. 2. *See* for later cases, for example, judgment of 11 September 2019, *Oana Mădălina Călin v Direcţia Regională a Finanţelor Publice Ploieşti – Administraţia Judeţeană a Finanţelor Publice Dâmboviţa and Others*, C-676/17, EU:C:2019:700, pp. 42–56; judgment of 19 October 2017, *Hansruedi Raimund v Michaela Aigner*, C–425/16, EU:C:2017:776, pp. 40–42; judgment of 14 September 2017, *The Trustees of the BT Pension Scheme v Commissioners for Her Majesty's Revenue and Customs*, C-628/15, EU:C:2017:687, pp. 57–58; judgment of 15 September 2011, *Ministre du Budget, des Comptes publics et de la Fonction publique v Accor SA*, C-310/09, EU:C:2011:581, pp. 78–79.)

53 Perelman, p. 41.

54 Strang, Johan. "Two Generations of Scandinavian Legal Realism." *RETFÆRD*, årgång 32, no. 1/124, 2009 warns against treating Scandinavian legal realism as a single movement, with one common purpose throughout the period of time in which its most important representatives were active.

(and several other legal concepts such as, for example 'positive law') among the Scandinavian legal realist scholars was rather harsh. Their aim is said to have been "to cure people, including lawyers, of their nonsensical ideas, thus liberating them from the religious and metaphysical stages of believing that . . . there are ideals of human rights or justice to be implemented by law."[55] In my experience, the spirit of Scandinavian legal realism still has an important influence on general Swedish legal thinking. The second problem regards the solution to increase justice by forging a common sense of justice. This would require one sense of justice to prevail over the other – silencing the other.[56] By proposing easier access to evidence as a means to increase access to justice, one disregards one of the fundamental requirements of justice itself: that of recognizing what is not equal. Both of these acts of injustice are examples of what Lyotard refers to as a *wrong*.[57]

The aim of this study is to suggest a concept[58] of justice which considers the complexity of the jurisdictional landscape of the EU and the role of evidence in the formation of the just judgment. It wishes to contribute to a better understanding of how the differences within a jurisdictional landscape may disturb the sought-for sturdiness of jurisdictional decision-making. 'Jurisdiction' is understood here in both its territorial and its procedural law aspects – in general application and in the singular[59] – as a "regulatory environment."[60] Jurisdiction is also a matter of force[61] connected to a territory and the spatio-temporal commonality, connected to that force. This

55 Bjarup, Jes. "Scandinavian Legal Realism." *The Philosophy of Law: An Encyclopedia*, edited by Mark Tebbit, Vol. 2, Routledge, 1999.

56 Lyotard, pt. 13, p. 123.

57 Lyotard, p. xi. Lyotard, himself, uses the word *tort* to distinguish from *dommage*, translated into English as 'wrong' and 'damages' (Le Différend, p. 9). *Tort* has also been translated into English 'tort,' *see* for example Douzinas, Costas, and Ronnie Warrington. " 'A Well-Founded Fear of Justice': Law and Ethics in Postmodernity." *Law and Critique*, vol. II, no. 2, 1991, p. 130.

58 With 'concept' is meant here a term to which is connected an idea. Etymologically, a 'concept' *grasps hold of* an idea. (Concept: *con+capere* (to grasp); "Originally in *Philosophy*: a general idea or notion, a universal; a mental representation of the essential or typical properties of something, considered without regard to the peculiar properties of any specific instance or example. Later often (frequently with *of*): the meaning that is realized by a word or expression."; "Concept, N." Oxford English Dictionary, Oxford UP, September 2023.) To the idea is connected a number of characteristics (– something we may find also in Lyotard's definition of the word: "*l'unité de la conscience de représentations liées*," Lyotard, Jean-François. "Judicieux dans le différend." *La Faculté de juger*, edited by Derrida, Jacques et al., Minuit, 1985, p. 195).

59 Douzinas, Costas. "The Metaphysics of Jurisdiction." *Jurisprudence of Jurisdiction,* edited by Shaun McVeigh, Routledge, 2016.

60 Joerges, Christian. "The Challenges of Europeanization in the Realm of Private Law: A Plea for a New Legal Discipline." *Duke Journal of Comparative & International Law,* vol. 14, no. 2, Summer 2004, pp. 149–196.

61 Weber, Max. *From Max Weber: Essays in Sociology*. Edited and Translated by H. H. Gerth, and C. Wright Mills, Routledge, 2014, p. 78; Derrida, pp. 972 ff.

means that jurisdiction is primarily understood in a formalistic sense, concerning the legislative power over a particular territory and the choice of court in international procedure.[62] Secondarily, it is understood as a matter of regimentation of culture as a spatio-temporal commonality.[63]

With the particular focus on cultural[64] differences within the EU this book wishes to contribute to the growing (and not new) critique of the integration through law course of action,[65] as well as the aim of an ever-closer union as a political ambition.[66] Perhaps it may be seen as a response to the request and prediction that international private and procedural law develop solutions to the ever-growing, ever-deepening global polycontexturality.[67] With a reference to the humanist liberal values, one might strive for mutual solidarity rather than an equality which disregards and thus erases both differences and freedom. As such, approximative justice considers differences between "*as-if* neutral spaces"[68] and questions whether

62 For example, in Regulation (EU) No 1215/2012 of the European Parliament and of the Council of 12 December 2012 on jurisdiction and the recognition and enforcement of judgments in civil and commercial matters (recast), OJ L 351, 20.12.2012, p. 1 (Brussels I); Council Regulation (EC) No 2201/2003 of 27 November 2003 concerning jurisdiction and the recognition and enforcement of judgments in matrimonial matters and the matters of parental responsibility, repealing Regulation (EC) No 1347/2000, OJ L 338, 23.12.2003, p. 1 (Brussels II); Regulation (EU) No 650/2012 of the European Parliament and of the Council of 4 July 2012 on jurisdiction, applicable law, recognition and enforcement of decisions and acceptance and enforcement of authentic instruments in matters of succession and on the creation of a European Certificate of Succession, OJ L 201, 27.7.2012, p. 107 (Succession Regulation).

63 Geertz, Clifford. *The Interpretation of Cultures: Selected Essays.* E-book, Basic Books, 1973, p. 5.

64 The word 'cultural' is used here with reference to the EU analysis of the problem: Explanatory Report to the opinion of the EP A5 73/2001.

65 As advocated by Cappelletti in 1985.

66 Everson, Michelle, and Christian Joerges. "Facticity as Validity: The Misplaced Revolutionary Praxis of European Law." *Research Handbook on Critical Legal Theory*, edited by Emilios Christodoulidis et al., Edward Elgar Publishing, 2019; Fischer-Lescano, Andreas, and Günther Teubner. "Regime-Collisions: The Vain Search for Legal Unity in the Fragmentation of Global Law." *Michigan Journal of International Law*, vol. 25, no. 4, Summer 2004, pp. 999–1046; Legrand, Pierre. "European Legal Systems are Not Converging." *International and Comparative Law Quarterly*, vol. 45, no. 1, Jan. 1996, pp. 52–81; Legrand, Pierre. "Sens et Non-Sens d'un Code Civil Européen." *Revue Internationale de Droit Comparé*, vol. 48, no. 4, Jan. 1996, pp. 779–812.

67 Joerges, Christian. "How is a Closer Union Conceivable under Conditions of Ever More Socio-Economic and Political Diversity Constitutionalising Europe's Unitas in Pluralitate." *European Law Journal*, vol. 24, 2018, pp. 257–267; Everson, Michelle, and Christian Joerges. "Reconfiguring the Politics-Law Relationship in the Integration Project through Conflicts-Law Constitutionalism." *European Law Journal*, vol. 18, no. 5, Sep. 2012, pp. 644–666; Watt, Horatia Muir. "Private International Law beyond the Schism." *Transnational Legal Theory*, vol. 2, no. 3, 2011, pp. 347–428. *Re* polycontexturality: Günther.

68 Primarily, Lyotard, p. 123, but also, Derrida, p. 961.

such a space can be created by political intent in the name of justice. In the exploration of these questions, this book rejects the dejected perception of the impossibility or irrelevance of justice of the legal realists – as it asks what may be understood as a common European sense of juridical justice today.[69] From the perspective of a legal and jurisprudential tradition that deleted the word justice from its vocabulary a century ago, the ambition to give the citizens of Europe a common sense of justice comes across as a rather important example of miscommunication between the legislators of the EU. The claim that the European Union rests on a common history and therefore shares common values[70] with the consequence that the forging of a common sense of justice should be an achievable goal risks being perceived as "charlemagnean."

The main contemporary theories of juridical justice may perhaps be said to focus on justice's external demands on law.[71] The focus in this book is the relation between evidence and justice, that is the relation between knowledge of the particular case and the just judgment and takes the perspective of the parties.[72] It therefore accepts as a point of departure the relative concept of juridical justice as self-referentiality, where law restricts what a just judgment may be.[73] Perelman argued that the distinction between an abstract concept of justice and that of the "innumerable situations" of concrete justice must be upheld in order to be able to put light on the specific difficulties that follow from the application of formal justice in the concrete situation.[74] Accordingly, it restricts itself to concrete justice, which takes place through the legal judgment. As will be developed in Chapter 2, such theories of justice may be found in Bentham, Hägerström, Hart, Ekelöf, Twining et al. and Luhmann who unite in their formalistic understanding of juridical justice as the correct application of law.

69 The expression 'juridical justice' is borrowed from Teubner and will be used to refer to a concept of justice which is relevant to law and as distinguished from justice relevant to other human practices. It is used synonymously to 'legal justice.'

70 Preamble and articles 2 and 6 TEU.

71 *See*, for example, Douzinas, Costas, and Adam Gearey. *Critical Jurisprudence: The Political Philosophy of Justice*. Hart Publishing, 2005 (p. 5 *re* external vs. internal); Åhrén, Mattias. *Indigenous Peoples' Status in the International Legal System*. OUP, 2016; Baxi, Upendra. "Towards a Climate Change Justice Theory." *Journal of Human Rights and the Environment*, vol. 7, no. 1, Mar. 2016, pp. 7–31; Torres, Gerald. "Environmental Burdens and Democratic Justice." *Fordham Urban Law Journal*, vol. 21, no. 3, Spring 1994, pp. 431–460. *Also*, Luhmann's justice as adequate complexity, in Law As a Social System, OUP.

72 *Re* 'judgment,' see Chapter 3.

73 Hart, H. L. A. "Positivism and the Separation of Law and Morals." *Harvard Law Review*, vol. 71, no. 4, (*The Harvard Law Review Association*) 1958, pp. 593–629.

74 Perelman, p. 41.

Aside from Wigmore's chart method, which illustrates one understanding of how inferences are made and how they should be arranged,[75] and the entertaining Nine Mile Walk story in Analysis of Evidence,[76] existing evidence theories primarily focus on the probability of the object of proof,[77] the credibility of the narratives[78] and, in respect of civil procedure, the standard and burden of proof.[79] Although some of these theories encompass several aspects to the problem of evidence in law, they have not paid just attention to the attribution of sense in the process of drawing conclusions. In Swedish jurisprudence, the closest theory of evidence and justice may be found in the theory of alternative hypotheses. This takes the plurality of deductions possible to make from an evidentiary fact into account but like other probability-based theories is proposed for criminal proceedings. The most important proponent for the consideration of alternative hypotheses in criminal proceedings in Sweden criticized the probability theories for being founded on fictive frequencies.[80] Approximative justice considers the calculation of probability irrelevant because there is no escaping fictive frequencies.

Approximative justice considers those cases which may not be determined and agrees with those who argue that the case as established is rather a selection of facts and inferences resulting from the judge's activity.[81] Therefore, it is argued here, to be just the judge must be aware of this, and humbled by it, in the way that a kindergarten teacher must seek the wisest forward-facing solution to a conflict rather than the "correct" reaction to the past.[82] This book suggests that this can only be done through approximation in two senses: approximation of the judge towards the parties, the judge's addressing themselves to the parties in the effort to genuinely hear them, and an approximation of the case, an approximative establishment of the case. The

75 Wigmore, John H. "Problem of Proof." *Illinois Law Review*, vol. 8, no. 2, 1913–1914, pp. 77–103; Schum, David. "A Science of Evidence: Contributions from Law and Probability." *Law, Probability and Risk*, vol. 8, 2009, pp. 197–231; *see also* Goodwin, p. 223.

76 Anderson et al., Chapter 1.

77 Ekelöf, P. O. "Free Evaluation of Evidence." *Scandinavian Studies in Law*, vol. 8, 1964, pp. 45–66; Cohen, L. Jonathan. *The Probable and the Provable*. Clarendon, 1977; Lindell, Bengt. *Sakfrågor och rättsfrågor: en studie av gränser, skillnader och förhållanden mellan faktum och rätt*. Iustus, 1987; Diesen, Christian. *Bevisprövning i brottmål*. Juristförlaget, 1994.

78 See, primarily, Wagenaar, Willem A. et al. *Anchored Narratives: The Psychology of Criminal Evidence*. Harvester Wheatsheaf, 1993.

79 See, for example, Heuman, Lars. *Bevisbörda och beviskrav i tvistemål*. 1st ed., Norstedts Juridik, 2005.

80 Diesen, Christian. *Utevarohandläggning och bevisprövning i brottmål*. Juristförlaget, 1993. Dissertation.

81 For example, Kennedy.

82 Oppenheimer, Sharifa. *Heaven on Earth: A Handbook for Parents of Young Children*. SteinerBooks, 2006, p. 202. *Also* Derrida, Jacques. *Marx Spöken: Skuldstaten, sorgearbetet och Den nya internationalen*. Translated by Jonas Magnusson, Daidalos, 2003, (Derrida, Specters of Marx), chapter 1.

judge as *bona mater hortensis*, maybe, rather than a superimposing machine who speaks the law in a vain attempt to meet the bull's eye – as if there were a bull's eye that could be hit. In this book the focus will be on the possibility of justice disregarding any possible disagreements as to the ethics of the substance, supposing as a hypothesis that juridical justice is the correct application of law. As it focusses on the factual side, the minor premise, it also restricts itself to the just judgment. It therefore hopes to contribute to the contemporary discourse on justice and law which is provoked to a large extent by internationalization and globalization.[83] This book takes the course of direction and seeking to lay out reasons against a superimposed common sense of justice: accept fragmentation, overcome the "harmony addiction."[84]

Bibliography

Åhrén, Mattias. *Indigenous Peoples' Status in the International Legal System.* OUP, 2016.

Anderson, Terence et al. *Analysis of Evidence.* 2nd ed., CUP, 2010.

Augenstein, Daniel, editor. *'Integration Through Law' Revisited: The Making of the European Polity.* Ashgate Pub., 2012.

Baxi, Upendra. "Towards a Climate Change Justice Theory." *Journal of Human Rights and the Environment*, vol. 7, no. 1, Mar. 2016, pp. 7–31.

Bentham, Jeremy. *Rationale of Judicial Evidence.* Edited by J. S. Mill, Vol. I, Hunt and Clarke, 1827.

Bjarup, Jes. "Scandinavian Legal Realism." *The Philosophy of Law: An Encyclopedia*, edited by Mark Tebbit, Vol. 2, Routledge, 1999.

Blanc, Emmanuel. *La Preuve judiciaire. Commentaire du Décret du 17 décembre 1973.* Librairie du Journal des notaires et des avocats, 1974.

Cappelletti, Mauro et al., editor. *Integration Through Law: Europe and the American Federal Experience.* de Gruyter, 1985.

Cohen, L. Jonathan. *The Probable and the Provable.* Clarendon, 1977.

Derrida, Jacques. "Force de loi: le Fondement mystique de l'autorité." *Cardozo Law Review*, vol. 11, nos. 5–6, Jul/Aug. 1990.

Derrida, Jacques. *Marx Spöken: Skuldstaten, sorgearbetet och Den nya internationalen.* Translated by Jonas Magnusson, Daidalos, 2003 (Derrida, Specters of Marx).

Diesen, Christian. *Utevarohandläggning och bevisprövning i brottmål.* Juristförlaget, Diss. Stockholm, 1993.

Diesen, Christian. *Bevisprövning i brottmål.* Juristförlaget, 1994.

Douzinas, Costas. "The Metaphysics of Jurisdiction." *Jurisprudence of Jurisdiction*, edited by Shaun McVeigh, Routledge, 2016.

Douzinas, Costas, and Adam Gearey. *Critical Jurisprudence: The Political Philosophy of Justice.* Hart Publishing, 2005.

83 Joerges, Christian, and Michelle Everson. "Law, Economics and Politics in the Constitutionalization of Europe." *Developing a Constitution for Europe*, edited by Erik O. Eriksen et al., Routledge, 2004, pp. 162–179; Fischer-Lescano, Andreas, and Günther Teubner. "Regime-Collisions: The Vain Search for Legal Unity in the Fragmentation of Global Law." *Michigan Journal of International Law*, vol. 25, no. 4, Summer 2004, pp. 999–1046.

84 Payne, Kim John. *Being at Your Best When Your Kids Are at Their Worst: Practical Compassion in Parenting.* Shambhala Publications, 2019, pp. 29–32. *Also*, Lyotard, pt. 146.

Douzinas, Costas, and Ronnie Warrington. "'A Well-Founded Fear of Justice': Law and Ethics in Postmodernity." *Law and Critique*, vol. II, no. 2, 1991, p. 130.

Ekelöf, P. O. "Free Evaluation of Evidence." *Scandinavian Studies in Law*, vol. 8, 1964, pp. 45–66.

Ekelöf, P. O. *Rättegång II*. 8th ed., Norstedts Juridik, 2010.

Ekelöf, P. O. et al. *Rättegång I*. 9th ed., Norstedts Juridik, 2016.

Everson, Michelle. "A Citizenship in Movement." *German Law Journal*, vol. 15, no. 5, Aug. 2014, pp. 965–984.

Everson, Michelle, and Christian Joerges. "Reconfiguring the Politics-Law Relationship in the Integration Project through Conflicts-Law Constitutionalism." *European Law Journal*, vol. 18, no. 5, Sept. 2012, pp. 644–666.

Everson, Michelle, and Christian Joerges. "Facticity as Validity: The Misplaced Revolutionary Praxis of European Law." *Research Handbook on Critical Legal Theory*, edited by Emilios Christodoulidis et al., Edward Elgar Publishing, 2019.

Fischer-Lescano, Andreas, and Gunther Teubner. "Regime-Collisions: The Vain Search for Legal Unity in the Fragmentation of Global Law." *Michigan Journal of International Law*, vol. 25, no. 4, Summer 2004, pp. 999–1046.

Gearey, Adam. *Law and Aesthetics*. Bloomsbury Publishing Plc, 2001.

Geertz, Clifford. *The Interpretation of Cultures: Selected Essays*. E-book. Basic Books, 1973.

Goodwin, Jean. "Wigmore's Chart Method." *Informal Logic*, vol. 20, no. 3, 2000, pp. 223–243.

Günther, Gotthard. "Life as Polycontexturality." *Wirklichkeit und Reflexion*, (first published in) edited by H. Fahrenbach, Festschrift für Walter Schulz, Pfullingen 1973, pp. 187–210, http://vordenker.de/ggphilosophy/gg_life_as_polycontexturality.pdf, 2014, p. 4.

Hart, H. L. A. "Positivism and the Separation of Law and Morals." *Harvard Law Review*, vol. 71, no. 4, 1958, pp. 593–629.

Heuman, Lars. *Bevisbörda och beviskrav i tvistemål*. 1st ed., Norstedts Juridik, 2005.

Joerges, Christian. "The Challenges of Europeanization in the Realm of Private Law: A Plea for a New Legal Discipline." *Duke Journal of Comparative & International Law*, vol. 14, no. 2, Summer 2004, pp. 149–196.

Joerges, Christian. "How Is a Closer Union Conceivable under Conditions of Ever More Socio-Economic and Political Diversity Constitutionalising Europe's Unitas in Pluralitate." *European Law Journal*, 24, 2018, pp. 257–267.

Joerges, Christian, and Michelle Everson. "Law, Economics and Politics in the Constitutionalization of Europe." *Developing a Constitution for Europe*, edited by Erik O. Eriksen et al., Routledge, 2004.

Kennedy, Duncan. *A Critique of Adjudication: Fin de Siècle*. Harvard UP, 1997.

Kramer, Xandra E. "The Structure of Civil Proceedings and Why It Matters: Exploratory Observations on Future ELI-UNIDROIT European Rules of Civil Procedure." *Uniform Law Review*, vol. 19, no. 2, Jun. 2014, pp. 218–238.

Legrand, Pierre. "European Legal Systems Are Not Converging." *International and Comparative Law Quarterly*, vol. 45, no. 1, Jan. 1996, pp. 52–81.

Legrand, Pierre. "Sens et Non-Sens d'un Code Civil Européen." *Revue Internationale de Droit Comparé*, vol. 48, no. 4, Jan. 1996, pp. 779–812.

Léonard, Sarah, and Christian Kaunert. "Beyond Stockholm: In Search of a Strategy for the European Union's Area of Freedom, Security, and Justice." *European Politics and Society*, vol. 17, no. 2, 2016.

Lévy-Bruhl, Henri. *La Preuve judiciaire. Essai de sociologie juridique*. Marcel Rivière, 1963.

Lindell, Bengt. *Sakfrågor och rättsfrågor: en studie av gränser, skillnader och förhållanden mellan faktum och rätt*. Iustus, 1987.
Luhmann, Niklas. *Law as a Social System*. OUP, 2004.
Lyotard, Jean-François. *The Postmodern Condition: A Report on Knowledge*. Translated by Geoff Bennington and Brian Massumi, Manchester University Press, 1984.
Lyotard, Jean-François. "Judicieux dans le différend." *La Faculté de juger*, edited by Jacques Derrida, et al., Minuit, 1985.
Lyotard, Jean-François. *The Different – Phrases in Dispute*. Translated by Georges Van Den Abbeele, University of Minnesota Press, 1988.
Lyotard, Jean-François. *Le Différend*. Minuit.
Normand, Jacques. *Le juge et le litige*. L.G.D.J., 1965.
Nylund, Anna, and Magne Strandberg, editors. *Civil Procedure and Harmonisation of Law: The Dynamics of EU and International Treaties*. Intersentia, 2019.
Oppenheimer, Sharifa. *Heaven on Earth: A Handbook for Parents of Young Children*. SteinerBooks, 2006, p. 202.
Payne, Kim John. *Being at Your Best When Your Kids Are at Their Worst: Practical Compassion in Parenting*. Shambhala Publications, 2019, pp. 29–32.
Perelman, Chaïm. *Justice et raison*. Editions de l'Université de Bruxelles, 1972.
Poché, Fred. *Penser avec Derrida: Comprendre la déconstruction*. Chronique sociale, 2007.
Schum, David. "Inference Networks and Their Many Subtle Properties." *Information and Decision Technologies*, vol. 16, 1990, pp. 69–98.
Schum, David. "A Science of Evidence: Contributions from Law and Probability." *Law, Probability and Risk*, vol. 8, 2009, pp. 197–231.
Storskrubb, Eva. *Civil Procedure and EU Law, A Policy Area Uncovered*. OUP, 2008, pp. 9–12.
Strang, Johan. "Two Generations of Scandinavian Legal Realism." *RETFÆRD*, årgång 32, no. 1/124, 2009.
Stürner, Rolf. "Principles of European Civil Procedure or a European Model Code? Some Considerations on the Joint ELI-UNIDROIT Project." *Uniform Law Review*, vol. 19, no. 2, Jun. 2014, pp. 322–328.
Teubner, Günther. "Self-Subversive Justice: Contingency or Transcendence Formula of Law?" *The Modern Law Review*, vol. 72, no. 1, 2009, pp. 1–23.
Torres, Gerald. "Environmental Burdens and Democratic Justice." *Fordham Urban Law Journal*, vol. 21, no. 3, Spring 1994, pp. 431–460.
Tournier, Clara. *L'intime conviction du juge de jugement*. ANRT, 2003. Lille thèses.
Wagenaar, Willem A. et al. *Anchored Narratives: The Psychology of Criminal Evidence*. Harvester Wheatsheaf, 1993.
Walter, Bruno. "Bruckner and Mahler." *Chord and Discord,* vol. 2, no. 9, 1948, p. 41, https://www.uv.es/~calaforr/walter.html. Accessed 31 Mar. 2022.
Watt, Horatia Muir. "Private International Law beyond the Schism." *Transnational Legal Theory*, vol. 2, no. 3, 2011, pp. 347–428.
Weber, Max. *From Max Weber: Essays in Sociology*. Edited and translated by H. H. Gerth and C. Wright Mills. Routledge, 2014.
Wigmore, John H. "Problem of Proof." *Illinois Law Review,* vol. 8, no. 2, 1913–1914, pp. 77–103.

Chapter 2

Obstructions of Knowledge

Introduction

Chapters 2 and 3 wish to present the theoretical presuppositions guiding the argument that justice in the concrete case must be understood as approximative. Whereas the current chapter will present the theoretical understanding of the relation between evidence and justice with a particular focus on evidence, the next chapter will switch focus towards the reasoning regarding the formation of a just judgment.[1] The role of the evidence in the formation of the legal judgment has been analyzed inspired by Lyotard's theory of knowledge and justice as presented in *The Differend*.[2] This chapter explores the theory of the differend and presents the terminology used throughout the book for the analysis of the differend in cases with cross-border evidence. The theory of the differend is here related to positive law notions of evidence and justice before introducing the impasses of justice – why justice trips on its own presuppositions and therefore struggles to take place – as laid out by Derrida in *Force of Law*.[3] Lyotard's differend is read here as another such impasse for the formation of a just judgment.

The Purpose of Evidence

The raison d'être of the EU Evidence Regulation on cross-border taking of evidence is the importance that the parties get access to justice regardless of the choice of jurisdiction within the EU.[4] Not only is the objective to give the

1 The expression 'formation of a judgment' here refers both to the internal process which in Swedish is referred to as *omdömesbildning*, and the external decision-making, external in the sense that a legal judgment must be communicated in order to have effect, and external also in that it leads to some (concrete) effect. Re 'formation of a judgment': "the formation of a judgment or the capacity to form a well-founded opinion on the basis of reasons and counter-reasons." (Key, Ellen. Folkbildningsarbetet särskilt med hänsyn till skönhetssinnets odling. K. W. Appelbergs boktryckeri, 1906, p. 15. The translation is my own.)

2 Lyotard, Jean-François. *The Differend – Phrases in Dispute*. Translated by Georges Van Den Abbeele, University of Minnesota Press, 1988. Both the original French version (Lyotard, Jean-François. *Le Différend*. Minuit, 1983) and the English translation have been studied.

3 Derrida, Jacques. "Force de loi: le Fondement mystique de l'autorité." *Cardozo Law Review*, vol. 11, nos. 5–6, Jul/Aug. 1990, pp. 949–1046.

4 Chapters 1, 4 and 10.

DOI: 10.4324/9781003495383-2

European citizens access to justice across borders, but they should also get *equal* access to justice.[5] As noted earlier, in some of the EU Member States the word 'justice' is not seen as a term relevant to law. One may ask then, why there is nevertheless evidence also in their judicial procedures. It appears, however, that the father of Scandinavian legal realism, Hägerström, understood justice to be the correct application of law to the case, i.e., the correct legal judgment.[6] This aligns with Bentham's perception that evidence and procedure aim at "rectitude of decision."[7] Justice as the correct application of law corresponds to the understanding of justice as treating equal cases equally[8] – a maxim held as a shared good, generally recognized; according to Perelman, "*[l]a notion de justice suggère à tous inévitablement l'idée d'une certaine égalité. Depuis Platon et Aristote, en passant par Saint Thomas, jusqu'aux juristes, moralistes et philosophes contemporains, tout le monde est d'accord sur ce point.*"[9] It seems also Scandinavian legal realists would agree with this.[10]

5 European Union: Council of the European Union. *Presidency Conclusions, Tampere European Council, 15–16 October 1999*, 16 Oct. 1999, Title VI, https://www.europarl.europa.eu/summits/tam_en.htm. Accessed 30 Nov. 2024.

6 Mindus, Patricia. *A Real Mind: The Life and Work of Axel Hägerström*. Springer Science & Business Media, 2009, pp. 152–153. *See also* Olivecrona, Karl. "The Legal Theories of Axel Hägerström and Vilhelm Lundstedt." *Scandinavian Studies in Law*, vol. 3, 1959, p. 132. Later generations of Scandinavian scholars, such as Swedish proceduralist Ekelöf, used the word 'justice,' in the instances that I have found also in the sense of correctness and rightness (rectitude). (For example, in Ekelöf, P. O. *Rättegång II*. 8th ed., Norstedts Juridik, 2010, p. 20.) In the extent that correct and right are senses of the term 'justice,' there can be no doubt that the concept of 'justice' has always been a valid term in Swedish procedural law jurisprudence also by the legal realists. Scandinavian legal realists may therefore have opposed the existence of any absolute and ideal justice but accepted a relative, limited legal sense of 'justice' – which they seem reluctant to refer to as justice.

7 Bentham, Jeremy. *Rationale of Judicial Evidence*. Edited by J. S. Mill, Vol. I, Hunt and Clarke, 1827, pp. 1–3, 548; Twining, William. *Theories of Evidence: Bentham and Wigmore*. Weidenfeld & Nicolson, 1984, p. 48. *See also* Twining, William. *Rethinking Evidence: Exploratory Essays*. 2nd ed., Cambridge University Press, 2006, pp. 104–105, where Twining explains that "rectitude of decision" is an unattainable ideal, nevertheless relevant for the theory of evidence, as it is – in the terminology of this thesis – the purpose-point of the evidence.

8 The phrasing "treat equal cases equally and unequal cases unequally" seems to be a conclusion derived at from reading different Aristotelean works, primarily Nicomachean Ethics, Book V and Politics; Euvrard, Jean-Louis. "Aristote." *Dictionnaire de la Justice*, edited by Loïc Cadiet, PUF, 2004, pp. 72 ss.; Westen, Peter. *Speaking of Equality: An Analysis of the Rhetorical Force of 'Equality' in Moral and Legal Discourse*. Princeton UP, 2014, p. 185.

9 Perelman, Chaïm. *Justice et raison*. Editions de l'Université de Bruxelles, 1972, p. 21. Whether the evidence should be predetermined by law or free is however a point on which *tout le monde n'est pas d'accord*. Bentham held that evidence must be free. In Swedish procedure, this has been a fact since before the reformed CJP of 1942, whereas the main rule in French civil procedure was that of regulated evidence until 2016, when the main rule and the exceptions shifted place. (Ordonnance n° 2016–131 du 10 février 2016 portant réforme du droit des contrats, du régime général et de la preuve des obligations, NOR: JUSC1522466R.)

10 Mindus, Section 5.4.

The access to justice doctrine is also to a large extent shared goods[11] – both within the EU and within the larger area encompassing the Contracting States of the European Convention of Human Rights (ECHR).[12] The access to justice doctrine consists of two main components: the right to a fair trial (6 ECHR and 47 CFR[13]) and the right to effective remedy (13 ECHR and 47 CFR).[14] Not only is it clear from these provisions that the fair trial and the effective remedy are closely interconnected, but it is also apparent that they consist of or are dependent on a number of other rights and principles. These have been developed in rulings from the European Court of Human Rights (ECtHR) mainly. Initially, it may be stated from this caselaw that access to justice consists of a right to access to a trial, and that this trial be fair.[15] A number of requirements are laid on the trial for it to be perceived as fair. One expression of the right to a fair hearing is the right to be heard which requires that the trial is adversarial in the sense that there is a real opportunity to oppose.[16] In case C-301/87, the EU Court established that "observance of the right to be heard is . . . a fundamental principle of Community law which must be guaranteed even in the absence of any rules governing the procedure in question."[17] It has been held that the right to be heard and

11 Limits to the commonality may be seen in the circumstance that the expression remains untranslated into the Swedish language – a sign, perhaps, of the discomfort Swedish lawyers have to use the Swedish word for justice *rättvisa* – for example in Bull, Thomas. "Rättighetsskyddet i Högsta förvaltningsdomstolen." *Svensk juristtidning*, 2017, p. 232; Ekelöf, P. O. "Access to Justice." *Svensk juristtidning*, 1981, pp. 109–120.

12 European Convention for the Protection of Human Rights and Fundamental Freedoms, as amended by Protocols Nos. 11 and 14, 4 November 1950, ETS 5.

13 Charter of Fundamental Rights of the European Union, OJ C 202, 7.6.2016, p. 389 (Consolidated); judgment of 22 December 2010, *DEB Deutsche Energiehandels- und Beratungsgesellschaft mbH v Bundesrepublik Deutschland*, C279/09, EU:C:2010:811, para. 59–62; judgment of 8 December 2011, *Chalkor AE Epexergasias Metallon v European Commission*, C-386/10 P, EU:C:2011:815, para. 52; judgment of 28 July 2011, *Brahim Samba Diouf v Ministre du Travail, de l'Emploi et de l'Immigration*, C-69/10, EU:C:2011:524, para. 42; judgment of 6 November 2012, *Europese Gemeenschap v Otis NV and Others*, C199/11, EU:C:2012:684, para. 48.

14 Explanation on Article 47 – Right to an effective remedy and to a fair trial, Explanations relating to the Charter of Fundamental Rights (OJ 2007 C 303, p. 17). It is stated that the national jurisdictions in the EU enjoy some discretion in respect of the form of the remedy but the CJEU has developed a doctrine in accordance with which EU Member States are to pay damages in case of their own breach of EU law. (Judgment of 19 November 1991, *Andrea Francovich and Others v Italian Republic*, joined Cases C-6/90 and C-9/90, EU:C:1991:428, para. 43.)

15 *Golder v the United Kingdom*, 21 Feb. 1975, Series A no. 18.

16 *Re* the adversarial principle, see for example also *Pellegrini v France*, 28541/95, para. 44, ECHR 1999-VIII; *Reinhardt and Slimane–Kaïd v France*, 23043/93, 22921/93, ECHR 1998-II, p. 666, para. 103–106; judgment of 22 November 2012, *M. M. v Minister for Justice, Equality and Law Reform, Ireland*, C-277/11, EU:C:2012:744, para. 87.

17 Judgment of 14 February 1990, *French Republic v Commission of the European Communities*, Case C-301/87, EU:C:1990:67, para. 29.

its corresponding responsibility of the judge to hear both parties, *audiatur et altera pars*, is of natural law calibre, supposedly going back to Hesiod and Aristophanes, thus making part of the "communal conscience" even before it took part of jurisprudence.[18] Following the principle of equality of arms stipulated in the *Neumeister* case, the right to present evidence must be equally divided between the parties in the sense that both parties must have the same means of access to evidence.[19] In the *Dombo Beheer* case, the ECtHR held "that each party must be afforded a reasonable opportunity to present his case – including his evidence – under conditions that do not place him at a substantial disadvantage vis-à-vis his opponent."[20] (A substantial disadvantage was found in the inability to hear a witness.[21]) In 1796, Villenave held that evidence is a means to establish the truth of a contested fact.[22]

The right to effective remedy[23] in turn requires that law be interpreted and applied so that the result of the application attributes to the law full effect.[24] Because of the fundamental legal requirement that equal cases be treated equally[25] the judge must know what the concrete case is. Justice in concrete is justice exercised in real-life situations.[26] To treat equals equally, and be able to deliver

18 Motulsky, Henri. "Le droit naturel dans la pratique jurisprudentielle: le respect des droits de la défense en procédure civile." *Écrits, études et notes de procédure civile.* Dalloz, 2010, p. 66.

19 *Neumeister v Austria,* 27 June 1968, para. 28–29, Series A no. 8; Rainey, Bernadette et al. *The European Convention on Human Rights.* 7th ed., Oxford UP, 2017, p. 263.

20 *Dombo Beheer B.V. v the Netherlands*, judgment of 27 October 1993, Series A no. 274, p. 19, para. 33; Fricero, Natalie. "Garanties de nature procédurale: équité, publicité, célérité et laïcité." *Droit et pratique de la procédure civile – Droit interne et européen,* (2017/2018), edited by Serge Guinchard, 9th ed. Dalloz, 2016, (212.21), pp. 814–815.

21 Dombo Beheer, para. 35; Settem, Ola Johan. *Applications of the 'Fair Hearing' Norm in ECHR Article 6(1) to Civil Proceedings: With Special Emphasis on the Balance Between Procedural Safeguards and Efficiency*. Springer, 2015, p. 350.

22 Villenave. *Des Jurés et de la conviction intime.* Malassis, 1796, p. 3. ("[l]a preuve est un moyen déterminé, par la loi, pour établir la vérité d'un fait contesté.")

23 *Al-Adsani v the United Kingdom*, 35763/97, para. 47, 54, ECHR 2001-XI; judgment of 15 May 1986, *Marguerite Johnston v Chief Constable of the Royal Ulster Constabulary*, 222/84, EU:C:1986:206; judgment of 15 October 1987, *Union nationale des entraîneurs et cadres techniques professionnels du football (Unectef) v Georges Heylens and others*, 222/86, EU:C:1987:442; judgment of 3 December 1992, *Oleificio Borelli SpA v Commission of the European Communities*, C-97/91, EU:C:1992:491.

24 Judgment of 5 October 2004, *Bernhard Pfeiffer and Others v Deutsches Rotes Kreuz, Kreisverband Waldshut eV*, Joined Cases C-397/01 to C-403/01, ECLI:EU:C:2004:584, para. 111–118; Skouris, Vassilios. "Effet Utile Versus Legal Certainty: The Caselaw of the Court of Justice on the Direct Effect of Directives." *European Business Law Review*, vol. 17, no. 2, 2006, pp. 241–255; *Re* the ECHR, see Reiertsen, Michael. *Effective Domestic Remedies and the European Court of Human Rights: Applications of the European Convention on Human Rights Article 13*. Cambridge UP, 2022.

25 The motto is included in statutory law: Article 6, Déclaration des Droits de l'Homme et du Citoyen de 1789; Protocol no. 12 to the Convention for the Protection of Human Rights and Fundamental Freedoms, Rome, 4 December 2000, ETS 177, as well as RF 1:9.

26 Perelman, p. 41.

a correct concrete legal judgment, thus giving the rule full effect, the parties' allegations must be proven.[27]

In sum, evidence is a means with two separate aims: to let the parties be heard and to give the judge knowledge of the case for the legal rule to come into effect. The right to a fair hearing as the right to be heard implies a right to present evidence. The right of access to justice thus raises a requirement that justice be concrete in the sense of a correct legal judgment. 'The correct application of law' indeed does seem like an adequate description of what juridical justice may be. (With 'justice in concrete' is henceforth meant the just legal judgment,[28] i.e., rectitude in the concrete decision.)

The Aporias

In such a traditional positive law notion then, justice takes place when the law is correctly applied. Evidence serves the *indirect* purpose of giving the judge knowledge of the case so that substantive law may be correctly applied but also the *direct* purpose of letting the party be heard. Whereas the objective of the aforementioned survey was to find what may be understood by justice within law and what evidence has to do with it, in the following, I will introduce the theoretical background against which the positivity is problematized. The aim of this negativity[29] is antithetically the same as in the preceding section, namely, to ask how juridical justice may be understood. It has been held that the objective of law is to realize social harmony.[30] It has also been held that one aim of law is to create security for the subjects, in order that they can live within the constraints of law, freely in their "safe positions."[31] For this security, with the doctrine of access to justice, one aspires for some predictability as freedom from the haphazard of arbitrariness through the treating of equals equally, through the correct application of law to the case. The concern here is to present how the understanding of the relation between justice and evidence alters when evidence is understood as a language act and how this impacts the possibility of the correct judgment. This book argues that with approximative justice social harmony and safe positions may however indeed be possible.

27 35:1 CJP, 6 and 9 CPC; Lyotard, pt. 28.

28 *Re* 'legal judgment,' see Chapter 3.

29 Cf. Cisney, Vernon, W. *Deleuze and Derrida. Difference and the Power of the Negative.* Edinburgh UP, 2018.

30 Motulsky, Henri. *Principes d'une réalisation méthodique du droit privé. La théorie des éléments générateurs des droits subjectifs.* préf. Paul Roubier, Sirey, 1948; Dalloz, 1991, p. 9.

31 Cf. Vilhelm Lundstedt as in Ekelöf, P. O. et al. *Rättegång I.* 9th ed., Norstedts Juridik, 2016, p. 21, note 23.

In *The Differend* Lyotard questions the possibility of objective knowledge arguing that there can be no consensus regarding knowledge.[32] Therefore, there can also be no consensus regarding the just judgment. Lyotard consequently seeks a sense of justice which may take place in a fragmented world.[33] This question is perhaps even more acute today, especially within the sphere of the EU – despite, or perhaps because of, the ambitions of furthering harmonization. Based on Lyotard's and Derrida's theories of justice as presented in *The Differend* and *Force of Law* the study seeks to explore how juridical justice struggles to take form. Together, Lyotard and Derrida present four aporias against the correct judgment as some form of "bull's eye justice."[34] *Aporia* is an experience of no passage[35] and is understood here as an end to reason in the sense that reason cannot reach any definitive answer as to the correct judgment. The first three aporias are presented by Derrida in *Force of Law* and present an "inherent and ultimately irresolvable paradox."[36] Lyotard's differend is understood here to constitute a fourth aporia but differs from Derrida's in that the differend is not understood here as a matter of paradox. Derrida's aporias of justice are all also explicitly concerned with a tension between the *law* and justice,[37] whereas Lyotard rather concentrates on the interplay between *knowledge* and justice.

The first two aporias of justice are read here to concern the rule, whereas the latter two are understood as concerning the facts.[38] As this thesis studies evidence (upholding the distinction between matters of law and matters of fact) these two paradoxical impasses of justice will be presented superficially in order to introduce the main ideas of Derrida's theory that are built upon in this book. Some arguments that I present here may support an understanding of justice as a correct interpretation of a rule, and others will not. In the

32 Carroll, David. "Rephrasing the Political with Kant and Lyotard: From Aesthetic to Political Judgments." *Diacritics*, vol. 14, no. 3, 1984, (Special Issue on the Work of Jean-François Lyotard), p. 75; Plonowska Ziarek, Ewa. *An Ethics of Dissensus, Postmodernity, Feminism, and the Politics of Radical Democracy*. Stanford UP, 2001, p. 85.

33 "Consensus is a horizon that is never reached." (Lyotard, Jean-François. *The Postmodern Condition: A Report on Knowledge*. Translated by Geoff Bennington and Brian Massumi, Manchester UP, 1984, p. 61.) *Also* "Lyotard's concern is to suggest how justice is to be understood in a situation where social interaction cannot be experienced as the easy exchange of experiences between equal parties, where the position of the other remains always irreducibly other, incapable of being assumed by the one who speaks, and where the one who speaks occupies many places at once." (Barron, Anne. "Lyotard and the Problem of Justice." *Judging Lyotard*, edited by Benjamin Andrew, Routledge, 1992, p. 31.)

34 This expression is inspired by Kahneman, Daniel et al. *Noise*. Harper Collins, 2021.

35 Derrida, p. 946; Cornell, Drucilla. *The Philosophy of the Limit*. Routledge, 1992, p. 71.

36 Cornell, p. 118.

37 Derrida, p. 923; Gehring, Petra. "The Jurisprudence, of the 'Force of Law'." *Derrida and Law*, edited by Pierre Legrand, Ashgate, 2009, p. 119; Svenungsson, Jayne. "Justice in the Prophetic Tradition." *Eco-Ethica*, vol. 6, 2017, p. 145.

38 Cornell, pp. 133–134.

extent that the interpretation of a rule can be correct, one can claim that the interpretation of evidence may also be correct. But in this book, it is argued that 'correct' must then also be understood as an approximation.

Derrida's approach to the question of justice focusses on the contradictory tension between the need for rule and restriction on the one hand and the need for freedom, autonomy and responsibility on the other, for there to be justice and a just judgment. The very first aporia is found in the impossibility to apply a rule without first choosing the rule.[39] Before the rule is chosen it is suspended – there is a gap between the rule and its application.[40] There is always a subject who chooses the rule; even when the case is clear and is (on the verge of being) a mere calculation,[41] the rule to apply would nevertheless need to be chosen by a subject – a person with autonomy and responsibility.[42] The second aspect of this constitutes the second aporia regarding the rule, namely, that the rule must also be interpreted, it must be given sense.[43] This sense is given to the rule in relation to a concrete and singular case.[44] This, again, requires a subject who can assume responsibility for the interpretation. Had the rule been a matter of calculation it would nevertheless first need to be chosen and then (re)interpreted in relation to the particular case.[45]

Interpretation means attribution of sense – an attribution which could have been another. The deliberation as to which rule to apply and how to interpret 'it' is a moment of suspense, a gap between the rule and its interpretation and application;[46] that is between abstraction and passivity on the one hand and the concrete of action on the other – a gap which is overcome only by action. These aporias are particularly salient in hard cases, where there is no previously determined relation between a rule and a type of case: the case is therefore also undecidable[47] – and yet the decision must be made.[48] In the concluding chapters, we will return to Derrida's theory of justice as we discuss how to manage, when forming a judgment, the void and lack of solid foundation of which the four aporias are a result.

Derrida's third aporia shifts the focus onto the singularity of the case, and the relation between knowledge thereof and justice. Derrida reasons that a just judgment recognizes the case's singularity ("treat equal cases equally and *unequal cases unequally*"[49]), but as singularity is irreducible[50] and the

39 Derrida, p. 960; Poché, Fred. *Penser avec Derrida: Comprendre la déconstruction.* Chronique sociale, 2007, p. 104.
40 Derrida, pp. 952, 992.
41 Derrida, pp. 960–964.
42 Derrida, pp. 960–964.
43 Derrida, p. 960; Cornell, p. 134; Cisney, pp. 256–260.
44 Derrida, p. 964.
45 Derrida, p. 960; Poché, p. 104.
46 Gehring, p. 124.
47 Derrida, p. 962.
48 Derrida, p. 966.
49 P. 19, n. 8.
50 Derrida, pp. 965, 1023.

investigation into the case cannot be eternal, the decision that is the legal judgment limits what details may be considered. Therefore, the singularity of the case cannot be fully recognized.[51] With his third aporia, Derrida thus brings the attention to the circumstance that justice takes place through the means of a concrete judgment – if at all.[52] Derrida claims that the judgment is made in the "urgency" which requires the judgment to be made.[53] (One runs out of time.[54]) The decision is a cut[55] that separates not only the chosen interpretation of the rule from those not chosen but also puts an end to the investigations and deliberations as to the identity of the case.[56] The decision comes as a halt and blocks the horizon of knowledge – one cannot see any further into the specifics of the case.[57]

It is understood here that when the horizon is blocked a Lyotardian differend occurs – a differend as the negation of (the relevance of) alternative senses.[58] This builds on an understanding of the horizon as itself a delimitation to the perception of reality.[59] Referring to its Greek etymology, Derrida explains that a horizon is both an opening and the limit of the opening.[60] As such it gives a perspective, a cut, a slice, of what lays ahead – a delimitation of unlimited (endless) progression or expectation.[61] With horizon two things are therefore involved: the look-out-point and the view. The look-out-point at which the judge is standing in a civil proceeding is the question what to do, that is, the determination of the legal consequence (which requires that a rule is chosen, interpreted and then applied). This question in turn depends on the question what the case is about, which is another look-out-point, namely, the look-out-point of judicial fact-finding. It is from this look-out-point that the evidence is perceived. When the judge investigates the case, there is an

51 Derrida, p. 949; *see also* Legrand, Pierre. "On the Singularity of Law." *Harvard International Law Journal*, vol. 47, no. 2, Summer 2006, p. 526 (specifically), Clark, Timothy. "Derrida: A Pragmatics of Singularity." *The Poetics of Singularity: The Counter-Culturalist Turn in Heidegger, Derrida, Blanchot and the Later Gadamer*, Edinburgh UP, 2005, p. 126.

52 Cisney, p. 259.

53 *Re* the *déni de justice* because of judiciary unsusceptible to urgency, see for example, Bogdan, Michael. "The Brussels/Lugano lis pendens rule and the 'Italian torpedo'." *Scandinavian Studies in Law*, vol. 51, 2007, pp. 89–98; Kenny, David, and Rosemary Hennigan. "Choice-of-Court Agreements, the Italian Torpedo, and the Recast of the Brussels I Regulation." *International and Comparative Law Quarterly*, vol. 64, no. 1, Jan. 2015, pp. 197–210.

54 17:9:2 CJP.

55 Derrida, p. 963; Cisney, p. 258.

56 Ne bis in idem! *Re* the identity of the case, see Ekelöf, P. O. *Processuella grundbegrepp och allmänna processprinciper: några problem inom den allmänna processrättsläran*. P.A. Norstedts & Söners Förlag, 1956, pp. 86 ss.

57 Derrida, p. 966; Gehring, p. 124.

58 Lyotard, pts. 40, 147, 179, 180.

59 Derrida, p. 966.

60 Derrida, p. 967.

61 Derrida, p. 967; *see also* Derrida, Jacques. *L'Autre Cap*. Minuit, 1997, p. 32.

awareness of both of these look-out-points. To this we will return after having first explained the evidence as a language act.[62]

Just as Lyotard's differend is understood here in relation to Derrida's third aporia, so is the third aporia understood in relation to Lyotard's theory examining the conditions for knowledge. Like the horizon is an opening that allows for new discoveries, as well as restricts what may be perceived, Lyotard's epistemological conditions not only help create knowledge, but also rule out knowledge. (Therefore they cause differends.[63]) According to Lyotard, these are conditions under which human lives are lived[64] and in that sense it is not the fault of humans that conflict occurs. The conflict simply isn't really between humans but between what Lyotard calls genres of discourse, and what is here referred to as human practices.[65] Lyotard perceives of everything that takes place (i.e., words, events, facts) as a phrase,[66] that is, a linguistic – and thus social[67] – entity.[68] This aligns with Wittgenstein's understanding of language, where language is not used as a manner of transferring thoughts about reality to others, but the entirety of reality.[69] What makes Lyotard's theory so useful for the understanding of evidence is that it concerns the sense that is attached not only to words (which we already understand as linguistic entities) or body language, but moreover to other human behavior as well as other circumstances, facts of any kind. As language is social, it positions us (humans) in relation to each other and to the situations that occur. I will argue that when evidence is taken across jurisdictional borders, it is also taken across linguistic borders – and to them belong also social borders.

Conditions for Knowledge – Obstructions of the Horizon[70]

Lyotard presents five components which are understood here to condition knowledge. These components are the phrase, the genre of discourse, the stakes, the concatenation and the phrase regimen. In this section, I introduce

62 P. 56 and Chapter 5.

63 Gualandi, Alberto. *Lyotard.* 2nd ed., Les Belles Lettres, 2004, p. 34.

64 Lyotard, pt. 193; Cf. de Man, Paul. "The Epistemology of Metaphor." *Critical Inquiry*, vol. 5, no. 1, 1978, pp. 13–30; Lévy-Bruhl, Henri. *La Preuve judiciaire.* Essai de sociologie juridique, Marcel Rivière, 1963.

65 Lyotard, pt. 198; Barron, p. 32.

66 Cf. Bennington, Geoffrey. *Lyotard: Writing the Event.* Manchester UP and Columbia UP, 1988, pp. 123 ff, who translates the French *phrase* into 'sentence.' Douzinas and Warrington also use the word 'sentence.' (Douzinas, Costas, and Ronnie Warrington. "'A Well-Founded Fear of Justice': Law and Ethics in Postmodernity." *Law and Critique*, vol. II, no. 2, 1991, pp. 115–147.)

67 Lyotard, pt. 193; Gane, Nicholas. *Max Weber and Postmodern Theory: Rationalization Versus Re-enchantment.* Palgrave Macmillan, 2002.

68 The word used is 'universe,' Lyotard, pt. 4; Bennington, pp. 125 ff.

69 Wittgenstein, Ludwig. *Filosofiska undersökningar.* Translated by Anders Wedberg, Thales, 2012 (Philosophical Investigations).

70 Derrida, p. 967.

my take on the first three of these components and their impact on the question of juridical justice. In the following chapter, I present how I have used them in the comparative study which follows in the chapters below, based also on my understanding of the phrase regimen. I illustrate them using the Machete and the Little Sweetheart experiences. In the presentation of the comparative method in Chapter 4, I explain how the concepts of 'phrase regimen' and 'concatenation' have inspired my comparative analysis of civil procedural fact-finding.

Evidence is here understood as a *language act*. The term 'language act' is inspired by Lyotard's 'phrase'[71] and will be understood to encompass both evidentiary means and evidentiary fact. With 'language act' will be understood anything that takes place,[72] that is every event,[73] every occurrence,[74] every uttering, every *thing*. As such, the language act is undetermined:[75] it "comes along"[76] (takes place[77]) and may attract[78] a referent, a sense, an addressor and an addressee.[79] The referent is "what the [language act] is about."[80] (–What are you talking about? – The contract.) The sense is the signification of the referent.[81] (–What about the contract? – It means that Mr X agreed to sell me a fully functioning tractor.) The addressee is "that to which or addressed to which this is signified"[82] about the referent. (–Why are you showing me this? – Because you are a judge and I want you to judge that Mr X must deliver to me a fully functioning tractor in accordance with the contract.) The addressor is that "in the name of which this is signified."[83] (–I am telling you this because I want a fully functioning tractor delivered or I want my money back.) From this we can see that sense (the agreement to sell/purchase a tractor) is related to all other instances,[84] whereas they in turn are not directly related to each another. There is no person directly connected to the referent, but only through the sense. The sense therefore holds a central role in the phrase universe.[85] For this reason, as will be developed further, *sense* encompasses meaning, signification, significance, purpose and intention

71 Lyotard, pts. 18, 25, 94, 104, 113; Malpas, Simon. *Jean-François Lyotard*. Routledge, 2003, p. 63.
72 Lyotard, pts. 37, 51; Sawyer, Dylan. *Lyotard, Literature and the Trauma of the Differend*. Palgrave Macmillian, 2014, p. 26.
73 *Re* the word 'event,' see Bennington, p. 9.
74 Lyotard, pts. 99, 113.
75 Lyotard, pts. 93, 180 (indeterminate).
76 Lyotard, pt. 184.
77 Lyotard, pts. 37, 51; Sawyer, p. 26.
78 Lyotard, pt. 76.
79 Lyotard, pts. 18, 25, 111.
80 Lyotard, pts. 25, 104.
81 Lyotard, pt. 74.
82 Lyotard, pt. 25.
83 Lyotard, pt. 25.
84 Lyotard, pts. 18, 25, 111, 123, 137–140; Malpas, p. 63.
85 Lyotard, pt. 18.

(at least). The language act is not something that is sent from one to another; the addressor and the addressee are not sender and receiver of the language act.[86] The language act is a situation,[87] composed of the instances, which consequently make part of the language act. The instances may be several[88] and/or equivocal,[89] as the language act presents one or more phrase universes.[90] This means that it may be impossible to identify with certainty either the sense, the referent, the addressor or the addressee or several of the instances.

This is what happened in the Little Sweetheart case; it was not possible to determine the sense of the picture, different addressees attributed different senses to it and ended up in a quarrel about this. There was no quarrel as to the ethics of the picture which was not based upon the sense that had first been attributed to it. The sense thus determined the ethics. It may be noted in this context that this theory does not question the existence of facts *per se*; it is not towards facts that one should be sceptical,[91] but towards a consensus regarding their senses – i.e., what sense to attribute to them, what inferences to draw from them. As the expression 'language act' used here resembles Searle's *speech act* a quick note may be useful to uphold the distinction.[92] Whereas with Searle, the focus seems to be the performativity of language and enunciations, Lyotard "converts" *all* events into language acts, and thus sees everything as language rather than certain use of language as also events. The choice of the expression 'language act' is to also refer to the two meanings of act: action and document, as in event and thing – as anything that takes place, and which impacts or may be used in human communication to carry meaning and function.[93] With 'language act' will be meant here any

86 Lyotard, pt. 18.
87 Lyotard, pt. 115.
88 Lyotard, pt. 25.
89 Lyotard, pt. 111.
90 Lyotard, pt. 18.
91 Comp. Twining, Rethinking Evidence, pp. 100–103, and perhaps specifically, p. 2: "sceptical *about what?*"
92 Searle, John, P. "What Is a Speech Act?" *Perspectives in the Philosophy of Language: A Concise Anthology*, edited by Robert J. Stainton, Broadview Press, 2000 (1965), p. 258. *Re* the term 'language act,' *see also* Derrida, Jacques. *Sovereignties in Question: The Poetics of Paul Celan*. Fordham UP, 2005, p. 83, where it is used in a general descriptive manner including the performative aspect of Austin, John. *How To Do Things With Words*. Clarendon Press, 1975, p. 6, and Searle, "What Is a Speech Act?" above in this note. *See also*, Ricœur, Paul, and Jean-Pierre Changeux. *La Nature et la Règle: Ce qui nous fait penser*. Odile Jacob, 1998; Abel, Olivier. *Paul Ricœur, Jacques Ellul, Jean Carbonnier, Pierre Chaunu: Dialogues*. Labor et Fides, 2012, p. 26, *as well as* Ricœur, Paul. *Le Discours de l'action*. Edited by Catherine Goldenstein et Jean-Claude Monod, Fonds Ricœur, 2015, where the expressions '*acte de parole*' or '*acte de discours*' are used in translation of 'speech act,' with references made by Ricœur to Searle and Austin. *See however, also*, Villaverde, Marcelino Agís. *Knowledge and Practical Reason: Paul Ricœur's Way of Thinking*. LIT Verlag Münster, 2012, pp. 138 and 180, where the expression 'language act' is used.
93 Lyotard, pts. 50–51; Sawyer, p. 26.

occurrence which is given sense by and to humans. Both the evidence and the whole case are therefore seen as language acts.

As a means used to point out or understood as pointing out the reality of a contested fact,[94] the *evidentiary* language act is an ostensive language act.[95] Lyotard writes that the ostensive language act includes deictics[96] – understood as designators of singularity.[97] As such they "are designators of reality . . . designating their origin as an extra-linguistic permanence."[98] He then clarifies that what is pointed to is not permanent at all.[99] To this, and more importantly to Lyotard's understanding of reality, we will return later. I will however hold, paraphrasing Lyotard, that evidence points out a reality "outside" of law – an extra-legal (or non-legal) reality[100] – which in the subsumption of the judgment is legally qualified.[101] When a language act comes along, several *human practices* compete in giving it sense.[102] Legal subsumption is law as a human practice imposing itself on the language act, or the cluster of language acts[103] which together constitute the case, thereby determining the legal sense of the case and the case as legal. The term 'human practice' is used to refer to an idea including such components as idiom,[104] mass of knowledge, discipline, library, vocabulary, semantics, etymology, habitual activity, social organism,[105] culture,[106] etc. A human practice is therefore understood as a genre of discourse within which knowledge is created and relativized.[107] Examples of human practices touched upon in this thesis are EU law, civil procedure, civil procedural fact-finding and non-legal[108] human practices

94 P. 21, n. 22.

95 Lyotard, pts. 28, 41, 49, 53, 54, 243.

96 For an analysis of the terms 'ostensive,' 'deictic' and 'demonstrative': Chung, Kyung-Sook. *Space in Tense: The Interaction of Tense, Aspect, Evidentiality and Speech Acts in Korean.* John Benjamins Publishing, 2012, p. 3.

97 I will use the term 'ostensive' to refer to a language act which contains (explicitly or not) a deictic such as *I, here, now.* (Lyotard, pt. 50, *also* pt. 73.)

98 Lyotard, pt. 50.

99 Lyotard, pt. 50.

100 Cf. Leclerc, Olivier. *Le Juge et l'expert: Contribution à l'étude des rapports entre le droit et la science.* L.G.D.J., 2005, p. 199.

101 Motulsky, Henri. "Prolégomènes pour un futur Code de procédure civile: la consécration des principes directeurs du procès civil par le décret du 9 septembre 1971." *Écrits, études et notes de procédure civile.* Dalloz, 2010, p. 293.

102 Lyotard, pt. 234.

103 Lyotard, pts. 82, 181. *See also* Welamson, Lars. "Civil - och straffprocessrätt 1980–1987." *Svensk juristtidning*, 1989, p. 521.

104 Lyotard, pt. 12.

105 Luhmann, Niklas. "Law as a Social System." *Northwestern University Law Review,* vol. 83, no. 1 & 2, 1988–1989, p. 140.

106 Geertz, Clifford. "Common Sense as a Cultural System." *The Antioch Review*, vol. 67, no. 4, Geertz at Antioch (Fall 2009), pp. 770–790.

107 The Postmodern Condition Lyotard, Jean-François. *The Postmodern Condition: A Report on Knowledge.* Translated by George Bennington and Brian Massumi, Machester UP, 1984, pp. 8–10; Malpas, pp. 20–21.

108 Luhmann, Niklas. *Law As a Social System.* OUP, 2004.

such as disciplines of science. Like a genre of discourse, a human practice can also be categorized as ontological,[109] logical,[110] dialogical,[111] of historic inquiry,[112] cognitive,[113] narrative,[114] tradition[115] etc., and they link phrases by imposing onto phrases its stake – the finality.[116] This is how they attribute sense to language acts.

What Lyotard refers to as the stakes, or the finalities,[117] of the genres of discourse are here referred to as *purpose-points*. From the perspective of the purpose-point the language act will be seen, and it is therefore a look-out-point which opens to the horizon, as mentioned earlier. The language act is understood and given sense in relation to the purpose-point of the "winning" human practice.[118] The purpose-point is the innate teleology of each human practice. Like a magnet the purpose-point will "turn" the language act so that the instance of the sense will face the purpose-point.[119] Because of their specific finalities, human practices are heterogenous – meaning they are untranslatable from one to the other.[120] The term 'purpose-point' is chosen to express the perspective which is both a point of departure and a destination for understanding and communication.

Little Sweetheart and the War of Human Practices

Following the theory here presented, the quarrel regarding the determination of the picture called Little Sweetheart, was a quarrel between different human practices, or between persons who apply different human practices to determine how the picture should be understood – what sense to attribute to it. This dispute was therefore, in the words of Lyotard a "civil war of language."[121] The Little Sweetheart case illustrates that several scientific areas of expertise may have contradicting views on how to determine a language act. Each human practice refers back to a large collection of research, theory and narrative, which may be illustrated with the library: the collection of books resulting from the research and specific to it, relevant for further research and thus circulation, recreation, of the theories, narrative and knowledge.[122] The

109 Lyotard, pt. 127.
110 Lyotard, pt. 129.
111 Lyotard, pt. 106.
112 Lyotard, pt. 76.
113 Lyotard, pt. 85.
114 Lyotard, pt. 89.
115 Cabbala as a tradition is mentioned as a genre of discourse, Lyotard, p. 106.
116 "The stakes bound up with a genre of discourse determine the linkings between phrases." (Lyotard, pt. 148, *see also* pts. 181, 183, 219; May, Todd. *The Political Philosophy of Poststructuralist Anarchism*. Penn State UP, 1994, pp. 109–110.)
117 Lyotard, pt. 40, for example.
118 Lyotard, pts. 181, 186, 191, 234.
119 Douzinas, Warrington, p. 122.
120 Lyotard, pt. 256.
121 Lyotard, pts. 198, 201.
122 Lyotard, pts. 234, 253, 260.

human practice is thus closed to itself[123] and will not be able to consider what is not relevant for its purpose-point. This means that each judgment, as a cognizance of reasons and counter-reasons,[124] refers to both previous judgments and the future, the finality of the purpose-point.[125] The horizon of knowledge is understood here to consist of a muddle of human practices, each with their own purpose-points.[126] The judge stands at the look-out-point of the human practice of law, looking to legally qualify[127] the relevant case as a slice of this muddle. In an eddying whirl, the human practice serves the purpose-point with relevant material which delivers the criteria to determine what is and what is not: is the picture in the children's book an expression of racism (in which case it is connected to theft of human beings, slavery and in general the worst of humanity, knowledge of which is created and spread in the aim of liberating human beings alive today from the shackles that were placed on their ancestors) or is it a pedagogical depiction which strengthens toddlers' innate love and curiosity (in which case it is connected to the psychology and pedagogy of toddlers aiming to help develop strong healthy individuals who possess the capacity to live at peace with one another)?

Whereas this may be understood as a war between human practices where the humans are mere pawns, lacking all personal responsibility,[128] it also risks leaving the judge in a state of agony where caught in the crossfire they nevertheless must render a judgment.[129] A correct and *therefore* just judgment. The power of those other human practices to render their judgments by imposing themselves on the case, to let them determine the case, is pushed back as the legal judgment is made; the horizon is blocked. This leads to the question how there can be a correct judgment when the facts are all interpreted and valued differently within different human practices (even if they are all cognitive). The differend is therefore held here to be the fourth aporia of justice. As noted earlier, the human practices and their purpose-points determine the sense of what takes place and is said in any situation.[130] As will be developed in relation to the comparative method later,[131] the sense of each language act is determined, as in delimited, in the following language

123 In *The Differend*, Lyotard speaks of genres of discourse and phrase regimen as heterogenous, *for example* pp. xi, xii, xiv, pts. 40, 77, 80, 222, 224. Cf. Luhmann, Niklas. "Operational Closure and Structural Coupling: The Differentiation of the Legal System." *Cardozo Law Review*, vol. 13, no. 5, Mar 1992, p. 1437.
124 P. 18, n. 1.
125 Consider Spanish *por* and *para*; both are involved in the formation of the judgment.
126 The muddle of human practices is understood here as "life as polycontexturality," as in Günther, Gotthard. "Life as Polycontexturality." *Wirklichkeit und Reflexion*, (first published in) edited by H. Fahrenbach, Festschrift für Walter Schulz, Pfullingen 1973, pp. 187–210, http://vordenker.de/ggphilosophy/gg_life_as_polycontexturality.pdf, 2014, p. 4.
127 Motulsky, Prolégomènes, p. 293.
128 Lyotard, p. 11 *Prétexte*, pts. 90, 151, 188.
129 Derrida, p. 945; Gehring, p. 128.
130 Lyotard, for example, pt. 181.
131 Chapter 4.

act link.[132] The final judgment of the procedure, the legal judgment, will be the last link in a particular chain of judgments. These links will concern the appraisal and interpretation of the evidentiary language acts, the claims and allegations, but also, of course, decisions regarding the procedure itself. If one were to adhere to linear thinking, one would consider the interpretation and application of the substantive law rule to follow, because its application takes place at a later stage in time. The idea of the purpose-point contradicts such chronology in thinking, it upsets the linearity of Chronos by creating a crochet-like texture of time.[133]

Linking is done onto the sense of the language act, and when linking happens, all other possible senses are disregarded. A differend is the circumstance that these negated interpretations represent other perspectives, other worldviews; other perceptions and experiences which are not presented, expressed or (re)cognized.[134] Negating them constitutes an injustice,[135] wherefore every judgment regarding how to interpret a language act is unjust. There can be no just judgment, judging is unjust.[136] These depressing impasses undeniably put a damper on the justice project. In the light of this, Derrida's hesitation to speak under the title "the Possibility of Justice" is understandable.[137] Also the Swedish legal realists' mocking the entire idea of justice as a legal matter may seem more reasonable than depressed, that is, more realistic than pessimistic. As in legal proceedings, the decision-making is in the hands of the judge,[138] anxiety risks imposing itself, paralyzing the whole enterprise. If justice and law are from a formalistic understanding the same,[139] it's the entire enterprise of law that risks being petrified. Fortunately, both Derrida

132 Cf. Lyotard, pt. 18; *see however* Gearey, Adam. *Law and Aesthetics.* Bloomsbury Publishing Plc, 2001, p. 60, note 7.

133 Cisney, pp. 177 ss. In this, Derrida's justice as deconstruction also coincides with the theory of the differend.

134 Lyotard, 40; Kant, Immanuel. *Kritik av det rena förnuftet.* Translated by Jeanette Emt, Thales, 2004. (Kant, Pure Reason), A68/B93. For a comment on Lyotard's reading of Kant in *The Differend, see* Piché, Claude. "The Philosopher-Artist: A Note on Lyotard's Reading of Kant." *Research in Phenomenology*, vol. 22, 1992, pp. 152–160; Carroll; Rasch, William. "In Search of the Lyotard Archipelago, or: How to Live with Paradox and Learn to like It." *New German Critique*, no. 61, 1994, pp. 55–75.

135 Cf. Ingram who equates the differend to an injustice. (Ingram, David. "The Kantianism of Arendt and Lyotard." *Judging Lyotard*, edited by Benjamin Andrew, Routledge, 1992, p. 137.)

136 Lyotard, p. xi. "In short, the differend is the inevitable precipitate of any system or any concept of self that attempts to impose a necessary order upon the contingency of events." (Dunn, Allen. "A Tyranny of Justice: The Ethics of Lyotard's Differend." *Boundary 2*, vol. 20, no. 1, (Duke UP), 1993, p. 196.)

137 Derrida, p. 920.

138 Expressed like that, it is a tautology – and yet, the fact is not self-evident. It is explored and explained in Kennedy, Duncan. *A Critique of Adjudication: Fin de Siècle.* Harvard UP, 1997. *Also*, Derrida, p. 961.

139 Pattaro, Enrico. "From Hägerström to Ross and Hart." *Ratio Juris*, vol. 22, no. 4, Dec. 2009, p. 538; Cf. Taruffo, Michele. "Notes for a Theory of Justice." *Justice, Morality and Society, A Tribute to Alexander Peczenik*, edited by Aulis Aarnio, Juristförlaget i Lund, 1997, p. 400; Derrida, p. 947.

and Lyotard offer a way forward, a move out of the freeze.[140] And both offer paradoxical solutions, equally congenial to their initial negativity: "Justice is an experience of the impossible. A will, a desire, a demand for justice whose structure wouldn't be an experience of aporia would have no chance to be what it is, namely, a call for justice."[141]

Bibliography

Abel, Olivier. *Paul Ricoeur, Jacques Ellul, Jean Carbonnier, Pierre Chaunu: Dialogues*. Labor et Fides, 2012.

Austin, John. *How to Do Things with Words*. Clarendon Press, 1975.

Barron, Anne. "Lyotard and the Problem of Justice." *Judging Lyotard*, edited by Benjamin Andrew, Routledge, 1992.

Bennington, Geoffrey. *Lyotard: Writing the Event*. Manchester UP and Columbia UP, 1988.

Bentham, Jeremy. *Rationale of Judicial Evidence*. Edited by J. S. Mill, Vol. I, Hunt and Clarke, 1827.

Bogdan, Michael. "The Brussels/Lugano lis pendens rule and the 'Italian torpedo'." *Scandinavian Studies in Law*, vol. 51, 2007, pp. 89–98.

Bull, Thomas. "Rättighetsskyddet i Högsta förvaltningsdomstolen." *Svensk juristtidning*, 2017, p. 216.

Carroll, David. "Rephrasing the Political with Kant and Lyotard: From Aesthetic to Political Judgments." *Diacritics*, vol. 14, no. 3, 1984, Special Issue on the Work of Jean-François Lyotard.

Chung, Kyung-Sook. *Space in Tense: The Interaction of Tense, Aspect, Evidentiality and Speech Acts in Korean*. John Benjamins Publishing, 2012.

Cisney, Vernon, W. *Deleuze and Derrida. Difference and the Power of the Negative*. Edinburgh UP, 2018.

Clark, Timothy. "Derrida: A Pragmatics of Singularity." *The Poetics of Singularity: The Counter-Culturalist Turn in Heidegger, Derrida, and the Later Gadamer*, Edinburgh UP, 2005, p. 126.

Cornell, Drucilla. *The Philosophy of the Limit*. Routledge, 1992.

de Man, Paul. "The Epistemology of Metaphor." *Critical Inquiry*, vol. 5, no. 1, 1978, pp. 13–30.

Derrida, Jacques. "Force de loi: le Fondement mystique de l'autorité." *Cardozo Law Review*, vol. 11, nos. 5–6, Jul./Aug. 1990, pp. 949–1046.

Derrida, Jacques. *L'Autre Cap*. Minuit, 1997.

Derrida, Jacques. *Sovereignties in Question: The Poetics of Paul Celan*. Fordham UP, 2005.

Douzinas, Costas, and Ronnie Warrington. "'A Well-Founded Fear of Justice': Law and Ethics in Postmodernity." *Law and Critique*, vol. II, no. 2, 1991, pp. 115–147.

Dunn, Allen. "A Tyranny of Justice: The Ethics of Lyotard's Differend." *Boundary 2*, vol. 20, no. 1 (Duke UP), 1993.

Ekelöf, P. O. *Processuella grundbegrepp och allmänna processprinciper: några problem inom den allmänna processrättsläran*. P.A. Norstedts & Söners Förlag, 1956.

Ekelöf, P. O. "Access to Justice." *Svensk juristtidning*, 1981, pp. 109–120.

Ekelöf, P. O. *Rättegång II*. 8th ed., Norstedts Juridik, 2010.

Ekelöf, P. O. et al. *Rättegång I*. 9 ed., Norstedts Juridik, 2016.

140 Cornell, pp. 71, 118.

141 Cf. Derrida, p. 947; Gehring, p. 126. Cf. Gearey, p. 51.

Euvrard, Jean-Louis. "Aristote." *Dictionnaire de la Justice*, edited by Loïc Cadiet, PUF, 2004.
Fricero, Natalie. "Garanties de nature procédureale: équité, publicité, célérité et laïcité." *Droit et pratique de la procédure civile – Droit interne et européen*, (2017/2018), 9th ed., edited by Serge Guinchard. Dalloz, 2016, 212.21, pp. 814–815.
Gane, Nicholas. *Max Weber and Postmodern Theory: Rationalization Versus Re-enchantment*. Palgrave Macmillan, 2002.
Gearey, Adam. *Law and Aesthetics*. Bloomsbury Publishing Plc, 2001.
Geertz, Clifford. "Common Sense as a Cultural System." *The Antioch Review*, vol. 67, no. 4 (Geertz at Antioch Fall) 2009, pp. 770–790.
Gehring, Petra. "The Jurisprudence, of the 'Force of Law'." *Derrida and Law*, edited by Pierre Legrand, Ashgate, 2009.
Gualandi, Alberto. *Lyotard*. 2nd ed., Les Belles Lettres, 2004.
Ingram, David. "The Kantianism of Arendt and Lyotard." *Judging Lyotard*, edited by Benjamin Andrew, Routledge, 1992.
Kahneman, Daniel et al. *Noise*. Harper Collins, 2021.
Kant, Immanuel. *Kritik av det rena förnuftet*. Translated by Jeanette Emt, Thales, 2004.
Kennedy, Duncan. *A Critique of Adjudication: Fin de Siècle*. Harvard UP, 1997.
Kenny, David, and Rosemary Hennigan. "Choice-of-Court Agreements, the Italian Torpedo, and the Recast of the Brussels I Regulation." *International and Comparative Law Quarterly*, vol. 64, no. 1, Jan. 2015, pp. 197–210.
Key, Ellen. *Folkbildningsarbetet särskilt med hänsyn till skönhetssinnets odling*. K. W. Appelbergs boktryckeri, 1906, http://runeberg.org/folkbildn/0027.html. Accessed 18 Sep. 2021.
Leclerc, Olivier. *Le Juge et l'expert: Contribution à l'étude des rapports entre le droit et la science*. L.G.D.J., 2005.
Legrand, Pierre. "On the Singularity of Law." *Harvard International Law Journal*, vol. 47, no. 2, Summer 2006.
Lévy-Bruhl, Henri. *La Preuve judiciaire*. Essai de sociologie juridique. Marcel Rivière, 1963.
Luhmann, Niklas. "Law as a Social System." *Northwestern University Law Review*, vol. 83, nos. 1 & 2, 1988–1989.
Luhmann, Niklas. "Operational Closure and Structural Coupling: The Differentiation of the Legal System." *Cardozo Law Review*, vol. 13, no. 5, Mar. 1992, p. 1437.
Luhmann, Niklas. *Law as a Social System*. OUP, 2004.
Lyotard, Jean-François. *The Differend – Phrases in Dispute*. Translated by Georges Van Den Abbeele, University of Minnesota Press, 1988.
Lyotard, Jean-François. *The Postmodern Condition: A Report on Knowledge*. Translated by Geoff Bennington and Brian Massumi, Manchester UP, 1984.
Lyotard, Jean-François. *The Differend – Phrases in Dispute*. Translated by Georges Van Den Abbeele, University of Minnesota Press, 1988.
Malpas, Simon. *Jean-François Lyotard*. Routledge, 2003.
May, Todd. *The Political Philosophy of Poststructuralist Anarchism*. Penn State UP, 1994.
Mindus, Patricia. *A Real Mind: The Life and Work of Axel Hägerström*. Springer Science & Business Media, 2009.
Motulsky, Henri. *Principes d'une réalisation méthodique du droit privé. La théorie des éléments générateurs des droits subjectifs*. préf. Paul Roubier, Sirey, 1948; Dalloz, 1991.
Motulsky, Henri. "Le droit naturel dans la pratique jurisprudentielle: le respect des droits de la défense en procédure civile." *Écrits, études et notes de procédure civile*. Dalloz, 2010.

Motulsky, Henri. "Prolégomènes pour un futur Code de procédure civile: la consécration des principes directeurs du procès civil par le décret du 9 septembre 1971." *Écrits, études et notes de procédure civile*. Dalloz, 2010.
Olivecrona, Karl. "The Legal Theories of Axel Hägerström and Vilhelm Lundstedt." *Scandinavian Studies in Law*, vol. 3, 1959.
Pattaro, Enrico. "From Hägerström to Ross and Hart." *Ratio Juris*, vol. 22, no. 4, Dec. 2009.
Perelman, Chaïm. *Justice et raison*. Editions de l'Université de Bruxelles, 1972.
Piché, Claude. "The Philosopher-Artist: A Note on Lyotard's Reading of Kant." *Research in Phenomenology*, vol. 22, 1992, pp. 152–160.
Plonowska Ziarek, Ewa. *An Ethics of Dissensus, Postmodernity, Feminism, and the Politics of Radical Democracy*. Stanford UP, 2001.
Poché, Fred. *Penser avec Derrida: Comprendre la déconstruction*. Chronique sociale, 2007.
Rainey, Bernadette et al. *The European Convention on Human Rights*. 7th ed., Oxford UP, 2017.
Rasch, William. "In Search of the Lyotard Archipelago, or: How to Live with Paradox and Learn to Like It." *New German Critique*, no. 61, 1994, pp. 55–75.
Reiertsen, Michael. *Effective Domestic Remedies and the European Court of Human Rights: Applications of the European Convention on Human Rights Article 13*. CUP, 2022.
Ricœur, Paul. *Le Discours de l'action*. Edited by Catherine Goldenstein et Jean-Claude Monod. Fonds Ricœur, 2015.
Ricœur, Paul, and Jean-Pierre Changeux. *La Nature et la Règle: Ce qui nous fait penser*. Odile Jacob, 1998.
Sawyer, Dylan. *Lyotard, Literature and the Trauma of the Differend*. Palgrave Macmillan, 2014.
Searle, John P. "What Is a Speech Act?" *Perspectives in the Philosophy of Language: A Concise Anthology*, edited by Robert J. Stainton, Broadview Press, 2000 (1965).
Settem, Ola Johan. *Applications of the 'Fair Hearing' Norm in ECHR Article 6(1) to Civil Proceedings: With Special Emphasis on the Balance Between Procedural Safeguards and Efficiency*. Springer, 2015, p. 350.
Skouris, Vassilios. "Effet Utile Versus Legal Certainty: The Caselaw of the Court of Justice on the Direct Effect of Directives." *European Business Law Review*, vol. 17, no. 2, 2006, pp. 241–255.
Svenungsson, Jayne. "Justice in the Prophetic Tradition." *Eco-Ethica*, vol. 6, 2017, pp. 135–149.
Taruffo, Michele. "Notes for a Theory of Justice." *Justice, Morality and Society, A Tribute to Alexander Peczenik*, edited by Aulis Aarnio, Juristförlaget i Lund, 1997.
Twining, William. *Theories of Evidence: Bentham and Wigmore*. Weidenfeld & Nicolson, 1984.
Twining, William. *Rethinking Evidence: Exploratory Essays*. 2nd ed., Cambridge University Press, 2006.
Villaverde, Marcelino Agís. *Knowledge and Practical Reason: Paul Ricoeur's Way of Thinking*. LIT Verlag Münster, 2012.
Villenave. *Des Jurés et de la conviction intime*. Malassis, 1796.
Welamson, Lars. "Civil-och straffprocessrätt 1980–1987." *Svensk juristtidning*, 1989, pp. 401–456.
Westen, Peter. *Speaking of Equality: An Analysis of the Rhetorical Force of 'Equality' in Moral and Legal Discourse*. Princeton UP, 2014.
Wittgenstein, Ludwig. *Filosofiska undersökningar*. Translated by Anders Wedberg. Thales, 2012 (Philosophical Investigations).

Chapter 3

Justice as Navigation

Introduction

Lyotard's skepticism towards the possibility of justice is founded in the violence of the discourse towards the occurrence, the case, the language act.[1] Lyotard may be said to share the negation of the possibility of an absolute and objective justice with Derrida (as well as with many of their predecessors[2]). We find in Lyotard a tension between the personal responsibility of the judge and their limited room to maneuver. He rejects the possibility of objectivity on account of the perpetual war[3] between different perspectives and their contexts, namely, what is here referred to as purpose-points and human practices. Lyotard's emphasis on the sharing of senses between the interlocutors raises a demand that the judge assume the responsibility to (properly) listen.[4] That which creates the paradox also offers a way forward. A paradox is also found in Derrida. As the judgment must be passed for justice to be rendered,[5] an urgency occurs demanding that the meditation on the sense of the case be interrupted.[6] At an acute moment, the judge must assume the power to cut, divide, separate what is from what is not. The judge must go from listening to acting.[7] Derrida emphasizes the personal responsibility of the judge.[8] The responsibility must be taken freely wherefore it is also a reason

1 Lyotard, Jean-François. *The Differend – Phrases in Dispute*. Translated by Georges Van Den Abbeele, University of Minnesota Press, 1988/Lyotard, Jean-François. *Le Différend*. Éditions de minuit. 1983, for example, pts. 93 and 263.

2 Chapter 2. *See also* Douzinas, Costas, and Adam Gearey. *Critical Jurisprudence: The Political Philosophy of Justice*. Hart Publishing, 2005.

3 Lyotard, pt. 198.

4 Lyotard, pt. 236.

5 Passing no judgment is *déni de justice*. (Derrida, Jacques. "Force de loi: le Fondement mystique de l'autorité." *Cardozo Law Review*, vol. 11, nos. 5–6, Jul/Aug. 1990, p. 966.)

6 Derrida, p. 966.

7 Poché, Fred. *Penser avec Derrida: Comprendre la déconstruction*. Chronique sociale, 2007, pp. 100–107.

8 The personal responsibility is more explicitly elaborated in Derrida, Jacques. *Politics of Friendship*. Verso, 1997, pp. 250 ss, as well as in Chapter 9 below. *See also* Cisney, Vernon, W. *Deleuze and Derrida. Difference and the Power of the Negative*. Edinburgh UP, 2018, pp. 256 ff; Poché, pp. 101–103.

DOI: 10.4324/9781003495383-3

why justice cannot be absolute and concrete.[9] It can however be approximative; it can involve the addressing of one's self toward the person who is being judged, or whose situation is under judgment[10] and one can assume the responsibility to listen and to attempt to be just towards the other and thus being just towards thinking.[11]

The access to justice doctrine connects to the traditional understanding of evidence according to which evidence is a means to truth[12] and knowledge.[13] As a means, evidence is a function, namely, that of giving knowledge about something else. The evidence itself is therefore only a stepping-stone on the way to what matters: the object of proof. What one does not know is the object of proof, whereas the proof itself is presented as apparent – something apparent which makes the obscure visible.[14] This means that when an inference is made based on evidence a connection is seen between them – a connection which allows one to see the object of proof thanks to the evidence. This connection over-bridges a gap.[15] This gap creates a problem which is particularly severe when evidence is taken across jurisdictional borders in the hope to increase access to justice across those borders. The previous chapter illustrates that the possibility for evidence to give the judge knowledge of the case is obstructed by the multiple senses that may be attributed to an evidentiary language act. In this chapter, a solution to the conundrum of achieving just judgments despite the lack of foundation is suggested.

The idea of common sense is central to approximative justice. One reason for this is the political ambition to give the citizens of the EU a "common sense of justice."[16] That aim is understood here to concern a shared *sense of justice* in the EU, as a feeling of what is just, as the German *Rechtsgefühl*, and

9 Perelman, Chaïm. *Justice et raison*. Editions de l'Université de Bruxelles, 1972; *see also* Cisney, p. 259.
10 Derrida, p. 923.
11 Lyotard, p. xii, pts. 202, 234, 236.
12 Villenave. *Des Jurés et de la conviction intime*. Malassis, 1796.
13 There is traditionally a distinction between truth and knowledge, via language, but this distinction is dissolved as I understand the theory of Lyotard in *The Differend*, through the idea of the *phrase*. My own adaptation ('language act') indeed considers this dissolution.
14 Etymologically, *evidence* stems from Latin *evidens*, meaning "obvious, apparent," in turn from *ex* and *videre*. Only from the 14th C, was the detour meaning of *means* added (to the English word): "appearance from which inferences may be drawn." "evidence, n." *OED Online*, Oxford University Press, September 2021, www.oed.com/view/Entry/65368; "Evidence." *Merriam-Webster.com Dictionary*, Merriam-Webster, https://www.merriam-webster.com/dictionary/evidence. Both accessed 14 Nov. 2021. If evidence is seen as possibly false, it either hinges on or becomes itself a matter of criminal law. In criminal procedure both trustworthiness and reliability of evidence are central concerns; this book hopes to contribute to the understanding of these matters in administrative, criminal or civil procedure by bringing the attention to the cross-border influence on those assessments. *See also* p. 117, n. 48 (in fine).
15 Lyotard, p. 123; Derrida, p. 953.
16 Chapter 1.

Swedish *rättskänsla*.[17] (It could of course also be read as a *common sense* of justice, as in commonsensical justice – and sometimes it might be.) Interestingly, the Scandinavian legal realists also understood of the term 'justice' an expression of a feeling void of any meaning wherefore it also lacks all argumentative power.[18] Lyotard may be said to agree on the point that justice is not a cognitive ontological matter: a judgment is validated as just "ethically by a feeling."[19]

Another importance of the expression 'common sense' in this work is the decisive role that the sharing of senses plays in communication and so for the possibility of a party to be heard – which happens when the addressee and addressor share the same idiom. Not only does the European access to justice doctrine presuppose the right to be heard for there to be a fair trial, but also in Lyotard's theory of justice is being heard imperative to avoid that a wrong be committed. For this, the sense of a language act must be able to be recovered in the idiom of the court. We therefore need an understanding of what makes such a sharing of senses possible – idiom being only a part of what determines the commonly shared sense of a language act. Our comprehension of 'common sense' is developed with the help of Patricia Cochran's *Common Sense and Legal Judgment*[20] where the references to common sense made in legal judgments are analyzed based on the theories of Thomas Reid, Antonio Gramsci and Hannah Arendt.

Judgment

Before discussing the just judgment, the word 'judgment' will be developed. The term 'judgment' is here distinguished from 'legal judgment.' With 'legal judgment' I mean the final judgment made in court after a court proceeding. The legal judgment is traditionally understood to consist of two stages: the establishment of the facts and the deciding of the legal consequence.[21] In

17 Lyotard, pts. 41, 181.

18 Ross, Alf. *On Law and Justice*. University of California Press, 1959, Chapter 12, On Justice; Pattaro, Enrico. "From Hägerström to Ross and Hart." *Ratio Juris*, vol. 22, no. 4, Dec. 2009, pp. 532–48; Mindus, Patricia. *A Real Mind: The Life and Work of Axel Hägerström*. Springer Science & Business Media, 2009, pp. 145, 154.

19 Lyotard, pts. 41, 181.

20 Cochran, Patricia. *Common Sense and Legal Judgment, Community Knowledge, Political Power, and Rhetorical Practice*. McGill-Queen's UP, 2017.

21 There may be other decisions which would justly be referred to as legal; they are, however, in this book not referred to as 'legal judgments'. Sometimes, the terms 'judicial decision-making' or 'adjudication' are used as synonyms of 'formation of a legal judgment'. However, both these alternative terms are used to emphasize the future (involving, sometimes, an action) that is the aim of the legal judgment as opposed to the internal mental process of linking two language acts. The distinction here held is found, albeit not as absolute correlates, in Swedish procedural terminology, distinguishing between *dom* (*legal judgment*) on the one hand and *beslut* and *slutligt beslut* (two types of *decisions*) on the other in CJP 17:1; and the general

this book the legal judgment is the concrete, tangible[22] outcome of the case, meaning that it is through the legal judgment that justice may take place. It is the imposition of the human practice of law on (the language act that is) the case, and in this imposition, the law qualifies the case legally.[23]

'Judgment' is used here to refer to any equation of one to another (a = b[24]). This is therefore an internal process of a human faculty.[25] It takes place through connecting two language acts by equating their sense;[26] where one singular instance is seen as being equal to previously perceived instances which have been equated with a particular word or concept.[27] The just judgment as the correct application is the correct answer to the question: is this or is this not equal to previously decided cases with the application of the rule?[28] Any judgment, legal or not, is made in relation to the past and to the future.[29] Like the legal rule, also the cognitive evidentiary language acts are understood on the basis of what has already been understood,[30] and in this process facts are established in relation to language. The language acts are also given a sense in accordance with the achieving of the purpose-point of the human practice; the purpose-point and the human practice impose themselves on the phrase in the establishment of the reality which is therefore a matter also of the future.[31] The criteria of the legal rule cannot help to determine however, whether the new single case is 'equal': that depends on the single case. What must be determined with the "fresh judgment"[32] is what this fresh case is.[33] Is it or is it not equal?

judgment in 40:7:3 CJP (*omdöme*) which is understood to correspond with the internal judgment. (Kant, Immanuel. *Kritik av det rena förnuftet*. Translated by Jeanette Emt, Thales, 2004. (Kant, Pure Reason), A68/B93.)

22 The Stockholm Programme – An open and secure Europe serving and protecting citizens, OJ C 115, 4.5.2010, p. 4.

23 12 CPC; Motulsky, Henri. "Prolégomènes pour un futur Code de procédure civile: la consécration des principes directeurs du procès civil par le décret du 9 septembre 1971." *Écrits, études et notes de procédure civile*. Dalloz, 2010, p. 293.

24 Frege, Gottlob. "On Sense and Nominatum." *The Philosophy of Language*, edited by A. P. Martinich, translated by Herbert Feigl, 2nd ed., OUP, 1990, p. 190; Lyotard, Jean-François. *Discourse, Figure*. Translated by Antony Hudekand Mary Lydon, University of Minnesota Press, 2011, pp. 103 ff.

25 Lyotard, p. 168; Kant, Immanuel. *Kritik av omdömeskraften*. Translated by Sven-Olov Wallenstein, Thales, 2003. (Kant, Critique of Judgment), § 40.

26 Chapter 2.

27 Kant, Pure Reason, A68/B93.

28 Kant, Pure Reason, A68/B93.

29 Kant, Pure Reason, A68/B93; Lyotard, pts. 155, 156, 160.

30 Kant, Pure Reason, A68/B93.

31 Lyotard, pt. 88: "Reality is not a matter of the absolute eyewitness, but a matter of the future."

32 Derrida, p. 961, quoting Stanley Fish in his article "Force." *Doing What Comes Naturally: Change, Rhetoric, and the Practice of Theory in Literary and Legal Studies*. Duke UP, 1989. *See also* Cornell, Drucilla. *The Philosophy of the Limit*. Routledge, 1992, p. 120.

33 Cf. 35:1 CJP. *See also* Gearey, Adam. *Law and Aesthetics*. Bloomsbury Publishing Plc, 2001, p. 61.

This is where the archipelago is illustrative.[34] For the judgment of a = b? is not binary.[35] The case to be subsumed under the legal rule consists of a cluster of language acts.[36] Each language act (evidence, allegations) contributes with one or more possible senses.[37] The sense or senses of each language act must be determined, which as noted, is done in relation to and under the constraints of the human practices and their purpose-points (it is also done under the constraints of the communicatory structure, which is the last condition for knowledge considered in this book and will be developed in the following chapter). As the Little Sweetheart case however shows this is not enough of an answer, since several human practices compete in attributing sense to a language act.[38] According to what criteria is the case then to be determined?[39] Each human practice may be correct within their sphere, according to its own mass of knowledge, idiom, purpose-point. If the judge has any agency, the question that remains is to determine which human practice has supremacy to determine the facts of the case.[40]

Lyotard likens the faculty of judgment to an admiral who navigates an archipelago between the different human practices like islands.[41] The archipelago is fragmented; it consists of a conglomerate of criteria that compete to be considered in order to determine what the evidence is, what the case is. As an admiral the judge must keep sailing – *navigare necesse est* – despite the uncertain conditions; the judge must proceed, must render a judgment. In the Little Sweetheart case, a judgment was rendered. The judge found the solution to that particular conflict in the lack of criminal intent. It was therefore not equal to the legal rule according to which the picture would be an expression of hate speech, and it could not be subsumed under it.[42] The case is unique, like all cases. It is only similar to other cases (with legal relevance or not) depending on the criteria chosen to analyze it. Even if one strives to disregard singularity in the name of equality and predictability, stability – law[43] – one cannot deny that the case is different from previous cases

34 Lyotard, pp. 130–135; Gualandi, Alberto. *Lyotard.* 2nd ed., Les Belles Lettres, 2004, p. 99.
35 *Re* Derrida's use of binarisms, see for example Cisney.
36 Kant, Pure Reason, A68/B93; Lyotard, pt. 82.
37 Chapter 2.
38 Lyotard, pt. 234.
39 According to what criteria is the carrying of a machete at a nightclub to be determined? According to what criteria is a picture in a children's book to be determined?
40 In the probability and preponderance of the evidence theories the applicable human practice is, peculiarly, statistics (without empirical foundations). Chapter 1.
41 Lyotard, p. 131; May, Todd. *The Political Philosophy of Poststructuralist Anarchism.* Penn State UP, 1994, p. 109; Rasch, William. "In Search of the Lyotard Archipelago, or: How to Live with Paradox and Learn to like It." *New German Critique*, no. 61, 1994, pp. 55–75.
42 Justitiekanslern, Decision of 18 Jan. 2013, Dnr 8473-12-32. The judgment could of course have been otherwise, where for example, the criminal intent would have been found to be proven in the picture itself.
43 Cf. the "safe positions" of Vilhelm Lundstedt as in Ekelöf, I, p. 21, note 23; Motulsky, Henri. *Principe d'une réalisation méthodique du droit privé. La théorie des éléments générateurs des droits subjectifs.* préf. Paul Roubier, Sirey, 1948; Reprint Dalloz, 1992, p. 9.)

but nevertheless must be compared to previous cases to decide if they are similar on the relevant criteria. Law strives to establish those relevant criteria, but each new language act, each new case as a cluster of language acts,[44] must be determined first by some cognitive human practice as a concrete fact, before the normative and hypothetical of the law can qualify it.

Navigating the Spatio-Temporal Commonality as Justice

The just judgment is here understood to be held to raise not only the requirement that the parties be heard, but also that people accept the judgment as just.[45] The differend is the impossibility of being heard because of the impossibility of being understood. Being heard presupposes that what is expressed in one language or one idiom is recognized in another; the just judgment presupposes that what the party means to say is also understood by the judge.[46] Whereas, in the Little Sweetheart case there was no general consensus regarding the sense of the picture (and the case was determined on another criterion: that of ill intent), in many cases, despite the conflict between the parties, there is a consensus regarding what senses are normally attributed to words, facts, behaviors etc. This is because there is a shared access to the idiom[47] between the addressor and the addressee, that is, the party and the judge. The same sense is attributed to the language acts – there is a *common sense*.

From the theories presented by Cochran two different aspects of 'common sense' are discernible: knowledge and reasoning. In evidence theory, one notes that a distinction is made between facts and commonplace generalizations,[48] where the former regards concrete circumstances and the latter regards abstract deductions about what *generally* takes place.[49] Common knowledge may be notorious[50] only to the court,[51] but normally covers the local area, such as a small town or a country.[52] Commonplace generalizations must also be seen as geographically relative (they are common in a particular place),

44 Lyotard, pt. 82.
45 Chapter 2.
46 Lyotard, pt. 78.
47 Lyotard, pt. 12.
48 Anderson, Terence et al. *Analysis of Evidence*. 2nd ed., CUP, 2010, Chapter 10; Edelstam, Henrik. *Sakkunnigbeviset*, Uppsala, 1991. Dissertation; *also* Malpas, Simon. *Jean-François Lyotard*. Routledge, 2003, pp. 64–65.
49 Lindell, Bengt. *Sakfrågor och rättsfrågor: en studie av gränser, skillnader och förhållanden mellan faktum och rätt*. Iustus, 1987, pp. 214–215.
50 The Swedish procedural rule regarding common/notorious knowledge aims primarily at restricting the burden of proof to that which is not commonly known. (35:2 CJP, commented further in the comparative chapters that follow.)
51 Lindell, Bengt. *Notorietet och kontradiktion*. Iustus, 2007, Chapter 4.
52 Lindell, Notorietet, p. 61.

as they may also include conclusions made on the basis of local knowledge[53] or local habits and traditions.[54] Commonplace generalizations thus involve a reasoning as to *why* something takes place or should take place based on what *normally* follows from some fact.[55] It is therefore also a matter of preconception. Knowledge and reasoning are two aspects of what in this book is referred to with a somewhat different terminology, so that what in the whole in Cochran is referred to as 'common sense' is here referred to as a 'spatio-temporal commonality.'

With *spatio-temporal commonality* is meant a human practice with its own mass of knowledge, reasoning and idiom. It develops organically[56] as a "product of history"[57] from everyday life experiences and creates a shared knowledge within a community.[58] The community is in turn shaped by this "community sense."[59] The spatio-temporal commonality is a "*social* phenomenon and therefore related to one's membership in social groups."[60] Adaptable as is the spatio-temporal commonality,[61] so too, are persons who move from one place to another accommodating and acclimatizing as they learn what the local spatio-temporal commonality gives, what the common understanding and common habits of a place are.

With 'common sense' is meant here a reasoning as to what 'makes sense' and so is indeed connected to the sense of the language act. Like all human practices, the spatio-temporal commonality has an idiom particular to it, namely, the idiom of ordinary language.[62] With 'idiom'[63] is understood a specific type of language, pertaining to a human practice, for example, the human practice here referred to as spatio-temporal commonality, but also Medicine and Law.[64]

53 Geertz, Clifford. "Local Knowledge: Fact and Law in Comparative Perspective." *Local Knowledge: Further Essays in Interpretive Anthropology*. Basic Books, 1983; Brush, Stephen B., and Doreen Stabinsky. *Valuing Local Knowledge: Indigenous People and Intellectual Property Rights*. Island Press, 1996.

54 The inferences made in the Nine Mile Walk illustrate this. (Anderson et al., Chapter 1.)

55 Geertz.

56 Cochran, p. 93.

57 Cochran, p. 91.

58 Cochran, for example, pp. 44, 133.

59 Cochran, p. 133.

60 Cochran, p. 91.

61 Cochran, p. 91.

62 Lyotard, pt. 229.

63 Lyotard, primarily pts. 12, 13, 21–24, 92, 93, 135, 151, *also* pp. 61–63.

64 Woodward, Ashley. "Testimony and the Affect-Phrase." *Rereading Jean-François Lyotard*, edited by Heidi Bickis and Rob Shields, Ashgate, 2013, p. 177, for a reading of the 'idiom' as encompassing both the genre of discourse/human practice and the phrase regimen/communicatory structure. The idiom is shared (Lyotard, pts. 78, 135) in contrast to idiolect (Lyotard, pts. 144, 145; Bennington, Geoffrey. *Lyotard: Writing the Event*. Manchester UP and Columbia UP, 1988, p. 123).

With this a distinction is made between 'idiom'[65] and 'language,' where idiom is used to refer to Swedish, French and English but also that of a human practice[66] (Medical French, Medical Swedish or Medical English). Language, in turn, is the phenomenon as such.[67] With 'common sense' is not meant therefore the biblical notion – but perhaps it is possible to connect it to the aesthetical (in particular with reference to communicability),[68] understanding common sense as "the 'folklore' of philosophy"[69] providing a theory of how to interpret the world.[70] Common knowledge, commonplace generalizations, notorious facts, preconceptions and the idiomatic common sense (all part of the spatio-temporal commonality) are "located in all kinds of knowledge and practices"[71] and functionally equivalent in the creation of knowledge of the case. Because much of the spatio-temporal commonality consists of tacit knowledge,[72] it *all* (not just the commonplace generalizations!) seeps in without notice and glues language acts together,[73] for example, an evidentiary language act to an object of proof, *as if*[74] there were no other objectively correct options. The judgment covers[75] the linking of language acts[76] under a coat-

65 The word 'idiom' seems to be a somewhat risky translation of the French *idiome*. According to the consulted dictionaries, *idiome* means "[t]out instrument de communication linguistique utilisé par telle ou telle communauté." *See also* the added comment: "C'est un terme très général qui recouvre aussi bien la notion de langue que les notions de dialecte, de patois, etc." It may be that the French word has a more general meaning than its English counterpart. I will use the word in the sense here indicated in the French dictionary.

66 Lyotard, pts. 93, 176, 251.

67 Lyotard's theory does not concern the difference between Swedish, French or English, but as it describes the walls raised against senses *within* language it also offers a theory for the walls raised *between* idioms. The concern here is (not only) that with a word (for example, 'ball') is meant something which in one idiom is expressed with two different words, depending on the properties (such as size) of it (Pierre Legrand. "Against A European Civil Code." *The Modern Law Review*, vol. 60, no. 1, Jan. 1997, p. 56.) – although this is also relevant here as well. This is after all one reason I went astray with the knife. My concern may be said to also be that a knife, a ball etc. may be used for so many different things, what a knife *is seen to be* depends on how it is used, which differs depending on the human practice. (Lyotard develops Wittgenstein's philosophy in Wittgenstein, Ludwig. *Filosofiska undersökningar*. Translated by Anders Wedberg, Thales, 2012 (Philosophical Investigations).)

68 Kant, Critique of Judgment, § 40; Lyotard, pp. 168–169. *See also* Lyotard, Jean-François. "Sensus communis." *Judging Lyotard*, edited by Andrew Benjamin, Routledge, 1992, p. 1.

69 Gramsci, as in Cochran, p. 95.

70 Cochran, p. 88.

71 Cochran, p. 127.

72 Lindell, Notorietet, pp. 36 ff, where Lindell refers to the 'invisible' part of the foundation for the judgment (and problematizes this in relation to the adversarial principle). *Also*, Fish, Stanley. "Fish v. Fiss." *Stanford Law Review*, vol. 36, no. 6, Jul. 1984, pp. 1325–1348.

73 Cf. Schum, David. "Inference Networks and Their Many Subtle Properties." *Information and Decision Technologies*, vol. 16, 1990, pp. 69–98 (as quoted in Goodwin, Jean. "Wigmore's Chart Method." Informal Logic, vol. 20, no. 3, 2000, pp. 223–243).

74 Lyotard, p. 123.

75 Lyotard, p. 123.

76 *Re* linking, see Chapters 5 and 6.

ing of spatio-temporal presuppositions. The spatio-temporal commonality sets law in relation to society[77] at large as the ordinary language[78] of everyday life.[79]

The admiral in the war of human practices must make the judgment what the case is. This is done on the basis of the criteria previously used to determine what is equal, because those are the criteria perceived as relevant.[80] By habit, by education, by learning and growing up. However, equating the case to previous cases is not to say that they are the same but similar – *as if* the same,[81] that is, *approximately* the same. The criteria we use to understand, passive as it is, are those that are the closest to us. There is a tension between being just to the single case by treating it as singular and by creating predictability by treating it like previous equal cases have been treated – *as if* they were equal.[82] These criteria are also "as if-objective," because other people around us use the same.[83] The international aspect however makes this determination more hazardous.

The Machete and the Spatio-Temporal Relativity

This may be illustrated with an analysis of the Machete case. As mentioned, when reading that a man from South America was carrying a knife to a disco, I imagined a typical Swedish carving knife. This section aims at presenting the conditions that led me to make such a mistake – a mistake which is easily made and difficult to avoid because one is often unaware of the pitfalls – because of indeterminacy one cannot be aware of them all. We

77 Lyotard, pts. 155, 156. *See also* pt. 195, regarding the interplay between the social and the judgment.
78 Lyotard, pts. 30, 91, 97, 101, 122, 146.
79 Lyotard, pt. 257.
80 Cf. Kant, Pure Reason, A68/B93.
81 Lyotard, p. 123.
82 Lyotard, p. 123, *also* pts. 9, 10, 57, 58.
83 Cf. SOU 1938:44, pp. 377–378, where it is specified regarding the judge's evaluation of evidence that the judge's "conviction must be objectively founded, meaning that it must be supported by reasons acceptable by other reasonable persons." ("Hans övertygelse måste vara objektivt grundad och sålunda stödjas på skäl, som kunna godtagas av andra förståndiga personer.") Cf. Kant, Critique of Judgment, § 40. *See also* Lindell, Bengt. *Civilprocessen.* 3rd ed., Iustus and Uppsala, 2012, pp. 116–117 *re* this "imaginary auditorium" that can verify the evaluation of the evidence. Lindell critically discusses this normative presupposition in Sakfrågor, p. 110 f. *See also* Ekelöf, P. O. et al. *Rättegång IV.* 7th ed., Norstedts Juridik, 2009, p. 160; Diesen, Christian, and Magne Strandberg. *Bevisprövning i tvistemål: Teori och praktik.* Norstedts Juridik, 2012, pp. 342–343; Nordh, Robert. *Bevisrätt C, Bevisvärdering.* Iustus, 2013, p. 39; Hassler, Åke. *Svensk civilprocessrätt.* Nord. bokh., 1963, p. 351. *Caselaw:* NJA 1998 s. 225 (primarily *re* the burden of proof and the standard of proof): NJA 2017 s. 1105; NJA 2014 s. 364; NJA 2012 s. 804; NJA 2009 s. 64; NJA 1975 s. 577. Lindell notes that there is no trace of 35:1:1 CJP in the caselaw, Notorietet, p. 61, which the preceding list confirms.

understand here a link between spatio-temporal commonality and Lyotard's idea of the archipelago, in which the human practices as areas of expertise pop up like islands, with their purpose-points as the highest point of the island, being as such both the look-out-point from which all is seen and the destination towards which all is drawn. The spatio-temporal commonality would then merely be common language and common knowledge – "the ungraded supply of phrases from all regimens and linkages from all genres"[84] – like the water between the islands. And in a geo-linguistically restricted space that figurative language may suffice. But this book is not limited to the relativity of facts from one human practice to another but seeks to illustrate the impact of this spatio-temporal commonality as a function to create a sense of objectivity, reason, rationality. It is therefore not satisfying to refer to it as the water surrounding the human practices on which the admiral judgment navigates. Although this is adequate, it is only one dimension. It does not cover the diagonality of cross-border evidence.[85]

In the case of evidence, the spatio-temporal commonality seeps in between the evidentiary language act and what it is equated to ontologically (a = b), as well as the evidentiary language act and the object of proof (a => b). The equating of two 'things' is the ordinary subsumption (one may be more general than the other), the inference drawn regarding the object of proof on the basis of the evidence is of course not the identical process – both are however a matter of attribution of sense and dependent on that sense. Therefore, sense is the key to both language and knowledge. More than the clear water of the archipelago, spatio-temporal commonality is like a muddy quagmire that filters and daubs all language acts which are presented to the human practice of law (the court, the judge) with sediment and peat[86] – regardless of their non-legal aspects.

In most cases the internal judgment is therefore "automatic" in the sense that the judge, responsible as they may be, is often not troubled with the judgment of what the evidence is and what the common inference is.[87] However, in cases where there are different human practices competing over the sense of a language act because, as in the Little Sweetheart case, there is no spatio-temporal commonality as to the sense of a particular language act, the judge must more forcefully grab the rudder and determine how to proceed. The judge will notice they are not able to rely on any given purpose-point like a North Star to guide the direction of the judgment and will need to take responsibility and judge what is what, whether a equals b.[88] It is the judge who casts the ship's gangplank over the abyss.[89] The imposition is inevitable;

84 Lyotard, pt. 229.
85 *Re* diagonal taking of evidence, Chapter 4.
86 Cochran, pp. 88 and 91.
87 Derrida, p. 955.
88 Lyotard, p. 135.
89 Lyotard, pp. 123, 130 ff., pts., 178, 180, 207, 217. *See also* Gearey, p. 60.

the aim is to make it as acceptable as possible. In the end, the parties must get out of the conflict and the judgment must not cause outrage neither among the parties nor the public.

Building on Lyotard's imagery, one may say I was navigating the Hispanic/Barcelonic waters with a nautical chart of a Swedish archipelago when I mistakenly interpreted the witness testimonials regarding the knives in the nightclub. Other circumstances of the case of the Barcelona fight, such as the fact that three generations of the man's family went together to the nightclub might have indicated to me that I was incapable of determining the context and so might have concluded that some other type of knife may have been used, but in my mind, there were no other adequate knives. The use of machetes was not an option as there simply is not enough vegetation for them to be of ordinary everyday use in Sweden or any other place I'd lived – I might have seen such machetes as things of the past the knowledge of which was only kept alive through the sagas of Hollywood blockbusters.

One may understand the archipelago therefore as a milieu,[90] an environment,[91] within which the senses are attributed, from different human practices.[92] Navigating between the human practices the admiral faculty of judgment comes to a halt by deciding when the case is sufficiently investigated,[93] what the case therefore must be and what legal consequence follows. The archipelago, environment etc. is full of language acts which take that place, and which are commonly known to the locals and offer senses to new-coming language acts as for free. The archipelago is not a neutral space, however, that the judge coolly sails. It is a geographical sphere,[94] with its proper mass of knowledge and its own idiom.

Muddy Justice

In the Machete example there is no conflict between different human practices as expertise (as opposed to the general, common, sometimes non-scientific knowledge of spatio-temporal commonality) but a confusion between presuppositions without any claim to scientific or otherwise expert knowledge. The judgments I made as to what type of knife was meant with the word

90 Lyotard's use of archipelago is indeed a comment to Kant's milieu. (Lyotard, p. 131 (*also* pt. 200).)

91 Joerges, Christian. "The Challenges of Europeanization in the Realm of Private Law: A Plea for a New Legal Discipline." *Duke Journal of Comparative & International Law*, vol. 14, no. 2, Summer 2004, pp. 149–196, where the expression 'regulatory environment' is used.

92 Lyotard, p. 131.

93 Even if there are formalized time-limits, such as 42:15, 42:15 a CJP, the rule must be chosen and interpreted etc., i.e., the first and second aporias presented in Derrida, p. 960; Cornell, p. 134; Cisney, pp. 256–260.

94 Piché, Claude. "The Philosopher-Artist: A Note on Lyotard's Reading of Kant." *Research in Phenomenology*, vol. 22, 1992, p. 153.

used in the witness testimonials in the case file, as well as the reason for carrying the knife (which showed not to be a knife at all in my mind, but a small sword!) was based on the habits and normality of the erroneous spatio-temporal commonality. It could have led to a very unjust legal judgment, had I had any adjudicative role.

When the legal judgment is accepted as just by people[95] it is understood here to be so because the establishment of the facts has been motivated in such a way that the person on the street, with their limited knowledge of different human practices, finds the motivation reasonable: it resonates with their spatio-temporal commonality and therefore seems based on common knowledge, common sense as in common interpretations and commonplace generalizations – common to that place. The spatio-temporal commonality allows for a judgment to *seem* correct, "as if"[96] it hit the bulls' eye. In other words, if the general public accepts the judgment, it is *de facto* correct. It is correct in retrospect (which means, as noted, that the justness of the judgment, when rendered, is a matter of the future[97]).

Cross-Border Justice – Navigating in a Maze

The judgment is then two things: it is a decision[98] and a human faculty.[99] As a human faculty judgment is a capability to navigate and find one's way through life's muddle of human practices, between the islands of human practices with the innumerable positions and perspectives to take.[100] Judgment as navigation means moving forward on an unstable surface, reading the environmental conditions and dealing with them to avoid capsizing. As a decision it is not a process or a voyage, but a halt. It is an obstruction, which, because of urgency,[101] halts the voyage.

The extent to which there is predictability in the legal judgment despite the indeterminacy of facts and their undecidability[102] is the extent to which it also may be perceived as 'correct' – because after it is rendered, it is accepted as just.[103] The only grounding in the domestic case – where both parties live their lives, run their business etc., on the territory covered by the jurisdiction of the court – is the muddy quagmire of spatio-temporal commonality, that

95 Teubner, Günther. "Self-Subversive Justice: Contingency or Transcendence Formula of Law?" *The Modern Law Review*, vol. 72, no. 1, 2009, pp. 1–23.
96 Lyotard, p. 123.
97 Lyotard, pt. 88.
98 Derrida, p. 963, but also (with reference to Walter Benjamin) p. 1023; Cornell, pp. 133 s.; Cisney, p. 258.
99 Lyotard, p. 168; Kant, Critique of Judgment, § 40.
100 Lyotard, pp. 130–135; Gualandi, p. 99.
101 P. 25, n. 53; p. 36, n. 5.
102 Derrida, p. 962.
103 Chapter 9.

space to which the judge and the parties all have access and therefore can hear one another. Unlike domestic cases, however, in a cross-border case, where evidence is foreign, the national judge is faced with a cognitive nothingness. This book presents justice as an approximation and an approach. As such it is tightly connected to the person of the judge who's therefore neither a mouth who speaks the law[104] nor a computer who calculates[105] the correct application of the law after having processed the probability of each object of proof.[106] To hear, to know, to judge, the Swedish judge will – by choice or by lack of choice – to some extent impose the Swedish spatio-temporal commonality, the senses of the human practice that they represent, namely, Swedish law and Swedish idiom.[107]

In this we find the problem with cross-border evidence. With Lyotard, both the word and the thing are attributed sense in the same manner as is a handshake (the signing of a deal?) and the carrying of a machete (common habit used for cutting down bush and beheading snakes in the back yard or sign of criminal intent, used in violence against another human being?), or a whiplash injury.[108] They are all language acts. When evidence is taken from one idiom, with all the complexity of language that Lyotard describes, to the context of another, there are several language barriers, the idiomatic being only one – the sense may not be recovered within the human practice that wins the war and thus attributes sense to the language act,[109] but instead some other sense is attributed and the former sense is lost in this translation. If it is just, like Lyotard claims, that the people govern the language acts, what people should govern in these cases – for justice to prevail?[110] Which spatio-temporal commonality is the evidence to be given sense in relation to? That of the court or that of the commonality sphere of the foreign party? The selection of relevance and sense of language acts is the neglect of other perspectives, other facts and other inferences.

The validation of one is the denial of others. Hearing is muting. This is why emotions get stirred up. Proposing that Little Sweetheart was an expression of hate when there was no such intent is to deny the competing explanations of love; it's to infringe on another's inner life and plant in them a thorn. This is not the thorn of racial hatred, but the thorn pinned by false accusation, of guilt sown into the conscience of the other on the basis of external expectations, external preconceptions, confused generalizations. The feeling of being wronged is planted in the person who was by others seen as the perpetrator.

104 de Montesquieu, Charles de Secondat baron. *De l'esprit des lois*. Vol. 1, Livre XI, Chap. VI, Lebigre frères, 1831, p. 305.
105 Derrida, pp. 946, 960.
106 P. 14, n. 77.
107 Lyotard, pts. 28, 37, 42, 160, 176.
108 As in the case NJA 1969 s. 311, discussed in the Medical Case Book example in Chapter 6.
109 Lyotard, pt. 78.
110 Lyotard, pt. 236.

The opposite applies to those who feel hurt by the picture. For Derrida the undecidability of the case causes anxiety.[111] The anxiety of the judgment is inevitable; there will always be a certain amount of subjectivity – of arbitrariness.[112] The judge will not be holding the scale and weigh the arguments and counterarguments[113] in order to deliver a judgment in accordance with the scale's verdict (that would be calculation, and not a free judgment). The judge must make the judgment. It is first an internal process, but it must be followed by an external decision-making. The lack of knowledge leaves the judgment to the judge, a judgment consisting in a choice of perspectives, of inferences to make, of senses to attribute to the language acts presented by the parties or collected on the initiative of the court itself.[114] If evidence is understood as connecting the law to the extra-legal reality and this extra-legal reality is sifted through the spatio-temporal commonality of the judge, then in the case of cross-border evidence the extra-legal reality will be sifted through a foreign spatio-temporal commonality. With the extra-legal reality consisting of a muddle of human practices, the horizon over which the judge as an admiral attempts to gaze may seem more like a maze.

Bibliography

Anderson, Terence et al. *Analysis of Evidence*. 2nd ed., CUP, 2010.

Bennington, Geoffrey. *Lyotard: Writing the Event*. Manchester UP and Columbia UP, 1988.

Brush, Stephen B., and Doreen Stabinsky. *Valuing Local Knowledge: Indigenous People and Intellectual Property Rights*. Island Press, 1996.

Cisney, Vernon, W. *Deleuze and Derrida. Difference and the Power of the Negative*. Edinburgh UP, 2018.

Cochran, Patricia. *Common Sense and Legal Judgment, Community Knowledge, Political Power, and Rhetorical Practice*. McGill-Queen's UP, 2017.

Cornell, Drucilla. *The Philosophy of the Limit*. Routledge, 1992.

de Montesquieu, Charles de Secondat baron. *De l'esprit des lois*, Vol. 1, Livre XI, Chap. VI, Lebigre frères, 1831.

Derrida, Jacques. "Force de loi: le Fondement mystique de l'autorité." *Cardozo Law Review*, vol. 11, nos. 5–6, Jul./Aug. 1990.

Derrida, Jacques. *Politics of Friendship*. Verso, 1997.

Diesen, Christian, and Magne Strandberg. *Bevisprövning i tvistemål: Teori och praktik*. Norstedts Juridik, 2012.

Douzinas, Costas, and Adam Gearey. *Critical Jurisprudence: the Political Philosophy of Justice*. Hart Publishing, 2005.

Edelstam, Henrik. *Sakkunnigbeviset*. Uppsala, 1991. Dissertation.

Ekelöf, P. O. et al. *Rättegång IV*. 7th ed., Norstedts Juridik, 2009.

111 Derrida, p. 962; Cornell, p. 134; Gehring, p. 124.

112 Cisney, p. 259.

113 Key, Ellen. *Folkbildningsarbetet särskilt med hänsyn till skönhetssinnets odling*. K. W. Appelbergs boktryckeri, 1906, p. 15.

114 This depends on the communicatory structure of the fact-finding; a matter studied comparatively in Chapter 6.

Fish, Stanley. "Fish v. Fiss." *Stanford Law Review*, vol. 36, no. 6, Jul. 1984, pp. 1325–1348.
Fish, Stanley. "Force." *Doing What Comes Naturally: Change, Rhetoric, and the Practice of Theory in Literary and Legal Studies*. Duke UP, 1989.
Frege, Gottlob. "On Sense and Nominatum." *The Philosophy of Language*, edited by A. P. Martinich, translated by Herbert Feigl, 2nd ed., OUP, 1990.
Gearey, Adam. *Law and Aesthetics*. Bloomsbury Publishing Plc, 2001.
Geertz, Clifford. "Local Knowledge: Fact and Law in Comparative Perspective." *Local Knowledge: Further Essays in Interpretive Anthropology*, Basic Books, 1983.
Gualandi, Alberto. *Lyotard*. 2nd ed., Les Belles Lettres, 2004.
Hassler, Åke. *Svensk civilprocessrätt*. Nord. bokh., 1963.
Joerges, Christian. "The Challenges of Europeanization in the Realm of Private Law: A Plea for a New Legal Discipline." *Duke Journal of Comparative & International Law*, vol. 14, no. 2, Summer 2004, pp. 149–196.
Kant, Immanuel. *Kritik av omdömeskraften*. Translated by Sven-Olov Wallenstein. Thales, 2003 (Kant, Critique of Judgment).
Kant, Immanuel. *Kritik av det rena förnuftet*. Translated by Jeanette Emt. Thales, 2004 (Kant, Pure Reason).
Key, Ellen. *Folkbildningsarbetet särskilt med hänsyn till skönhetssinnets odling*. K. W. Appelbergs boktryckeri, 1906, http://runeberg.org/folkbildn/0027.html. Accessed 18 Sep. 2021.
Lindell, Bengt. *Sakfrågor och rättsfrågor: en studie av gränser, skillnader och förhållanden mellan faktum och rätt*. Iustus, 1987.
Lindell, Bengt. *Notorietet och kontradiktion*. Iustus, 2007.
Lindell, Bengt. *Civilprocessen*. 3rd ed., Iustus and Uppsala, 2012.
Lyotard, Jean-François. *The Differend – Phrases in Dispute*. Translated by Georges Van Den Abbeele, University of Minnesota Press, 1988.
Lyotard, Jean-François. "Sensus communis." *Judging Lyotard*, edited by Andrew Benjamin, Routledge, 1992.
Lyotard, Jean-François. *Discourse, Figure*. Translated Antony Hudek and Mary Lydon, University of Minnesota Press, 2011.
Malpas, Simon. *Jean-François Lyotard*. Routledge, 2003.
May, Todd. *The Political Philosophy of Poststructuralist Anarchism*. Penn State UP, 1994.
Mindus, Patricia. *A Real Mind: The Life and Work of Axel Hägerström*. Springer Science & Business Media, 2009.
Motulsky, Henri. "Prolégomènes pour un futur Code de procédure civile: la consécration des principes directeurs du procès civil par le décret du 9 septembre 1971." *Écrits, études et notes de procédure civile*. Dalloz, 2010.
Nordh, Robert. *Bevisrätt C, Bevisvärdering*. Iustus, 2013, p. 39.
Pattaro, Enrico. "From Hägerström to Ross and Hart." *Ratio Juris*, vol. 22, no. 4, Dec. 2009.
Perelman, Chaïm. *Justice et raison*. Editions de l'Université de Bruxelles, 1972.
Piché, Claude. "The Philosopher-Artist: A Note on Lyotard's Reading of Kant." *Research in Phenomenology*, vol. 22, 1992.
Poché, Fred. *Penser avec Derrida: Comprendre la déconstruction*. Chronique sociale, 2007.
Rasch, William. "In Search of the Lyotard Archipelago, or: How to Live with Paradox and Learn to like It." *New German Critique*, no. 61, 1994, pp. 55–75.
Ross, Alf. *On Law and Justice*. University of California Press, 1959.

Schum, David. "Inference Networks and Their Many Subtle Properties." *Information and Decision Technologies*, vol. 16, 1990, pp. 69–98.
Teubner, Günther. "Self-Subversive Justice: Contingency or Transcendence Formula of Law?" *The Modern Law Review*, vol. 72, no. 1, 2009, pp. 1–23.
Villenave. *Des Jurés et de la conviction intime*. Malassis, 1796.
Wittgenstein, Ludwig. *Filosofiska undersökningar*. Translated by Anders Wedberg. Thales, 2012 (Philosophical Investigations).
Woodward, Ashley. "Testimony and the Affect-Phrase." *Rereading Jean-François Lyotard,* edited by Heidi Bickis and Rob Shields, Ashgate, 2013.

Chapter 4

Comparing Civil Procedural Fact-Finding

Introduction

In the preceding I have presented the evidentiary language act. I have also presented the human practice and its purpose-point as well as the particular type of human practice that is the spatio-temporal commonality. In this chapter I will present the last of the conditions for knowledge to which Lyotard's theory has inspired. It is also what will serve as the structure for the comparison in which I analyze the effects of the cross-border travel of evidence and its capacity to contribute to justice. The expression 'cross-border' is primarily used to refer to situations of international law, in particular private international law. Cross-border evidence is consequently such that has been brought from one jurisdiction to another. It may be held that any taking of evidence involves a crossing of borders, namely borders of different human practices. This point is not developed in this thesis, as the aim here is to analyze the suitability of cross-border taking of evidence in international private law proceedings in the EU.

The legal judgment is an unavoidable imposition of the human practice of law on the extra-legal reality.[1] It is argued in this book that to make the imposition of law on the extra-legal reality as harmless as possible, the legal judgment must seek to harmonize with its environment.[2] For evidence to fill its role as communicator between the law and the extra-legal reality, the law and the extra-legal reality must attribute to the evidence the same sense. This book studies the conditions for this to be achieved when evidence is taken across jurisdictional borders. In order to detect possible differences[3] within the jurisdictional landscape of the EU, two civil procedural

1 Chapters 2 and 3.

2 Cf. Ramshaw, Sara. "Jamming the Law: Improvisational Theatre and the 'Spontaneity' of Judgment." *Law Text Culture*, vol. 14, no. 1, 2010, pp. 133–159.

3 Legrand, Pierre. "Paradoxically, Derrida: For a Comparative Legal Studies." *Cardozo Law Review*, vol. 27, no. 2, Nov. 2005, pp. 631–718.

DOI: 10.4324/9781003495383-4

fact-finding[4] systems to which the Evidence Regulation[5] is applicable have been compared: the Swedish and the French. There are two main aims with the comparison. One is to find possible sources of miscommunication when evidence is taken across national jurisdictional borders. This serves as immediate assessment of the suitability of the Evidence Regulation to help increase access to justice, as understood as a positive law matter.[6] This is however a purpose serving the more distant purpose of assessing the possibility of a common sense of justice in the EU.

When evidence is included in the case material, it is, to my understanding, taken from another human practice, which has given it sense first. This means that as the language act has taken place, it keeps taking place; it is not reborn at each given moment, nor does it "die," ossified as a link of the past onto which new language acts are connected in a chain, each new link being the current link, each previous a matter of the past.[7] This is possibly a deviation from Lyotard's radicality,[8] but if nothing else, I understand this to be a condition for the comparison carried out in this thesis, and thus a condition to make visible my point. Therefore, the evidence is referred to in the rather traditional sense as a connector of previously occurring circumstances to the present – and even to the future[9] as the evidence takes place in the foundation of the judgment. Nevertheless, the gap[10] between language act 1 (that is, 'a' earlier) and language act 2 ('b' earlier) is at the core of this thesis.[11] This is dealt with by holding on to the understanding of the language act as that

4 Fact-finding is an expression used here to encompass both procedural law and substantive law in the extent that it concerns the administration and interpretation of evidence.
5 Regulation (EU) 2020/1783 of the European Parliament and of the Council of 25 November 2020 on cooperation between the courts of the Member States in the taking of evidence in civil or commercial matters (taking of evidence) (recast), OJ L 405, 2.12.2020, p. 1.
6 Cf. Legrand, Pierre. "Siting Foreign Law: How Derrida can help." *Duke Journal of Comparative & International Law*, vol. 21, no. 3, Spring 2011, p. 598.
7 Cf, Cisney, Vernon, W. *Deleuze and Derrida. Difference and the Power of the Negative.* Edinburgh UP, 2018, p. 221 regarding Derrida's understanding of this holding on to the past as well as the future in each judgment.
8 See, for example, Bennington, Geoffrey. *Lyotard: Writing the Event.* Manchester UP and Columbia UP, 1988, pp. 128–133; Curtis, Neal. "The Politics of Creation: Lyotard, Castoriadis, Malraux." *Rereading Jean-François Lyotard*, edited by Heidi Bickis and Rob Shields, Ashgate, 2013, p. 140.
9 See, however, Curtis. *Also*, Bentham, Jeremy. *The Works of Jeremy Bentham.* Vol. 7 (Rationale of Judicial Evidence Part 2). William Tait, 1843, Chapter 2 (Online Library of Liberty, https://oll.libertyfund.org/titles/bowring-the-works-of-jeremy-bentham-vol-7-rationale-of-judicial-evidence-part-2). Accessed 3 Dec. 2024.
10 Lyotard, Jean-François. *The Differend – Phrases in Dispute.* Translated by Georges Van Den Abbeele, University of Minnesota Press, 1988/Lyotard, Jean-François. *Le Différend.* Éditions de minuit. 1983, p. 123. Chapter 3.
11 Carroll, David. "Rephrasing the Political with Kant and Lyotard: From Aesthetic to Political Judgments." *Diacritics*, vol. 14, no. 3, 1984, Special Issue on the Work of Jean François Lyotard, pp. 74–88, p. 75; Bennington, pp. 124, 132.

which 'comes along' and 'takes place' and which attracts the addressor and addressee, by which, consequently, the language act itself does not change (despite the change of its contextual universe).[12] Language act 1 thus opens its universe not only to the referent and the sense but also to the addressor, who "passes" the language act on to the addressee,[13] who in turn attaches to the language act *both* a sense and referent that the conditions, that is, the human practice and the communicatory structure, allow.

Procedure as Communicatory Structure

Before describing the comparative method, the impact of the fourth and fifth conditions of Lyotard's theory of knowledge on the determination of the case must be presented: the concatenation (i.e., linking, which was introduced briefly in Chapter 2) and the phrase regimen. The phrase regimen concerns what may be understood as the grammar[14] regimenting which types of phrases are accepted, structuring them, requiring them to follow a certain order.[15] Phrase regimen may be for example cognitive or exclamative, interrogative, prescriptive or "reasoning, knowing, describing, recounting, questioning, showing, ordering, etc."[16] The phrase regimen, in short, regulates how to link language act 1 and language act 2. For its regimenting the flow of language acts it is referred to here as a communicatory structure. Procedural law does this. It decides *what* phrases may or must come, *from whom* what phrases may or must come, *when* different types of phrases may or must come etc.

The rules of procedure are thus understood as a grammar regimenting the communication which builds the knowledge about the particular court case. As such, procedural law is understood in this thesis as a phrase regimen and referred to as a *communicatory structure*.[17] The pointing of the evidence, as an ostensive language act, implies four links in a chain of language acts: extra-legal reality – the evidence – the allegations which claim that there is a real and concrete case that corresponds to the antecedent of the substantive law rule – the antecedent of the legal rule.[18] It is understood here that through this linking the law and the outside-of-law are connected.[19] The

12 Lyotard, pts. 111, 184.
13 Lyotard, pt. 47.
14 Bennington, pp. 131–132.
15 Lyotard, pt. 115.
16 Lyotard, p. xii, *see also* pts. 65, 179, 186, 204.
17 Wigmore's chart is understood here as an analysis of the non-chronological phrase regimen of evidence. Chapter 1; n19.
18 Cf. Bentham, Jeremy. *The Works of Jeremy Bentham*. Vol. 7 (Rationale of Judicial Evidence Part 2). William Tait, 1843, Chapter 1; Ekelöf, P. O. et al. *Rättegång IV*. 7th ed., Norstedts Juridik, 2009, IV, pp. 21–22; Lindblom, P. H. "Processens arkitektur." *Vänbok till Torleif Bylund*, edited by Torbjörn Andersson and Bengt Lindell, Iustus, 2003, pp. 171–260, p. 172.
19 The "translation" between the *probandum* and the *probans*, as well as between the criteria of the law and the allegations is thus understood here as instances of linking. (Jeremy.

communicatory structure thus allows and disallows certain language acts, like the human practices, also causing differends: some language acts will not be allowed, their senses will not be heard.

To understand the interrelations between the human practices, the communicatory structures and the purpose-points we may use a game metaphor. A human practice may be understood as a *category of games*, and the purpose-point of the human practice may be understood as the *object of the game*, what the game is about. When games share the same object, they belong to the same human practice. Rules within human practices concern the *tactics* for winning the game.[20] If the communicatory structure thus regulates the possible modes of playing, the purpose-point determines whether you play well, rather than whether you are playing the game at all (or another game).[21] The purpose-point may for example be to convince, to entertain or to gain money.[22] If the aim is to gain money, there might be more than one game to play. Casino gaming would, according to this theory, be one human practice; the rules of Blackjack and Roulette could be seen as two different communicatory structures. In Blackjack, once the croupier has dealt, the next act is for the players to look at their cards. If a player says "(I) stand" or waves their hand horizontally, the croupier turns the card dealt for themself and either takes more cards in accordance with the rules for the dealer or rests. If the player says "hit," "double (down)," "split" or "surrender" (or gives a signal with the meaning equivalent to any of these words) the dealer will respond to that in accordance with the rules of the game. But if the player says "drop," it won't fall within the rules of the game, and therefore won't make any sense, it is not a possible way of linking – it won't make part of the game and by doing so the player is simply not playing the game but carrying out some other form of action. In Roulette, the player must bet on white or black; if the player says "Always bet on black"[23] although it is perhaps not the most common phrasing, it will make sense to the croupier; if he says "Always bet on pink," the player will however not thereby be making a move within the game. Roulette and Blackjack are games with their own rules, and so they are communicatory structures. They share the same stake: to gain money; therefore, they make part of the same human practice.

Rationale of Judicial Evidence, specially applied to English practice. Edited by J. S. Mill, Vol. III, Hunt and Clarke, 1827, p. 18; Wigmore, John H. *The Principles of Judicial Proof*. Little, Brown, and Co., 1913, pp. 27 f; Ekelöf, P. O. "Free Evaluation of Evidence." *Scandinavian Studies in Law*, vol. 8, 1964, pp. 45–66; Twining William. *Theories of Evidence: Bentham and Wigmore*. Weidenfeld & Nicolson, 1984, p. 29.)

20 Lyotard, 185; *Re* procedural law as tactics, see Westberg, Peter. "Processtaktik och bevisbörda i dispositiva tvistemål." *Festskrift till Per Henrik Lindblom*, edited by Torbjörn Andersson and Bengt Lindell, Iustus, 2004, pp. 731–754.

21 Lyotard, 185.

22 Lyotard, 10.

23 As recommends Wesley Snipe's character in Kevin Hook's 1992 action film *Passenger 57*.

Diagonal Taking of Evidence

Like civil procedural fact-finding rules constitute a communicatory structure, so is the EU Evidence Regulation a communication structure for the cross-border taking of evidence. The main rule of the Evidence Regulation is that of cooperation.[24] In line with the objective of faster and simpler procedures,[25] the national courts are granted the power to contact each other directly.[26] Direct contact between the national courts is a significant change in the international regulation of judicial cooperation. The direct exchange of services between the courts in different Member States is an important means of speeding up the cooperation process.[27] The possibilities for a requested court to refuse to take evidence for a court in another Member State are limited to situations where, according to national law, a person has a right to refuse to be heard as a witness, that is, doctors, clergymen and other people in such professions.[28] Other than that, only if the request falls outside the scope of the regulation or the requesting court has not met with the requirements of the regulation is it possible to refuse the execution of a request.[29]

Evidence is primarily taken in accordance with the legal provisions for the taking of evidence in the jurisdiction of the requested court.[30] In that situation each court applies their "own" rules, in accordance with its national

24 Recitals 2, 3, 4, 29 Evidence Regulation; Opinion of 18 July 2007, *Tedesco*, C-175/06, EU:C:2007:451.

25 Recitals 8–11 Evidence Regulation (1206/2001). In *Lippens* (judgment of 6 September 2012, *Lippens*, C-170/11, EU:C:2012:540) the Court of Justice left it to the forum court to choose the simpler procedure (and thus upheld procedural autonomy). In *ProRail* (judgment of 21 February 2013, *ProRail*, C-332/11, EU:C:2013:87) the ruling was likewise in favor of simplicity, albeit in that case simplicity meant that the expert of the forum court would have access to the territory of the requested state (and the investigation would take place cross-border).

26 Article 3 Evidence Regulation, Recital 15 and article 2 Evidence Regulation (1206/2001).

27 European Union: Council of the European Union. *Presidency Conclusions, Tampere European Council, 15–16 October 1999*, 16 Oct. 1999, Title VI, p. 34, https://www.europarl.europa.eu/summits/tam_en.htm. Accessed 30 Nov. 2024.

28 Article 16.1 Evidence Regulation; judgment of 17 February 2011, *Werynski*, C-283/09, EU:C:2011:85, para. 51, 53.

29 Article 16.2 Evidence Regulation.

30 Article 12.2 Evidence Regulation. Exceptionally, the requesting court may take evidence directly on the territory where the evidence is found. This is another main invention of the Evidence Regulation (Articles 19–21 Evidence Regulation; judgment of 21 February 2013, *ProRail*, C-332/11, EU:C:2013:87). Direct taking of evidence may only take place on a voluntary basis which means that no coercive measures may be taken in order for evidence to be given to the requesting court representative. (Article 19.2 Evidence Regulation.) When evidence is taken directly by the court of the main proceeding, the forms pursuant to the legislation of the main are applied. (Article 19.3 Evidence Regulation.) This is an important step "forward" for the fact-finding in civil procedure in the courts of the EU, and it has been called a minor revolution. (Lebeau, Daniel, and Marie-Laure Niboyet. "Regards croisés du processualiste et de l'internationaliste sur le règlement CE du 28 mai 2001 relatif à l'obtention

procedural autonomy and the *lex fori regit processum principle.*[31] This means that the evidence is taken from one extra-legal environment,[32] before it is inserted in the communicatory structure of another legal human practice in accordance with which the evidence will be appraised and the case will be adjudicated. This reveals a perception of evidence, procedure and substantive law as independent of each other, where a correct judgment as the correct legal effect (consequence), giving effect to substantive law is achievable regardless of the form of procedure according to which the case is determined – as if the (effective) remedy were not dependent on the (fair) trial. This is however not always how procedure has been understood in the history of international private and procedural law,[33] and it does not reflect the relationship between the communicatory structure and the human practice. Communicatory structures and human practices are on the contrary connected, as the casino gambling illustration hopes to visualize.

Following the communicatory structure of the Evidence Regulation, cross-border taking of evidence is understood here as a *diagonal* taking of evidence. With 'diagonal' is here meant the relation between one judiciary and an extra-legal area of competence outside of the competence of this judiciary.[34] The Evidence Regulation serves as a communicatory structure regimenting the grammar of the national civil procedures as communicatory structures of the national legal systems; a grammar book for the translation of grammar,[35] respecting the identity of the different legal cultures. It is, in short, a communicatory structure for communicatory structures. The diagonality also indicates that other borders are involved: two horizontal and two vertical borders are implied. The legal qualification of a case is already a cross-border exercise, crossing the border between the legal/normative human practice and the cognitive. Evidence's extra-legal factual sense and its legal relevance/sense place the evidentiary language act at the crossing. Such crossing already takes place on

des preuves civiles à l'étranger." *Gaz. Pal.*, vol. 6, 2003, p. 225; Fartunova-Michel, Maria. *La preuve dans le droit de l'Union européenne.* Bruylant, 2013, p. 375.)

31 Spiro, Erwin. "Forum Regit Processum (Procedure Is Governed by the Lex Fori)." *The International and Comparative Law Quarterly*, vol. 18, no. 4, Oct. 1969, pp. 949–960; Font I Segura, Albert. "A EC Reading of the Principle Lex Fori Regit Processum." *Anuario Espanol de Derecho Internacional Privado,* 1, 2001, pp. 283–313.

32 Luhmann, Niklas. *Law As a Social System.* OUP, 2004.

33 Garnett, Richard Lyndon. *Substance and Procedure in Private International Law.* 1st ed., OUP, 2012.

34 It is inspired by Schmid, Christoph. "Vertical and Diagonal Conflicts in the Europeanisation Process." *Private governance, democratic constitutionalism and supranationalism,* edited by Christian Joerges and Olivier Gerstenberg, European Commission, 1998, p. 185; Joerges, Christian, and Michelle Everson. "Law, Economics and Politics in the Constitutionalization of Europe." *Developing a Constitution for Europe,* edited by Erik O Eriksen et al, Routledge, 2004, pp. 162–179.

35 "Lost in translation" is a frequent occurrence between grammars. For example, there are declinations in one language that cannot be found in another, and the same goes for conjugation.

loose grounds, but it is done under a consensus of a spatio-temporally relative as-if neutral space which is abandoned through the crossing between French law and Swedish spatio-temporal commonality and vice versa.[36]

Comparative Structure

The comparative study of this thesis is carried out in three steps following the road of the evidentiary language act from the extra-legal environment to the legal judgment. The legal judgment is the purpose-point of civil procedure, whereas determination of the case is the purpose-point of the evidentiary language act and the civil procedural fact-finding. The first comparative aspect to study how the purpose-points are determined in the law of civil procedure. The purpose-point of the evidence is studied as the actual object of proof and destination of the evidence. It is understood that it is towards this that the parties direct their evidence, and it is from this point that the judge understands the evidence, i.e., what the evidence is meant to show or support, what sense it may be given on the basis of its purpose in the proceedings. Being evidence is a function, therefore all evidence has a telos.[37] The function it is to fill thus determines the evidence.

Before comparatively studying the extra-legal human practices, which may contribute with senses to the determination of the cluster of language acts that constitute the case,[38] the civil procedural fact-finding systems are compared. The judicial fact-finding system structures the communication between the parties and the court in such a way that only certain language acts reach the final stage and are allowed to make part of the cluster constituting the case. The second comparative aspect to the proceedings is the concatenation of language acts, the communicatory structure. Procedural rules organize the evidence and other arguments in relation to each other. The linking structure of language acts follows fact-finding rules, which determine who may contribute to the case material (who may be heard decides whose perspectives may contribute to the assembly of language acts) and hierarchize the evidence. The concatenation may be chronological or achronological. When they are achronological they may be seen to pertain to the deliberations following the proceeding.[39]

The last perspective on the civil procedural shaping of the evidentiary language act is the non-legal but cognitive aspect of the evidence. It asks what knowledge the evidence may contribute to and sees civil procedure as not only a scheme for communication between the parties and the judge but also

36 Chapter 3.

37 Bentham, Jeremy. *Rationale of Judicial Evidence*. Edited by J. S. Mill, Vol. I, Hunt and Clarke, 1827, pp. 39 ff.

38 Lyotard, pt. 82.

39 NJA 1982 s. 175 I and II, *see also* Welamson, p. 538; Westberg, Peter. *Anskaffning av bevisning i dispositiva tvistemål*. Norstedts Juridik, 2010, pp. 622–623; Wigmore, John H. "Problem of Proof." *Illinois Law Review*, vol. 8, no. 2, 1913–1914, pp. 77–103.

between the law and non-legal human practices. Like the purpose-point, this involves a question of relevance: what circumstances and sources of knowledge are considered relevant in the different judicial fact-finding systems? The assessment of relevance is an assessment of causality and inference: what is the cause of a man carrying a sword to a night-club? In the eyes of many, there is criminal intent, but what if the carrying of a sword for some men is more like the carrying of a handbag for many women? Is the fact that the machete was carried at all a relevant circumstance in order to determine the criminal intent at the particular moment? The matter of relevance in relation to the law may be divided into two levels: first, the level of the human practice of law, and second, what are seen as relevant circumstances within that non-legal human practice.

The study does not differentiate between substantive and procedural law in the extent that this impacts the evidence. Each of the three analyses asks questions whose answer may be regulated in substantive or procedural law, as classified in the applicable national law. I have however taken the perspective of civil procedure, with the effect that in the extent that a matter may be both substantive and procedural, it will be referred to as procedural (the fact-finding in itself being a process). With 'substantive law' will be meant such a provision whose legal consequence is the concern of the legal judgment. The intention is to assess the tangible effects on justice that the application of the Evidence Regulation may have. As I have not come across relevant caselaw that is directly applicable I have elaborated mediately relevant caselaw in the ambition to concretize the collision between the Swedish and the French civil procedural fact-finding systems and their impact on the sense of the evidence. The cases developed fall within the applicability of the Evidence Regulation and therefore follow the structure of this regulation. National provisions regarding the national applicability of the regulation, national (geographical or material) jurisdiction in terms of internal organization of the national judiciary, and the procedural and evidentiary law that thereafter becomes applicable have been considered.[40]

The Boundaries of Imagination

The Evidence Regulation offers its own horizon – the examples in the comparison fall within the restrictions that the scope of the regulation constitutes. The Evidence Regulation is applicable in civil and commercial matters.[41] The

40 According to article 3.2 Evidence Regulation the Member States are to draw up a list of courts competent to take evidence in accordance with the regulation. In Sweden, all courts are competent to make requests for taking evidence in accordance with the EU regulation. (2 § Lag (2003:493) om EG:s förordning om bevisupptagning i mål och ärenden av civil eller kommersiell natur.) The first instance courts execute requests made by courts in other Member States. (5 §) The French judge is authorized to send a request for the taking of evidence to foreign courts. (733 CPC)

41 Article 1 Evidence Regulation. The notion 'civil or commercial matters' has been used within the framework of the Hague Conference since 1905 without any definition thereof ever

notion 'civil and commercial matters' has been defined for the purposes of other EU private international law documents by the Court of Justice[42] but has, as of yet, not been defined by the Court – specifically – for the purpose of the Evidence Regulation. The Commission writes in its Practice Guide for the Application of the Regulation on the Taking of Evidence that "it will apply to litigation based on civil and commercial law, consumer law, employment law and even competition law as far as private proceedings are concerned."[43] Not only matters covered by the Brussels I Regulation are covered[44] by the Evidence Regulation but also

> matters relating to the status or legal capacity of natural persons, rights in property arising out of a matrimonial relationship, wills and succession; bankruptcy, proceedings relating to the winding-up of insolvent companies or other legal persons, judicial arrangements, compositions and analogous proceedings.[45]

In the Practice Guide for the Application of the Regulation the Commission clarifies that the regulation applies to "all civil and commercial proceedings whatever the nature of the court or tribunal in which they are taking place."[46]

Neither the concept of 'evidence' nor the concept of 'taking of evidence' are defined in the regulation or in the preparatory documents.[47] The concept of

being developed. (Convention du 17 juillet 1905 relative à la Procédure Civile.) When the 1970 Hague Convention was developed a definition of the notion was discussed. With reference to the over 60 years without significant problems regarding the interpretation having occurred because of the missing definition, it was considered wisest not to define the concept at all. (Rapport de la Commission Spéciale, Ph. W. Amram, Actes et documents de la Onzième session, Conférence de la Haye, Tome IV, Obtention des preuves à l'étranger, 1968.)

42 Judgment of 14 October 1976, *LTU v Eurocontrol*, 29–76, EU:C:1976:137; judgment of 16 December 1980, *Netherlands v Rüffer*, 814/79, EU:C:1980:291; judgment of 14 November 2002, *Gemeente Steenbergen v Luc Baten*, C-271/00, EU:C:2002:656.

43 Practice Guide for the Application of the Regulation on the Taking of Evidence, drawn up by the Commission Services in consultation with the European Judicial Network in Civil and Commercial Matters, pp. 5–6; *see also* article 1.2 Brussels I.

44 Brussels I; judgment of 28 April 2005, *St Paul Dairy*, C-104/03, EU:C:2005:255 *re* the interplay between the Brussels I and the Evidence Regulations. *For further reading, see* Forner Delaygua, Joaquín J. "The Impact of the Enforcement Directive on the Brussels I Regime." *International Litigation in Intellectual Property and Information Technology*, edited by Arnaud Nuyts, Kluwer Law International, 2008, pp. 268–269; Hess, Burkhard. "Preservation and Taking of Evidence in Cross-Border Proceedings – Comparative Remarks in the Context of IP Litigation." *International Litigation in Intellectual Property and Information Technology*, edited by Arnaud Nuyts, Kluwer Law International, 2008, p. 294; von Hein, Jan. "Drawing the Line between Brussels I and the Evidence Regulation." *European Legal Forum*, no. 1, 2008, pp. 1–35.

45 Practice Guide, p. 5.

46 Practice Guide, p. 5.

47 Practice Guide, p. 6; Opinion of 18 July 2007, *Tedesco*, C-175/06, EU:C:2007:451, pt. 40.

'evidence' is however explained in the Practice Guide to include "for instance hearings of witnesses of fact, of the parties, of experts, the production of documents, verifications, establishment of facts, expertise on family or child welfare."[48] The examples in the comparative study encompass such evidence. The notion *taking* of evidence is not commented as such in the Practice Guide, nor has it been defined by the Court of Justice. However, in the *Tedesco* case, before the case was withdrawn, the advocate general rendered their opinion on the interpretation of the notion.[49] In their opinion, the notion taking of evidence must be interpreted independently, in order to reach the aim that is the raison d'être of the regulation.[50] The advocate general prescribes that the expression 'taking of evidence' be interpreted with regard to "the wording, legislative history, scheme and purpose of the Regulation."[51] They continue by stating that the purpose of the regulation is the simplification and acceleration of the cooperation between courts "applied to as many judicial measures for obtaining information as possible."[52] A systematic

48 Practice Guide, p. 6. Fartunova-Michel considers the possibility that the lack of mention of the notion of evidence could be due to "the natural connection" between evidence and procedure which would justify Member State competence over the rules of evidence through which the application of EU law in the national legal systems would be possible. (Fartunova-Michel, Maria. *La preuve dans le droit de l'Union européenne*. Bruylant, 2013, p. 83) Cf. Villenave. *Des Jurés et de la conviction intime*. Malassis, 1796. Villenave, who wrote in French, did not use the word evidence (or its French (non)equivalent *évidence*) but *preuve*. *Évidence* (Fr) is not equivalent to *evidence* (Eng) as the French word concerns the quality of something that is evident. *Preuve* has its own etymology (*Preuve* from *probare (probo)* meaning to test, verify, accept, recognize, assess. *Probare* from *probus*, meaning good, virtuous, https://www.etymonline.com), but with time it seems that the two words have come to coincide – both in French and in English. Swedish law does not seem to have had a concept equivalent to *preuve/proof*. *See also*, p. 37, n. 14.

49 Opinion of 18 July 2007, *Tedesco*, C-175/06, EU:C:2007:451. As Jan von Hein notes, until the AG delivered their opinion there was no "authoritative ruling" concerning the applicability of the Evidence Regulation, and as the case was withdrawn and the opinion so thoroughly prepared, the opinion may "serve as the next best thing" to such an authoritative ruling from the Court. (von Hein, p. 60, n. 44.)

50 Opinion, para. 41–42. The case in the national (Italian) court regarded infringements in intellectual property rights. The Italian court requested, in accordance with the normal procedure in Italy, a so-called *descrizione*, which is a description of the product that allegedly constituted an infringement of the intellectual property rights. (Para. 10.) The *descrizione* is performed by a bailiff. (Para. 1) The English authority considered this procedure to be "search and seizure of goods and documents" (para. 17) and thus excluded from the scope of the regulation. (Monthly summary of Council acts, of 4 July 2001, Document No 10571/01, statement 54/01, p. 16; Opinion, pt. 68.)

51 Opinion, para. 42. *Also* Initiative of the Federal Republic of Germany with a view to adopting a Council Regulation on cooperation between the courts of the Member States in the taking of evidence in civil and commercial matters, OJ 2000 C 314, 3.11.2000.

52 Opinion, para. 43.

interpretation indicated that the notion covers not only the hearing of witnesses but also "documents and other objects" as well as expert evidence.[53]

Some guidance as to the content of the notion 'taking of evidence' may additionally be found in the historical development behind the EU Evidence Regulation. The regulation is a furthering of the pre-existing international cooperation between national courts in the taking of evidence across borders. The Hague Conventions of 1905 and 1954[54] were drafted in French, and it is from this language that translations have been made – or otherwise phrased: other language versions are translations from the French original. The French term for 'taking of evidence' is in these documents *tout acte d'instruction.*[55] In that concept is included the hearing of witnesses, the swearing of an oath, expertise, inspections on sight or of accountancy books.[56] Also expert reports in family and child custody matters are included.[57] The Evidence Regulation thus seems to correspond to its international law precedents. It may be noted, however, that the matter of the scope of the notion has not sufficiently been clarified by the EU legislative or judiciary institutions. Requests for the taking of evidence in the form of DNA and blood samples for the use in family law matters are of concern as the interpretation of the notion differs between the Member States.[58] In this thesis, focus has been on the cross-border problematic of the *understanding* of the evidence, including its capacity to let the party be heard and the judge acquire knowledge. The procedural terminology and regulations regarding the taking are therefore not of immediate concern here.

Bibliography

Bennington, Geoffrey. *Lyotard: Writing the Event.* Manchester UP and Columbia UP, 1988, pp. 128–133.

Bentham, Jeremy. *Rationale of Judicial Evidence.* Edited by J. S. Mill, Vol. I, Hunt and Clarke, 1827.

53 Opinion, para. 44. In subsequent cases, the Court has clarified that the methods for cross-border taking of evidence in the regulation are not exhaustive, and that other means for cooperation in the same aim are allowed. (*Lippens*, para. 33; *ProRail*, para. 46.)

54 Convention du 17 juillet 1905 relative à la procédure civile; Convention du 1er mars 1954 relative à la procédure civile. Convention of 18 March 1970 on the Taking of Evidence Abroad in Civil or Commercial Matters replaced the Hague Convention of 1905.

55 Article 8 Convention du 17 juillet 1905 relative à la procédure civile; Convention du 1er mars 1954 relative à la procédure civile.

56 . . . "auditions de témoins, de prestation de serment, d'expertise, de déscente sur les lieux d'examen de livres d'un commerçant." (Explanations to the 1905 Hague Convention).

57 Practice Guide, p. 6.

58 Report from the Commission to the Council, the European Parliament and the European Economic and Social Committee on the application of the Council Regulation (EC) 1206/2001 of 28 May 2001 on cooperation between the courts of the Member States in the taking of evidence in civil or commercial matters, COM(2007) 769 final, Brussels, 5.12.2007, p. 2.

Bentham, Jeremy. *Rationale of Judicial Evidence, Specially Applied to English Practice*. Edited by J. S. Mill, Vol. III, Hunt and Clarke, 1827.

Bentham, Jeremy. *The Works of Jeremy Bentham*. Vol. 7 (Rationale of Judicial Evidence Part 2). William Tait, 1843. Online Library of Liberty, https://oll.libertyfund.org/titles/bowring-the-works-of-jeremy-bentham-vol-7-rationale-of-judicial-evidence-part-2. Accessed 3 Dec. 2024.

Carroll, David. "Rephrasing the Political with Kant and Lyotard: From Aesthetic to Political Judgments." *Diacritics*, vol. 14, no. 3, 1984, Special Issue on the Work of Jean-François Lyotard, pp. 74–88.

Cisney, Vernon, W. *Deleuze and Derrida. Difference and the Power of the Negative*. Edinburgh UP, 2018.

Curtis, Neal. "The Politics of Creation: Lyotard, Castoriadis, Malraux." *Rereading Jean-François Lyotard*, edited by Heidi Bickis and Rob Shields, Ashgate, 2013.

Ekelöf, P. O. "Free Evaluation of Evidence." *Scandinavian Studies in Law*, vol. 8, 1964.

Ekelöf, P. O. et al. *Rättegång IV*. 7th ed., Norstedts Juridik, 2009, IV.

Fartunova-Michel, Maria. *La preuve dans le droit de l'Union européenne*. Bruylant, 2013.

Font I Segura, Albert. "A EC Reading of the Principle Lex Fori Regit Processum." *Anuario Espanol de Derecho Internacional Privado*, vol. 1, 2001, pp. 283–313.

Forner Delaygua, Joaquín J. "The Impact of the Enforcement Directive on the Brussels I Regime." *International Litigation in Intellectual Property and Information Technology*, edited by Arnaud Nuyts, Kluwer Law International, 2008.

Garnett, Richard Lyndon. *Substance and Procedure in Private International Law*. 1st ed., OUP, 2012.

Hess, Burkhard. "Preservation and Taking of Evidence in Cross-Border Proceedings – Comparative Remarks in the Context of IP Litigation." *International Litigation in Intellectual Property and Information Technology*, edited by Arnaud Nuyts, Kluwer Law International, 2008.

Joerges, Christian, and Michelle Everson. "Law, Economics and Politics in the Constitutionalization of Europe." *Developing a Constitution for Europe*, edited by Erik O. Eriksen et al., Routledge, 2004, pp. 162–179.

Lebeau, Daniel, and Marie-Laure Niboyet. "Regards croisés du processualiste et de l'internationaliste sur le règlement CE du 28 mai 2001 relatif à l'obtention des preuves civiles à l'étranger." *Gaz. Pal.*, vol. 6, 2003.

Legrand, Pierre. "Paradoxically, Derrida: For a Comparative Legal Studies." *Cardozo Law Review*, vol. 27, no. 2, Nov. 2005, pp. 631–718.

Legrand, Pierre. "Siting Foreign Law: How Derrida Can Help." *Duke Journal of Comparative & International Law*, vol. 21, no. 3, Spring 2011.

Lindblom, P. H. "Processens arkitektur." *Vänbok till Torleif Bylund*, edited by Torbjörn Andersson and Bengt Lindell, Iustus, 2003.

Luhmann, Niklas. *Law As a Social System*. OUP, 2004.

Lyotard, Jean-François. *The Differend – Phrases in Dispute*. Translated by Georges Van Den Abbeele, University of Minnesota Press, 1988.

Ramshaw, Sara. "Jamming the Law: Improvisational Theatre and the 'Spontaneity' of Judgment." *Law Text Culture*, vol. 14, no. 1, 2010, pp. 133–159.

Schmid, Christoph. "Vertical and Diagonal Conflicts in the Europeanisation Process." *Private Governance, Democratic Constitutionalism and Supranationalism*, edited by Christian Joerges and Olivier Gerstenberg, European Commission, 1998.

Spiro, Erwin. "Forum Regit Processum (Procedure is Governed by the Lex Fori)." *The International and Comparative Law Quarterly*, vol. 18, no. 4, Oct. 1969, pp. 949–960.

Twining, William. *Theories of Evidence: Bentham and Wigmore*. Weidenfeld & Nicolson, 1984.

Villenave. *Des Jurés et de la conviction intime*. Malassis, 1796.

von Hein, Jan. "Drawing the Line between Brussels I and the Evidence Regulation." *European Legal Forum*, no. 1, 2008, pp. 1–35.

Westberg, Peter. "Processtaktik och bevisbörda i dispositiva tvistemål." *Festskrift till Per Henrik Lindblom*, edited by Torbjörn Andersson and Bengt Lindell, Iustus, 2004.

Westberg, Peter. *Anskaffning av bevisning i dispositiva tvistemål*. Norstedts Juridik, 2010.

Wigmore, John H. *The Principles of Judicial Proof*. Little, Brown, and Co., 1913.

Wigmore, John H. "Problem of Proof." *Illinois Law Review*, vol. 8, no. 2, 1913–1914, pp. 77–103.

Chapter 5

The Unbearable Inconstancy of Objects of Proof

Introduction

Evidence serves the double purpose of letting the party be heard, on the one hand as an independent form of procedural justice, and on the other hand giving the judge knowledge about the case, so that the judge may render a correct legal judgment by correctly applying substantive law and rendering substantive justice.[1] When evidence is taken across borders, does this impact what may be heard through the means of evidence and what knowledge may be given to the judge? The comparison that is introduced in this chapter aims at answering this question. This chapter is about the perspectives and the horizons of the different forms of civil procedure. The reality of the case consists of a swarm of senses[2] and the purpose-point of the human practice will be the perspective from which those senses will be seen – and others will not be seen.[3] The circumstance that some senses will be unknown (disregarded, neglected, ignored) is what Lyotard calls a 'differend.' Only senses which contribute to reaching the purpose-point will contribute to the swarm of senses of the reality of the case.[4] Lyotard describes the purpose-point as a canonical language act, phrased as a question.[5] If one subscribes to the traditional Aristotelian motto held to be of general consensus, on a theoretical level all legal judgments concern the distinction between equal/non-equal – equal to a statutory rule or equal to a previous case. The canonical question would therefore be phrased as the binary "Is this case equal or non-equal to the rule/previous cases subsumed under the rule?"[6]

1 Chapter 2.
2 Lyotard, Jean-François. *The Differend – Phrases in Dispute*. Translated by Georges Van Den Abbeele, University of Minnesota Press, 1988/Lyotard, Jean-François. *Le Différend*. Éditions de minuit. 1983, pt. 82.
3 The expression purpose-point is inspired by Lyotard's *stake* (*enjeu*, in French). Chapter 2.
4 Lyotard, pt. 179.
5 Lyotard, *for example*, pts. 186, 210, 212.
6 This may be seen also in Luhmann's binary code: Luhmann, Niklas. *Law As a Social System*. OUP, 2004, pp. 19 ff, 140.

DOI: 10.4324/9781003495383-5

As the formation of the legal judgment takes place two human practices may be said to be the winning,[7] that is, determinant, human practices: that of the law and that of cognition.[8] Legal qualification is what happens when the law imposes[9] itself on the case, which is established according to the fact-finding rules of procedure. The purpose-point of law will then be "imprinted"[10] on the language acts which constitute the case. The whole of the case will therefore be perceived from this point. Before this point, each language act will, however, have aimed to be considered in the construction of the reality of the case.[11] This fact-finding process has its own purpose-point: the establishment of the case. In jurisprudence, these two points are spoken of as the "frame of the case"[12] – what the judgment must be about and what the court therefore cannot exceed. They constitute the last two links of judicial procedure.[13]

The human practice of civil procedure has various possible purposes.[14] Andersson summarizes the findings made by Swedish jurisprudence regarding the different purposes of civil procedure as being the protection of individuals' rights, behavioral guidance, prevention, reparation, conflict resolution and "legal peace."[15] Andersson categorizes these objectives[16] of civil procedure

7 Lyotard, pt. 40.

8 Lyotard, pt. 176, *also* pts. 47–48, 85.

9 Cf. however, Lyotard, pt. 179, where the language is less offensive as the human practice "inspires" a mode of linking.

10 Lyotard, pt. 180, where the genre of discourse (here 'human practice') "imprints" its stakes (here 'purpose-point').

11 Lyotard, pt. 28.

12 For example, Nordh, Robert. *Processens ram i tvistemål: om yrkande och grunder, ändring av talan m.m.* 4th ed., Iustus, 2019. *See also* Schlag, Pierre, and Amy J Griffin. *How to Do Things with Legal Doctrine.* University of Chicago Press, 2020, Chapter 2, where the framing discussed seems to better correspond with how the word 'horizon' is used here.

13 This is a simplification, of course – partially because the language acts may be split into smaller parts, but also because the if-clause of the substantive law rule also plays a determining role as link in the concatenation. It is not found here, however, to serve as the purpose-point of either the individual judicial proceeding as a whole or as the purpose-point of the fact-finding.

14 Cadiet, Loïc et al., *Théorie générale du procès.* 3rd ed., PUF, 2020, Première partie is entirely devoted to the function of procedure, summarizing that the function is to "render justice" by expressing the law, p. 51. The matter is analyzed and discussed extensively in Swedish discourse, in terms of the function or the objectives of civil procedure, for example in Lindblom, P. H. "The Role of the Supreme Courts in Scandinavia." *Scandinavian Studies in Law*, vol. 39, 2000, pp. 325–366, and Lindblom, P. H. "The Growing Role of the Courts and the New Functions of Judicial Process – Fact or Flummery?" *Scandinavian Studies in Law*, vol. 51, 2007, pp. 281–310; Andersson, Torbjörn. *Rättsskyddsprincipen.* Uppsala, Iustus, 1997, Chapter 5. Dissertation; Lindell, Bengt. *Civilprocessen.* 3rd ed., Iustus and Uppsala, 2012, pp. 21–36.

15 Andersson, p. 224.

16 – Or functions, as they are often referred to – a term which has a different, more random and matter-of-factual connotation than what is meant with 'stake' in Lyotard's *The Differend.*

as *external* vs. *internal* in order to differentiate between the perspectives of society's needs for and uses of civil procedure, as a societal institution, and those of the parties.[17] Andersson finds that the judges' perception of the purpose of civil procedure impacts their rationale to choose a particular interpretation and application of both procedural and substantive law rules.[18] The political aims of a substantive law rule seem to encourage or require a certain interpretation of the rule.[19] Andersson's observation appears to confirm Lyotard's theory that what's at stake with a human practice determines the senses that are given to language acts within a particular practice. In other words, the purpose-point determines the sense and significance of a language act, be it a rule, an allegation or a piece of written evidence.

In the following, the two "levels" of purposes are sought in Swedish and French civil procedure: that of the judgment and that of the evidence. If the purpose-points in the direction of which the evidentiary language acts are linked differ, the evidentiary language acts will not be given the same sense in the different proceedings.[20]

The Purpose-Point of the Judgment

Swedish civil procedure divides cases into two types: cases amenable to out-of-court settlement and cases which are not.[21] The parties in both forms of Swedish civil procedure initiate the proceedings[22] and delimit the issue and the extent of the judgment by their claims.[23] In Swedish civil procedure, in no cases may the court render a judgment that exceeds the claims of the parties. This is particularly visible in child custody cases. The situation may be that one parent (1) claims sole custody, while the other (2) claims that the shared custody remain. The judgment may therefore only be whether parent 1 should be granted sole custody, or whether they should not. If sole custody is denied parent 1, the shared custody that was the outset, remains. If on the other hand both parents claim sole custody, it is not possible for the court to impose shared custody.[24] In this sense, the legal judgment is the answer to

17 Andersson, p. 228; Lindblom, The Role of the Supreme Courts, p. 334, referring to Andersson's *internal/external* as *private/public.*

18 Andersson, p. 289.

19 Andersson, pp. 283–284.

20 Lyotard, pt. 195.

21 17:3 CJP, is one example where they are treated differently.

22 42:1 CJP; Prop. 1986/87:89, p. 24; NJA 2003 s. 239; Lindell, Civilprocessen, pp. 272–273; Ekelöf, P. O. et al. *Rättegång V.* 7th ed., Norstedts Juridik, 2010, p. 22.

23 17:3 CJP; Prop 1942:5, pp. 411, 421–422; SOU 1938:44, p. 213. General caselaw: NJA 1993 s. 751; NJA 1993 s. 13; NJA 2003 s. 58; NJA 2013 s. 455; NJA 2007 s. 571; RH 1993: 119. Hassler, Åke. *Svensk civilprocessrätt.* Nord. bokh., 1963, p. 22.

24 6:4, 6:5 FB; Prop. 2005/06:99, pp. 86–87; Prop. 2004/05:137, p. 62; NJA 2007 s. 382; NJA 2006 s. 26, NJA 2003 s. 372; NJA 1999 s. 451; RH 2015:60; NJA 2014 s. 307; NJA 1998 s. 675; NJA 1987 s. 48; RH 2005:38.

the binary question. The French Code de procédure civile (CPC) likewise prescribes, in accordance with the principle of party autonomy,[25] that the parties in all forms of civil procedure at first instance level, initiate the proceedings[26] and delimit the issue and the extent of the judgment by their claims.[27] Both in Swedish and French civil proceedings, the parties initiate the action and delimit the issue and the extent of the judgment by their claims.[28] As the purpose-point of the proceedings, the parties' claims constitute the destination as well as the look-out-point of the issue.

The Purpose-Point of the Evidence

The civil procedural fact-finding systems of France and Sweden may, in terms of purpose-point, be divided into three different categories. In Swedish cases amenable to out-of-court settlement, only alleged facts expressly invoked may be used as grounds in the formation of the judgment.[29] The judges are therefore also restricted in their choice of substantive rule, to not only the claims but also those alleged facts that have been expressly invoked.[30] When the court is bound by the invoked alleged facts, these are the objects of proof in the sense that they are what's at stake with the evidence. In these cases, there is no point for the parties to prove a fact that they do not invoke as a reason for the judgment. It is indeed one of the exceptions[31] allowing the Swedish courts to deny the evidence, and thus restricting the parties' right to

25 Bolard, Georges. "La Matière du procès et le principe du dispositif." *Droit et pratique de la procédure civile – Droit interne et européen*, edited by Serge Guinchard, 9th ed., (2017/2018). Dalloz, 2016, 221.11, p. 849; Motulsky, Henri, "La cause de la demande dans la délimitation de l'office du juge." *Écrits, études et notes de procédure civile*. Dalloz, 2010, p. 104; Normand, Jacques. *Le juge et le litige*. L.G.D.J., 1965, pp. 39 ff: Lagarde, Xavier. *Réflexion critique sur le droit de la preuve*. L.G.D.J., 1994, pp. 34–35.

26 1 CPC; Bolard, p. 886; Motulsky, Henri. "La Réforme du Code de procédure civile par le Décret du 13 octobre 1965 et les principes directeurs du procès." *Écrits, études et notes de procédure civile*. Dalloz, 2010, p. 131.

27 4 and 5 CPC; Blanc, Emmanuel. *La Preuve judiciaire. Commentaire du Décret du 17 décembre 1973*. Librairie du Journal des notaires et des avocats, 1974, p. 16 s.; Bolard, 221.31–221.39, pp. 850–852. French doctrine distinguishes between the *objet de la demande* and the *cause de la demande*: Motulsky, La cause de la demande, p. 106; Motulsky, La Réforme du Code de procédure civile, p. 131; Bolard, 221.40–221.44, pp. 852–854.

28 17:3 CJP; RH 2009:50 (where the first instance court was criticized for having regarded evidentiary information that had come to the court's knowledge but had not been invoked by the parties); 4 CPC; Cadiet, Loïc, and Emmanuel Jeuland. *Droit judiciaire privé*. 10th ed., LexisNexis, 2017, p. 497.

29 17:3 CJP; Boman, Robert. *Om åberopande och åberopsbörda i dispositiva tvistemål*. P.A. Norstedt & Söners Förlag, 1964, pp. 7–8.

30 *iura novit curia;* Cadiet, Jeuland, p. 472.

31 35:7 CJP.

present evidence.[32] Thus, the link directly connected to the substantive law rule is the invoked allegations. The allegations are here understood as the descriptive language act which the ostensive evidentiary language act points to. The purpose-point of the evidence is to establish the truth-value[33] of the allegations. In other words, the purpose-point of the evidence is to verify[34] the alleged facts that have been explicitly invoked by the parties.

In Swedish cases not amenable to out-of-court settlement, the court may supplement the evidence presented by the parties by requesting further investigations.[35] In, for example, child custody cases – which are not amenable to out-of-court settlement[36] – the best interest of the child is a general condition which must always be considered.[37] The judges also possess investigative measures and are free to base the judgment on all facts that have come to their knowledge during the proceedings – even those that the parties have not specifically invoked.[38] The French judge is also free in this regard.[39] Whereas Swedish civil procedure is divided into cases depending on the extent of party disposition over the subject-matter, in terms of the purpose-points of procedure, French evidence law in civil procedure is divided into two "regimes," or systems: one where the evidence is regulated (this will be referred to as '*régime légal*'), and one where the evidence is free (this will be referred to as

32 The list in 35:7 CJP is exhaustive. The reason to keep to a minimum the situations in which the court may declare evidence inadmissible is held to primarily be to restrain the court from taking a stance in the matters of fact until the totality of the evidence has been presented – so as not to restrict the parties' right to present their case and be heard. (Westberg, Peter. *Anskaffning av bevisning i dispositiva tvistemål*. Norstedts Juridik, 2010, pp. 622–623; Ekelöf, P. O. et al. *Rättegång IV*. 7th ed., Norstedts Juridik, 2009, p. 38; Nordh, Robert. *Bevisrätt A: allmänna bevisfrågor: om ansvaret för bevisning, vittne, syn, sakkunnig m.m.* Iustus, 2009, p. 26.)

33 35:1 CJP, 6 and 9 CPC; Lyotard, pt. 28. Frege, Gottlob. "On Sense and Nominatum." *The Philosophy of Language*, edited by A. P. Martinich, translated by Herbert Feigl, 2nd ed., OUP, 1990, p. 190. *Also* Tarski, Alfred. "The Semantic Conception of Truth and the Foundations of Semantics." *The Philosophy of Language*, edited by A. P. Martinich, 2nd ed., OUP, 1990, p. 49.

34 Lyotard, pts. 10, 41, where the word used is "validate," "verify." See Chapter 9, below.

35 35:6 CJP, 42:19 CJP.

36 6:19 FB; 17:3 CJP; Cegrell Karlander, Isa. *Officialprincipen i migrationsprocessen: Domstolens utredningsansvar*. Uppsala, 2021, p. 49. Dissertation.

37 Art. 3, UN Commission on Human Rights, *Convention on the Rights of the Child.*, 7 Mar. 1990, E/CN.4/RES/1990/74; 6:2a FB. *See also*, Grahn-Farley, Maria. *Barnkonventionen. En kommentar*. Studentlitteratur, 2019.

38 42:18 CJP. The principle of immediacy requires that only what has been before the parties and the court immediately (and therefore in principle orally) may be included in the foundation for the legal judgment. (17:2 CJP) As will be shown in Chapter 7, in these types of cases, the Swedish judge may themselves add evidence to the case and expose it to the parties under the adversarial principle. (Article 6 ECHR)

39 7 CPC; Normand, Jacques. "Procédure civile." *JCl.*, Fasc 152, no. 13, as indicated in Aynès, Augustin, and Xavier Vuitton. *Droit de la preuve, Principes et mise en œuvre processuelle*. 2nd ed., LexisNexis, 2017, p. 139, 85.

'*régime libre*').[40] Within the *régime libre* the French judge may add evidence to the material on which they will construct the case.[41] The parties' burden of allegation is thus a formal requirement to clarify and verify the applicability of the legal rule to which the parties refer their claims. The French judge is however free to base the judgment on all the facts that have been entered into the debate or can be found in the case file, even those that the parties have not specifically invoked.[42]

Lagarde[43] identifies a distinction between facts that have been expressly invoked, which must be taken into consideration by the judge in the foundation of the judgment, and the facts retrieved[44] from the case material. Ekelöf makes a similar distinction in regards of Swedish procedural theory in that between immediately and mediately relevant circumstances.[45] Immediately relevant circumstances are referred to as 'legal facts' and are those that, in Motulsky's terms, constitute a substantive right,[46] in other words, those circumstances that give the judge reasons to conclude in favor of a claim. Mediately relevant circumstances are those that support the immediate ones, i.e., evidentiary facts.[47] Lagarde draws his distinction however between facts that

40 Aynès, Vuitton, p. 93; Croze, Hervé. *Procédure civile. Technique procédurale civile.* 6th ed., LexisNexis, 2017, p. 202.

41 The Medical Case Book example in Chapter 6 discusses the implications when in a cross-border evidence situation one of the jurisdictions may investigate a case and thus seek evidence, whereas the other jurisdiction depends entirely on the evidence and allegations submitted by the parties.

42 Cass. soc., 5 déc. 2012, n° 11–21.113, *Bull. Civ.* V, n° 325, in which case the *tribunal de prud'hommes* included information that it had itself searched for on the internet, in the foundation for the judgment without subjecting the information to the parties according to the principle of contradiction. *See also* Cass. civ. 1e, 28 janv. 2015, N° 13–27.125, *Bull. Civ.* 2015, I, n° 21 regarding the inclusion and communication of common knowledge in the case material, Cass. civ. 2e, 15 nov. 1995, n° 93–19.324, *Bull. civ.* II N° 281 p. 166 (*re* the delimitation of the issue as to what has been communicated in writing as opposed to claims made orally at the hearing), Cass. Civ. 3e, 20 nov. 1985, n° 84–13.353, *Bull civ.* III n° 153 p. 116 (*re* the judge's power to consider facts that have been entered into the case material albeit not expressly invoked, so called *faits adventices*); Aynès, Vuitton, p. 85 (*re* the judge's power to found the judgment on all facts entered into the case material, invoked or not); Bolard, 221.51 s, p. 744–745.

43 Lagarde, p. 104.

44 –Not derived! The facts must have been explicitly mentioned in the debate so as to meet the requirements of the principle of contradiction. *See also* Bolard, 221.52, on this point.

45 Ekelöf, P. O. *Processuella grundbegrepp och allmänna processprinciper: några problem inom den allmänna processrättsläran.* P.A. Norstedts & Söners Förlag, 1956, p. 57.

46 Motulsky, *Principes d'une réalisation méthodique du droit privé*, Sirey, 1948; Dalloz, 1991 as quoted by Bolard, 221.81, p. 857.

47 Ekelöf, Processuella grundbegrepp, p. 57. The distinction between 'evidentiary fact' and 'legal fact' is analyzed for Swedish purposes in Lindblom, P. H. "Processens arkitektur." *Vänbok till Torleif Bylund*, edited by Torbjörn Andersson and Bengt Lindell, Iustus, 2003, pp. 171–260, with a focus on the confusion between legal fact (which may be abstract as well as concrete), and evidentiary fact which may also be object of proof in relation to another evidentiary fact.

have been expressly invoked and those that have not been expressly invoked but likewise may be immediately relevant and used as such.[48]

All matters of fact that come to the knowledge of the French judge, in all types of cases within the *régime libre*, may be used for the judge to motivate his judgment. In these types of cases, the evidence therefore does not necessarily have to respond to the allegations but to the claims (both forms of civil procedure require the parties to formulate allegations, that is, descriptive language acts "with cognitive value"[49]). In cases not amenable to out-of-court settlement, as well as cases within the *régime libre*, the purpose-point must be seen to be the legitimacy of the parties' claims. If the judgment concerns the question: "What (who) is right?" the following question ("that depends . . .") will in the Swedish cases amenable to out-of-court settlement be "Is it true?" (which is a binary question regarding the parties' allegations), in the French *régime libre* and Swedish cases *not* amenable to out-of-court settlement the question is (the more open non binary): "What happened?" In these – French as well as Swedish – cases the links directly attached to the substantive law rule are the evidentiary language acts.

In matters within the *régime légal*,[50] where the evidence is regulated, things look a bit different. In those cases, between the evidence on the one hand and the rule relevant to the parties' claims on the other, there is a rule regarding the form of the evidence.[51] Therefore, the purpose-point of the evidence is to prove that it shares the sense of that rule; if the evidence rules require that an agreement be proven with a written contract, the purpose-point of the evidentiary language act is to prove that it has the sense of a written contract. Only thereafter does the interpretation of the detailed content of the written contract become relevant. The interpretation may at that point be proven with any means; any language act will be accepted as evidence and assessed freely by the judge.[52] Such evidence is then linked to the interpretation of the written content, not to the language act of the agreement as such or to the allegations. The allegations will be a link further away. The written content on the other hand will be given sense from the perspective of the allegations.

48 See also, regarding the Swedish discourse, Ekelöf, IV, p. 15.

49 Lyotard, pt. 176; 42:2 CJP, 6 CPC.

50 Although there are cases where the evidence is regulated also in Swedish civil procedure, it does not constitute its own "regime" within evidence law but is rather understood as ad-hoc exceptions of formality requirements within the law of obligations, *see* The Will example in Chapter 6.

51 1359 CC; Rapport au Président de la République relatif à l'ordonnance n° 2016–131 du 10 février 2016 portant réforme du droit des contrats, du régime général et de la preuve des obligations, JORF n°0035 du 11 février 2016; Aynès, Vuitton, pp. 230 ff.

52 As noted earlier, it is not, however, possible to add content to the contract through testimonial evidence or other. The intricacies of the distinction between adding content to a contract and merely interpreting it are discussed in Samuelsson, Joel. *Tolkning och utfyllning*. Iustus, 2008.

In Swedish law, the formality requirements on wills[53] as well as those for real-estate purchases[54] are perceived as the formal requirement for the legal act to be binding rather than rules of evidence. In regulating that the form for the legal act[55] must be the written, the form also by consequence becomes the means of pre-constituted evidence.[56] The two coincide in the same language act. The referent of the ostensive language act is itself the ostensive language act. The French law seems to make this distinction clearer as it regulates the forming of a legal act separately from the proving of it.[57] If the evidentiary language act must, for reasons of communicatory structure, point to the interpretation of the wording of the contract, this constitutes an important restriction in the freedom of the parties to present evidentiary language acts. It means that the reality that the evidentiary language acts can construct is limited, first, to what may share the sense of 'contract' and second, to what sense may be given to the wording of the contract – whereas when the evidence is free regarding the agreement, the restriction is set by the allegations that there was an "agreement." Thereafter, the parties are free to present evidence in the form of witness testimonials, photos, notes etc. of their choice with the aim of giving the court a sense of a reality that corresponds with the perceived realities of the parties.

The Car Purchase Contract

Let us imagine a dispute about a car purchase between a French seller and a Swedish buyer which is tried in a French court. If the conflict concerns the purchase, from French law perspective, it concerns an *acte juridique* – an act taken with the purpose of creating a legal effect.[58] From the study earlier we know that the ultimate purpose-point is the legitimacy of the parties' claims,[59] for example whether the car should be delivered. If the value of the car is above 1500 €,[60] and if the case is tried in the French court under French law, it falls under the *régime légal* and the evidence is regulated so that a particular means of evidence must be presented in order to prove an

53 10:1 ÄB.

54 4:1, 20:7 JB; NJA 2000 s. 747; NJA 2012 s. 1095; NJA 1997 s. 336.

55 It is indeed the direct translation of the Swedish *rättshandling*. *Re* the Swedish extent of the concept, see Fridström Montoya, Therése. *Homo iuridicus: Den kapabla människan i rätten.* Iustus, 2017.

56 1359 CC. In Swedish law this does not follow from any explicit provision, but in French law it does.

57 For example, Titres III and IV CC regarding the formation of the legal act and Titre IV bis CC regarding the evidence of the legal acts.

58 1364 CC; Aynès, Vuitton, p. 230. *Actes juridiques* are voluntary acts, which are performed with the intention of acquiring a specific legal effect. (Cornu, Gérard. "Acte juridique." *Vocabularie juridique*, 9th ed. Quadrige PUF, 2011, p. 22.)

59 Chapter 5.

60 Décret n° 2004–836 du 20 août 2004 portant modification de la procédure civile.

alleged fact.[61] In the French *régime légal* the principle of legality implies that a prescribed means of evidence must be used in order to prove a certain allegation.[62] This means of evidence is pre-constituted in accordance with rules of formality.[63] Consequently, it is a written means of evidence. The evidence is conclusive ("perfect"),[64] and the judge's role is to verify the formality requirements and to establish the legally relevant facts, which are the objects of proof.[65] The main burden of proof rule is applicable: the person who alleges something must prove it.[66] The Swedish buyer will need to present a written contract of the purchase in order to win the case. This is foreign to Swedish evidence law, however, only in the extent that the French court is prohibited from accepting any other means of evidence. The Swedish court would likely assess the contract as such as evidence of a binding agreement between the parties.

If a written contract is presented as evidence in the French court, this is a "perfect" means of proof,[67] the evidentiary value of which the judge is not free to estimate. What remains is that the piece of paper presented as a contract must be interpreted to be just that. The *content* of the contract must also be interpreted.[68] Interpretation is an activity by the addressee, that is, the judge, once the contract is presented as evidence in the court.[69] When the means of evidence is regulated, one may say that the ultimate purpose-point of the evidence is to prove that it is the means of evidence that is prescribed. This is however not likely to be a point of conflict between the parties. As the interpretation of the contract can be proven with any means, a more accurate perspective to analyze this would be to say that the pre-constituted written evidence is the actual purpose-point of the rest of the evidence. This means that the rest of the evidence and the arguments are directed towards the written content of the pre-constituted evidence, that is, the contract. All other

61 1359 CC.
62 1359 CC.
63 1365–1367 CC.
64 1371–1372 CC.
65 285–316 CPC.
66 9 CPC establishes that each party must prove the necessary facts in order to win the case. (Aynès, Vuitton, p. 68.) The same principle is expressed in 1353 CC, in matters concerning contractual obligations. (Civ. 1e, 26 janv. 2012, n° 10–28.356, *Bull. civ.* I, n° 13; Lacroix-Andrivet, Jean-Paul. "Preuves à conserver." *Droit et pratique de la procédure civile – Droit interne et européen*, edited by Serge Guinchard, 9th ed., (2017/2018). Dalloz, 2016, 111.12, p. 70; Carbonnier, Jean. *Droit civil*. Vol. I, 1st ed. Quadrige PUF, 2004, p. 336.)
67 1369–1372 CC; The reform of 2016 shifted the weight of the *régime libre* and *régime légal*, so that the *régime libre* became the main rule. From a Swedish perspective, this would have possibly implied an abolishment of such an institute as "perfect proof." This was however not the case. For a recent use of this expression in French caselaw, see Cass. civ. 1e, 10 mars 2021, N° 19–22.117, 19–22.656, Non publié.
68 1188–1192 CC.
69 Lyotard, pt. 46 (*in fine*).

evidence which may be relevant in relation to the claims will nevertheless, because of the communicatory structure, be judged as inconsistent.[70] They will fall to the side, not heard.

Had the case been tried in a Swedish court, it would be tried as a case amenable to out-of-court settlement. Swedish law of evidence is based on liberty. The parties are free to present the evidence they choose to support their allegations. The court is in turn free to evaluate the evidence, albeit in harmony with laws of rationality and objectivity.[71] Even when the element is estimated to lack all evidentiary value, it is still categorized as evidence within the structure of civil procedure.[72] In the preparatory works, it is likewise stated that there should be no regulation regarding the source of knowledge "for the search for truth."[73] In accordance with Swedish law, the truth in this case would regard whether the parties had reached an agreement.[74] The principle of evidentiary freedom would therefore have prevailed with the consequence that the parties would have been able to present any means of evidence which they found to be of value to establish the case. In cases amenable to out-of-court settlement, there is, however, another sieve: that of the invoked allegations[75] with the effect that the parties must explicitly invoke the alleged facts on which they wish that the court establish the case and the court is restricted to determine the legitimacy of the claims based on the invoked allegations. The purpose-point is therefore the alleged facts, which are alleged *legal facts*, that is, facts that are immediately relevant because they are the translation of the hypothetical of the substantive law rule into an allegation of fact.[76] All the evidentiary language acts which point to the verification or falsification of the *allegations* are therefore relevant. A written contract presented as evidence is assessed alongside other evidence rather than serving as its primary reference point. This is because both the contract and the other evidence point to the same purpose-point. The allegations may broaden or delimit the scope of the agreement in comparison to what may follow from the written content of the contract, and so oral evidence may, for example, support allegations that the agreement contained details not noted in the written pre-constituted evidence. In the French court, the contract would therefore serve as object of proof in relation to the rest of the

70 Lyotard, pt. 40.

71 SOU 1938:44, pp. 377–378.

72 Prop. 1942:5, p. 331. *See also* 35:7 CJP according to which "evidence" may be disallowed on the basis of its lacking relevance or effect.

73 Prop. 1942:5, p. 218; *See also* Lindell, Civilprocessen, pp. 45–46, where he distinguishes between juridical and "real" truth.

74 1:1 AvtL.

75 17:3 CJP.

76 Kallenberg, Ernst. Svensk civilprocess. Bd 2.1, Gleerup, 1927, p. 541; Lindell, Bengt. *Sakfrågor och rättsfrågor: en studie av gränser, skillnader och förhållanden mellan faktum och rätt*. Iustus, 1987, p. 33.

evidentiary language acts. The other evidence would be auxiliary[77] or counterevidence[78] in relation to the content of the contract. In the Swedish court, on the other hand, all the evidence might sort as auxiliary or counterevidence to the written contract in relation to the explicitly invoked alleged legal facts.

Conclusion

At this point we can detect the beginning of different formations of chains constructing the matters of fact of the case. In all types of cases, the claims constitute the purpose-point of the judgment, what the judgment is about, what the individual civil proceeding is about, the purpose of processing, in short: what's at stake.[79] From here the linking differs in three manners.

The evidentiary language act is, from the point of view of the law (i.e., as a legal as opposed to a cognitive matter), divided into two language acts: the means and its intelligible content.[80] This distinction is relevant in the cases where evidence is regulated in an extent that it is not in other types of cases. When the evidence is regulated, the object of proof immediately connected to the means of proof is the evidentiary law rule, which in its turn is connected to the allegations of the parties. The evidence here must answer the question whether what is presented is what is requested in the evidentiary law rule. The question in this case is: "Does x ["this piece of paper"](presented as evidence) refer to the same referent as y (by law required means of evidence)?"[81] From the perspective of the judge, when the evidence is regulated, the chain between the evidence and the aims of the evidence is developed as follows: party claims – substantive law rule criteria – allegations *in conjunction with*

77 Ekelöf, P. O. "My Thoughts on Evidentiary Value." *Evidentiary Value: Philosophical, Judicial, and Psychological Aspects of a Theory*, edited by Peter Gärdenfors et al., Gleerups, 1983, p. 11; Schum, David. "A Science of Evidence: Contributions from Law and Probability." *Law, Probability and Risk*, vol. 8, 2009, pp. 197–231; Bolding, P. O. *Går det att bevisa?: Perspektiv på domstolsprocessen.* Norstedts, 1989, p. 20 (*hjälpfakta*). (Ekelöf translates the term into German as *Hilfsfaktum*.)

78 Bentham, Jeremy. *A Treatise on Judicial Evidence.* J. W. Paget, 1825, p. 44; *also* Bentham, Jeremy. *Rationale of Judicial Evidence: Specially Applied to English Practice.* Vol. V, Hunt and Clarke, 1827, pp. 21, 348, 400.

79 Lyotard, pts. 22, 30 ff.

80 Prop. 2004/05:131, pp. 165 ff; Ekelöf, IV, p. 256; Lindell, Civilprocessen, p. 488; 1365 CC. It is possible to consider the distinction between means of evidence as referent of the language act and the intelligible content of the evidence as the sense of the language act, but this risks blurring the distinction between the evidence and the ultimate object of proof. (Wigmore, John H. *Treatise on the System of Evidence in Trials at Common Law: Including the Statutes and Judicial Decisions of All Jurisdictions of the United states.* Little, Brown, and Co., 1904, § 267.) I prefer, therefore, to see the means and the content as two separate language acts.

81 Lyotard, pts. 47–48, 56, 66, 69. Cf. Frege, On Sense and Nominatum, p. 190; *see also* Lyotard, Jean-François. *Discourse, Figure.* Translated by Antony Hudek and Mary Lydon, University of Minnesota Press, 2011, p. 103 ff.

evidentiary law rule criteria – means of evidence. Therefore, the parties must present means which may be subsumed under the evidentiary law rule, the content of which may be connected to the substantive law rule, the consequence of which corresponds to the claims and wishes of the party.

In Swedish matters *not* amenable to out-of-court settlement as well as French matters under the *régime libre* the judges may found the legal judgment on anything that has entered into the debate, i.e., that it has been subject to contradiction by the opponent parties.[82] In these matters the linking is: party claims – substantive law rule – intelligible content of the evidence.

In Swedish cases amenable to out-of-court settlement the criteria must be specified by the parties' allegations which must be verified by the evidence.[83] The judge is bound by the invoked allegations and each invoked allegation must be proven, in order to be accepted by the judge and for the rule to apply.[84] When the allegations are binding on the judges, as is the case in Swedish matters amenable to out-of-court settlement, the evidence must help the judges determine the question whether the allegations are true. In Swedish matters amenable to out-of-court settlement, the chain is: party claims – substantive law rule – allegations – intelligible content of the evidence.

In the language of the legal judgment, we find that the frame of the proceedings are the following syllogisms:

1. If the allegations are true (and there is a substantive legal rule that corresponds) then the claims are legitimate (amenable to out-out-court settlement).
2. If the evidence indicates it (and there is a substantive legal rule that corresponds to what the evidence indicates) then the claims are legitimate (not amenable to out-of-court settlement + *régime libre*).
3. If the evidence corresponds to the prescribed form and its content corresponds to the claims (and there is a substantive legal rule that corresponds to the claims) then the claims are legitimate (*régime légal* + regulated form for obligation).

The parties must phrase allegations in all cases but only in Swedish cases amenable to out-of-court settlement are these allegations the second link to the claims. The cross-border implication is that a piece of evidence, such as a contract, responds to the invoked allegations in Sweden, but to a legal rule regarding forms of evidence in France. The sense of the evidentiary fact will not be assessed because it is transmitted in a format not recognized by the communicatory structure connecting the last two links (the two purpose-points) of the judicial proceedings. Whether the differences matter

82 16 CPC; Aynès, Vuitton, p. 93.
83 17:3 CJP.
84 Lyotard, pt. 28; 6 CPC.

in the outcome of the singular case is another matter, for in the end, it is the court as addressor of the legal judgment who decides what is and what is not the sense of that which is presented by the party as a contract.

It is however held in this thesis that justice is both the journey and its destination. Only if the parties have been heard can there be procedural justice; only if the judge has openly addressed themselves toward the parties to sincerely attempt to take in what each party has to say can there be procedural justice.[85] If the parties have not been heard it is also not possible to determine the case; it is not possible to know what senses have not been expressed, and therefore it is not possible to know whether the swarm of senses of which the judge constructs the case makes the case construction robust.[86] An unstable case construction means that the case is not properly investigated – or as expressed in French law: it is not put in a state to be adjudicated.[87] Moreover, only if the parties have been heard can there be a way to assess whether the legal judgment, that which determines the legal consequence and may bring substantive law (whether EU or national) into effect in the concrete case, is just in retrospect.[88]

If one does not follow the map, one cannot know if one has reached the destination. Parties from different legal environments travel with different maps – they travel with the maps they normally use and will expect to express themselves on the points and in the manner that is normal in their spatio-temporal commonality. In a citizen's every-day life, the legal and the non-legal language acts, that is, the every-day language acts which may be given a legal sense and those which may not, are all equally part of the spatio-temporal commonality. A procedure where the parties have not been heard cannot be said to give access to justice.

It is the link that follows that gives the previous its sense. The purpose-point is the overall purpose of the human practice which imposes itself on the language act – one language act at a time. In a judicial proceeding the purpose-point is the legal judgment – which regards the claims in the legal orders compared – and the judgment concerns whether the claims are justified. This depends on another human practice than the legal, namely, the cognitive/descriptive[89] where language acts concern the reality of the

85 With procedural justice is meant here a form of procedure which meets the requirements of Article 6 ECHR and is the result of such a procedure. In that sense it seems to correspond to Rawls' 'procedural justice'; Rawls, John. *A Theory of Justice*. Original ed., Belknap and Harvard UP, 2005.

86 These thoughts are further developed primarily in Chapter 8. *Re* robustness, see, for example, Ekelöf, IV, pp. 187–189.

87 Cf. "mise en état d'être jugée," 1564–1–5 CPC.

88 Lyotard, pt. 88.

89 I will not uphold the distinction between cognitive and descriptive language acts (Lyotard, pt. 176, *also* Lindell, Sakfrågor, section 1.3.1).

referent.[90] This means that the evidentiary language act itself serves as agglutinating factor. The dualism is yet again confused; to say that a = b, that is, to link, requires a third. Lyotard explains that to prove, one must first mean something, then describe it and, as a last step, show it.[91] This is done by presenting first a descriptive language act and then an ostensive language act, both being able to have the same referent.[92]

The sense is given to the evidence by the addressee. Standing at the purpose-point of the particular proceeding, the court thus considers, more or less consciously, the purpose-point of the evidence in their understanding of the same. Like a magnet, the purpose-point turns the language act so that its instance of the sense faces the purpose-point. The addressee, however, will also give the evidence a sense that conforms with the horizon of the human practice that the evidence may be said to emanate from, that is, which human practice it gives information about, by indicating it.[93] The evidence is brought into the practice of law from the external environment, which consists of a muddle of innumerable human practices.[94] In this chapter, the linking of language acts illustrates what is already known: what serves as *factum probandum* and what is *factum probans* is relative: in relation to one *factum probandum* one fact is *probans* but in relation to another *probandum* – in a chain of evidence.[95] Each *factum probandum* is a purpose-point. In the following chapter the cross-border implications of different concatenations in the proceedings of the forum court and the requested court will be studied. Thereafter follows the last comparative chapter, in which the relation between law and other human practices is studied.

Bibliography

Andersson, Torbjörn. *Rättsskyddsprincipen*. Uppsala and Iustus, 1997. Dissertation.

Aynès, Augustin, and Xavier Vuitton. *Droit de la preuve, Principes et mise en œuvre processuelle*. 2nd ed., LexisNexis, 2017.

Bentham, Jeremy. *A Treatise on Judicial Evidence*. J.W. Paget, 1825.

Bentham, Jeremy. *Rationale of Judicial Evidence: Specially Applied to English Practice*. Vol. V. Hunt and Clarke, 1827.

Bolard, Georges. "La Matière du procès et le principe du dispositif." *Droit et pratique de la procédure civile – Droit interne et européen*, edited by Serge Guinchard, 9th ed., (2017/2018). Dalloz, 2016.

Bolding, P. O. *Går det att bevisa?: Perspektiv på domstolsprocessen*. Norstedts, 1989.

Boman, Robert. *Om åberopande och åberopsbörda i dispositiva tvistemål*. P. A. Norstedt & Söners Förlag, 1964.

Cadiet, Loïc, and Emmanuel Jeuland. *Droit judiciaire privé*. 10th ed., LexisNexis, 2017.

90 Lyotard, pts. 47–48.

91 Lyotard, pt. 41.

92 Lyotard, pt. 65.

93 Lyotard, pts. 56, 59, 93.

94 Chapter 3.

95 Cf. Lindblom, Processens arkitektur.

Cadiet, Loïc et al. *Théorie générale du procès*. 3rd ed., PUF, 2020, Première partie.
Carbonnier, Jean. *Droit civil*. Vol. I, 1st ed. Quadrige PUF, 2004.
Cegrell Karlander, Isa. *Officialprincipen i migrationsprocessen: Domstolens utredningsansvar*. Uppsala, 2021. Dissertation.
Cornu, Gérard. "Acte juridique." *Vocabularie juridique*, 9th ed. Quadrige PUF, 2011.
Croze, Hervé. *Procédure civile. Technique procédurale civile*. 6th ed., LexisNexis, 2017.
Ekelöf, P. O. *Processuella grundbegrepp och allmänna processprinciper: några problem inom den allmänna processrättsläran*. P.A. Norstedts & Söners Förlag, 1956.
Ekelöf, P. O. "My Thoughts on Evidentiary Value." *Evidentiary Value: Philosophical, Judicial, and Psychological Aspects of a Theory*, edited by Peter Gärdenfors et al., Gleerups, 1983.
Ekelöf, P. O. et al. *Rättegång IV*. 7th ed., Norstedts Juridik, 2009.
Ekelöf, P. O. et al. *Rättegång V*. 7th ed., Norstedts Juridik, 2010.
Frege, Gottlob. "On Sense and Nominatum." *The Philosophy of Language*, edited by A. P. Martinich, translated by Herbert Feigl, 2nd ed., OUP, 1990.
Fridström, Montoya. *Therése. Homo iuridicus: Den kapabla människan i rätten*. Iustus, 2017.
Grahn-Farley, Maria. *Barnkonventionen. En kommentar*. Studentlitteratur, 2019.
Hassler, Åke. *Svensk civilprocessrätt*. Nord. bokh., 1963.
Kallenberg, Ernst. *Svensk civilprocess*. Bd 2.1. Gleerup, 1927.
Lacroix-Andrivet, Jean-Paul. "Preuves à conserver." *Droit et pratique de la procédure civile – Droit interne et européen*, edited by Serge Guinchard, 9th ed., (2017/2018). Dalloz, 2016.
Lagarde, Xavier. *Réflexion critique sur le droit de la preuve*. L.G.D.J., 1994.
Lindblom, P. H. "The Role of the Supreme Courts in Scandinavia." *Scandinavian Studies in Law*, vol. 39, 2000.
Lindblom, P. H. "Processens arkitektur." *Vänbok till Torleif Bylund*, edited by Torbjörn Andersson and Bengt Lindell, Iustus, 2003.
Lindblom, P. H. "The Growing Role of the Courts and the New Functions of Judicial Process – Fact or Flummery?" *Scandinavian Studies in Law*, vol. 51, 2007, pp. 281–310.
Lindell, Bengt. *Sakfrågor och rättsfrågor: en studie av gränser, skillnader och förhållanden mellan faktum och rätt*. Iustus, 1987.
Lindell, Bengt. *Civilprocessen*. 3rd ed., Iustus and Uppsala, 2012, pp. 21–36.
Luhmann, Niklas. *Law as a Social System*. OUP, 2004.
Lyotard, Jean-François. *The Differend – Phrases in Dispute*. Translated by Georges Van Den Abbeele, University of Minnesota Press, 1988.
Lyotard, Jean-François. *Discourse, figure*. Translated by Antony Hudek and Mary Lydon, University of Minnesota Press, 2011.
Motulsky, Henri. "La cause de la demande dans la délimitation de l'office du juge." *Écrits, études et notes de procédure civile*. Dalloz, 2010.
Motulsky, Henri. "La Réforme du Code de procédure civile par le Décret du 13 octobre 1965 et les principes directeurs du procès." *Écrits, études et notes de procédure civile*. Dalloz, 2010.
Motulsky, Henri. *Principes d'une réalisation méthodique du droit privé. La théorie des éléments générateurs des droits subjectifs*. préf. Paul Roubier, Sirey, 1948; Dalloz, 1991.
Nordh, Robert. *Bevisrätt A: allmänna bevisfrågor: om ansvaret för bevisning, vittne, syn, sakkunnig m.m.* Iustus, 2009.
Nordh, Robert. *Processens ram i tvistemål: om yrkande och grunder, ändring av talan m.m.* 4th ed., Iustus, 2019.

Normand, Jacques. *Le juge et le litige.* L.G.D.J., 1965.
Normand, Jacques. "Procédure civile." *JCl., Fasc 152, n° 13, as indicated in Aynès, Augustin and Xavier Vuitton. Droit de la preuve, Principes et mise en œuvre processuelle.* 2nd ed., LexisNexis, 2017.
Rawls, John. *A Theory of Justice.* Original ed., Belknap and Harvard UP, 2005.
Samuelsson, Joel. *Tolkning och utfyllning.* Iustus, 2008.
Schlag, Pierre, and Amy J. Griffin. *How to Do Things with Legal Doctrine.* University of Chicago Press, 2020.
Schum, David. "A Science of Evidence: Contributions from Law and Probability." *Law, Probability and Risk*, vol. 8, 2009, pp. 197–231.
Tarski, Alfred. "The Semantic Conception of Truth and the Foundations of Semantics." *The Philosophy of Language*, edited by A. P. Martinich, 2nd ed., OUP, 1990.
Westberg, Peter. *Anskaffning av bevisning i dispositiva tvistemål.* Norstedts Juridik, 2010.
Wigmore, John H. *Treatise on the System of Evidence in Trials at Common Law: Including the Statutes and Judicial Decisions of All Jurisdictions of the United States.* Little, Brown, and Co., 1904.

Chapter 6

Mr Ernest Changes His Mind

Structuring Evidence

Introduction

In the previous chapter two levels of purpose-points were sought in order to establish what the evidence is aiming at, what it is supposed to support. Initially it was found that in all the types of cases compared, the ultimate purpose-point is that of the legitimacy of the claims. What happens when the case is legally qualified is that the law as a practice 'imposes' itself on the matters of fact. Only what is relevant to determine the legitimacy of the claims will be seen as relevant, as having any sense in the context of a specific proceeding. At a closer look, it may therefore be found that there is a chain of purpose-points, the judgment is the connection of two links; the claimed legal consequence as link 1 and the facts of the case, as link 2[1] – but that link 2 varies depending on the form of procedure. The lower-level purpose-point was found to vary between three different forms of procedure. The Car Purchase Contract case makes visible that these forms of procedure do not apply equally to the different types of cases in the two legal orders compared: a contract is not established with the same fact-finding method in both Sweden and France. The consequence of this divergence may be that what is perceived as object of proof on the one hand and evidence on the other varies between the forms of proceedings.

Whereas the previous chapter sought two purpose-points which connect to each other in a concatenation of language acts, this chapter investigates the impact of the communicatory structure. The communicatory structure is understood as the order in which the evidentiary language acts are further linked and how this structure determines what senses are possible to attribute to the evidence – what is consistent and what is impertinent.[2] In line

1 Lyotard, Jean-François. *The Differend – Phrases in Dispute.* Translated by Georges Van Den Abbeele, University of Minnesota Press, 1988/Lyotard, Jean-François. *Le Différend.* Éditions de minuit. 1983, pt. 240. Bennington, Geoffrey. *Lyotard: Writing the Event.* Manchester UP and Columbia UP, 1988, pp. 124, 132. At a closer look one sees that the substantive law rule is inserted in-between links 1 and 2.

2 Lyotard, pt. 40; Douzinas, Costas and Ronnie Warrington. "'A Well-Founded Fear of Justice': Law and Ethics in Postmodernity." *Law and Critique*, vol. II, no. 2, 1991, pp. 115–147, p. 122.

DOI: 10.4324/9781003495383-6

therewith is analyzed the impact on the evidentiary language act of the rules regulating how evidence may be introduced in the procedure. In the comparison in this chapter, it will be asked what restrictions the two procedural law orders as communicatory structures raise against the presentation of an evidentiary language act.

The procedural and evidentiary law conditions for that purpose are studied comparatively for a cross-border analysis. The comparison contains two illustrations of how the communicatory structure of civil procedural fact-finding will impact the sense of the evidence and therefore the determination – and outcome – of the case. In the Medical Case Book illustration, I study the impact of who may act as an addressor in the fact-finding process, and thus add evidentiary language acts the senses of which may contribute to the judge's construction of the case. The Will illustration concerns the order in which the evidence is structured: what evidence is auxiliary and what is immediately connected to the ultimate object of the proof? It studies, therefore, how the same evidentiary language act is perceived as link 1 in one procedure and as link 2 in another, and vice versa.

Evidence Links

Evidence is spoken of as means as well as fact.[3] Examples of means of evidence are witness testimonials, (the written form of) a contract or a will etc.[4] As a means, evidence conveys a message;[5] as fact, evidence is an event or a state, which is the intelligible content of the means.[6] From an evidentiary fact another fact is inferred, which in relation to the evidentiary fact is the object of proof (*probans – probandum*). This constitutes a chain: the means of evidence conveys a message regarding a fact or state, which in turn serves as evidence of another fact or state, namely, the object of proof. It is this double meaning of the word evidence which is so well captured by Lyotard's theory of the phrase, and which is here referred to as 'language act.' The object of proof in turn is a concrete legal fact, as expressed in the allegations, which are connected to the criteria of the antecedent of the legal rule – spoken of

3 1354 CC; Bentham, Jeremy. *Rationale of Judicial Evidence.* Edited by J. S. Mill, Vol. I, Hunt and Clarke, 1827. *Also* Lindblom, P. H. "Processens arkitektur." *Vänbok till Torleif Bylund*, edited by Torbjörn Andersson and Bengt Lindell, Iustus, 2003, pp. 171–260.

4 Comp. "Written evidence" refers to the linguistic signs or figures, which transmit a written intellectual content. (Fitger et al. "Rättegångsbalken." *Kommentaren till 38 kap.* JUNO, 2020.)

5 1365 CC; Ekelöf, P. O. et al. *Rättegång IV.* 7th ed., Norstedts Juridik, 2009, p. 15, *also* p. 257; Lindell, Bengt. *Civilprocessen.* 3rd ed., Iustus and Uppsala, 2012, p. 488; *See also* Prop. 2004/05:131, pp. 165 ff.

6 "Written evidence" refers to the linguistic signs or figures, which transmit a written intellectual content. (Fitger et al. "Rättegångsbalken." *Kommentaren till 38 kap.* JUNO, 2020.) *Re* French law: 1364, 1381 CC; 199 CPC.

as abstract legal facts.[7] It was shown in the previous chapter that allegations presented by the parties are not necessarily what constitutes the last link on the chain in terms of ultimate object of proof, but it will be understood here that when a claim is made, it presumes an allegation of a right, and this allegation will take the same place in the chain as the allegations of fact expressly made (both may be given the sense of cognitive language acts). As Wigmore advised, evidence may be sorted schematically so that each alleged fact is supported by a "net" of evidentiary facts connected through the inferences that are made from one evidentiary fact[8] to another.[9] Depending on their position, they serve as evidentiary fact or auxiliary fact,[10] having immediate or mediate relevance for the establishment of the object of proof.[11] The evidence is thus connected in links.

According to Lyotard, *all* language acts are connected in links.[12] Even silence, or the "non-response," is a language act, as it is also given a meaning (–And you say *nothing*!?).[13] Wigmore's chart[14] is a method for analyzing how the evidentiary language acts that have already been collected are connected and together help us to understand the case so that it may be properly subsumed under the substantive law rule, in the formation of the legal judgment. The formation of the chain of language acts (which link may connect onto which other) depends on what is here called the communicatory structure.[15] The communicatory structure allows for pertinent language acts to connect, but it disallows others as inconsistent.[16]

7 Boman, Robert. "Om mellandom och omröstningar om omständigheter." *Festskrift till Welamson*, edited by Olle Höglund and Lars Welamson, Norstedts, 1987, p. 86; Lindell, Bengt. *Sakfrågor och rättsfrågor: en studie av gränser, skillnader och förhållanden mellan faktum och rätt*. Iustus, 1987, p. 27; Lindblom, Processens arkitektur, p. 174.
8 Wigmore, John H. *The Principles of Judicial Proof*. Little, Brown, and Co., 1913, p. 746.
9 Wigmore, John H. "Problem of Proof." *Illinois Law Review*, vol. 8, no. 2, 1913–1914, pp. 77–103; Schum, David. "A Science of Evidence: Contributions from Law and Probability." *Law, Probability and Risk*, vol. 8, 2009, pp. 197–231; *see also* Goodwin, Jean. "Wigmore's Chart Method." *Informal Logic*, vol. 20, no. 3, 2000, p. 223.
10 Ekelöf, P. O. "My Thoughts on Evidentiary Value." *Evidentiary Value: Philosophical, Judicial, and Psychological Aspects of a Theory*, edited by Peter Gärdenfors, et al., Gleerups, 1983, p. 11.
11 Bentham, Jeremy. *Rationale of Judicial Evidence: Specially Applied to English Practice*. Vol. V, Hunt and Clarke, 1827, pp. 28–29, *also* Vol I, pp. 69, 258; Ekelöf, My Thoughts on Evidentiary Value, p. 11, note 2; Ekelöf, IV, p. 15; Lindblom, Processens arkitektur, pp. 171–260.
12 Lyotard, pts. 40, 41, 102, 184. *Re* linking, *see also* Sawyer, Dylan. *Lyotard, Literature and the Trauma of the Differend*. Palgrave Macmillian, 2014, p. 27.
13 Lyotard, p. xii, pts. 22, 105. Moreover, silence is at the heart of the differend, as it may be (but doesn't have to be) the non-recognition of the utterance or act of the other.
14 Wigmore, Problem of Proof; Schum, A Science of Evidence; *see also* Goodwin, p. 223.
15 Lyotard, p. 94, pts. 21, 78, 185.
16 Lyotard, pt. 40.

An illustration may again be the anecdote of the machete: as the man in the night-club pulled a machete out from his pocket, the opponent responded by pulling *his* machete out from his pocket. Pulling a knife out from a pocket may under certain circumstances, such as in front of a person with whom one has a long-lasting conflict be understood as an offensive act. It is thus a language act which is given the sense of expressing aggression. A pertinent response is then to pull one's own knife out. This would then likewise be interpreted as an aggressive act. There are however other possible pertinent ways to respond to the first knife (–Put that away!). There are also inconsistent responses, which are responses that make no sense in the context (–What smithery made that fine piece of armor? Or why not: –Well! There it is, the knife Elisa gave you[17]).

Through rules regarding the pertinence of responses, communicatory structures restrict the content of communication. Chronology is however not required; the communicatory structure is applicable on logic as well as cognitive-historical language acts;[18] it is thus applicable on the Wigmorean chart of evidence – when the evidence is already collected and the totality of the case material is being assessed at the deliberations – as well as the chronological order of the events and the chronological order in which the events are recounted.[19] Like a communicatory structure, civil procedural fact-finding structures the information that is included in the foundation of the legal judgment, but this is done chronologically during the course of the proceedings.[20] Civil procedural fact-finding thus restricts the language acts that are included in the case material and the foundation of the judgment by rules regulating the different instances.[21]

The addressee instance is regulated in the role of the judge; as the addressor of the legal judgment, all language acts during the proceedings are ultimately directed to the judge, who is therefore the addressee. Through rules regarding the object of proof, the sense is regulated. The totality of the material will depend on the communicatory structure. In the example of the contract in the previous chapter, the rules requiring that the evidence take written form imply a rejection of oral evidence for that particular object of proof (namely, the *existence* of a contract, as opposed to its specific content). In other words, oral evidence cannot legally effectively have the sense of evidence of a contract which must be proven with the written form of evidence. The example of the contract therefore illustrates both the end of the chain, what the evidence is ultimately about, and the impact of the communicatory structure

17 Lyotard, pt. 82.
18 Lyotard, pts. 30, 97.
19 Lyotard, pt. 193.
20 Bennington, pp. 123 ff.
21 Lyotard, pts. 18, 25, 111, 123, 137–140; Malpas, Simon. *Jean-François Lyotard*. Routledge, 2003, p. 63.

regulating the referent of the evidentiary language act, regimenting the senses that may contribute to the determination of the reality of the case.[22]

Through rules regarding the means of evidence, the referent is regulated. In a system where the evidence is free, admissibility is the main rule. What needs detailed regulation in statute are therefore quite naturally the exceptions. In both France and Sweden, the main rule is that the evidence is free.[23] The primary difference between French and Swedish regulations regarding the admissibility of evidence may be said to consist in the perception of the exceptions. In France, the exceptions constitute a regime of their own, with a coherent structure. In Sweden, the exceptions are relatively ad hoc, responding to situations where the main rules do not seem appropriate or possible to follow.[24]

Whereas both Swedish and French laws see a contract as concluded and binding as soon as one party has expressly accepted the offer of the other party[25] (no written note needs to be taken) according to the main rule in French law, it is nevertheless the notes and signatures that make the contract regarding a value above a certain limit valid in court.[26] The constituent of the right, what gives the judge the possibility to judge in accordance with a claim (as was discussed in the previous chapter), is therefore either a meeting of minds or the signing of a paper with notes, depending on the communicatory structure. This means that the line between substantive law (here, contract law) and acts regulated thereby (contracts), on the one hand, and the evidence of such acts (signed and perhaps dated notes, witness testimonials, calendar notes, emails etc.), on the other hand, is drawn differently between the two legal orders.

In cross-border cases, the court's decision on the matter of applicable substantive law consequently has immediate implications on the parties' right to present evidence and thus be heard. When the evidence is regulated, the evidentiary means and the object of proof (for example, the binding contract) are seen as coinciding in the same language act. The means does not have any external referent: it is itself the referent.[27] In this sense it is like a coin or a token, as its value lies within itself and is not meant to allow for free spirited interpretations – on the contrary: the purpose-point of such regulations may be said to be to *restrict* the freedom and thus create more stringent foreseeability. The addressee is restricted to determine the sense of the evidence with reference to the evidentiary law rule. In contrast, when the evidence is free, the addressee determines with reference to their general knowledge, specialist

22 Lyotard, pts. 82, 88.
23 Prop. 1942:5, p. 218; 1358 CC; Ordonnance n°2016–131 du 10 février 2016 – art 4.
24 For example, 10:1 ÄB, 4:1, 20:7 JB.
25 1:1 AvtL and 1113 CC.
26 1359 CC.
27 Cf. Lyotard, pts. 47–48, 56, 66, 69.

knowledge and other specific knowledge[28] that has been included in the case material, whether what the parties have presented as evidence is indeed evidence of what they allege. The assessment regards whether that language act can be seen to share the same sense as the object that it is to prove. The referent is thus unregulated.

Through burden of proof rules, the addressor instance is regulated.[29] The main principle that the person who alleges something also bears the burden to present the evidence in support of the allegation, carries with it that the plaintiff[30] in Swedish courts presents their written evidence already with the summons.[31] The case is thus "driven" by the plaintiff. For tactical reasons the defendant may present only evidence that works counter to the allegations and evidence put forward by the plaintiff.[32] What Lyotard therefore shows is that every little thing relates to another and by referring to these little things as phrases he can show that often there is a referent, an addressor and an addressee in relation to whom this referent has sense (whether real or not), and so he presents a theory according to which not only law and legal text is interpreted but so are facts. In that sense there is no distinction between them. The impact of different rules regarding who may act as addressor in the fact-finding process of a cases on the sense of the evidence and the determination of the case will now be studied through the example of a cross-border torts case. In Swedish law, following the principle of evidentiary freedom the burden of proof is not regulated. It is therefore entrusted to caselaw and jurisprudence.[33] The main rule in French civil procedure is that the party who claims something shall prove it. Each party must prove the necessary facts in order to win the case.[34]

28 Cf. commonplace generalizations, and specialist generalizations, Edelstam, Henrik. *Sakkunnigbeviset*, Uppsala, 1991. Dissertation. section 7.2.

29 Lyotard, pt. 10.

30 Lyotard uses the word 'plaintiff' to refer to "[o]ne who suffers a damage and can proceed with a litigation . . . while one who suffers the wrong of a differend is called a *victim*." (Woodward, Ashley. "Testimony and the Affect-Phrase." *Rereading Jean-François Lyotard*, edited by Heidi Bickis and Rob Shields, Ashgate, 2013, p. 172.) I use the legal definition of 'plaintiff' and disregard Lyotard's use of the word.

31 42:2:4 CJP.

32 Ekelöf, IV, pp. 180 ff; Lindell, Sakfrågor, sections 4.4, 4.5; Nordh, Robert. *Bevisrätt C, Bevisvärdering*. Iustus, 2013, pp. 61–63. Evidence which lacks such a function, and for this reason does not aim at an object of proof of which the solution of the case depends, will be seen as redundant, irrelevant, and may therefore be rejected. (35:7 CJP)

33 SOU 1938:44, p. 379; NJA 2018 s. 617; NJA 2017 s. 1105; NJA 2014 s. 364; NJA 2012 s. 804; NJA 2009 s. 64; NJA 1975 s. 577; Ekelöf, IV, pp. 78–81; Lindell, Civilprocessen, pp. 535–546, where Lindell discusses the interplay between the burden of proof and the standard of proof.

34 9 CPC; Carbonnier, Jean. *Droit Civil*. Vol. I, 1st ed. Quadrige PUF, 2004, p. 336; Aynès, Augustin, and Xavier Vuitton. *Droit de la preuve, Principes et mise en œuvre processuelle*. 2nd ed., LexisNexis, 2017, Chaptire 2. The same principle is expressed in 1353 CC, *re* matters concerning contractual obligations. (Civ. 1e, 26 janv. 2012, n° 10–28.356, *Bull. civ.* I, n° 13; Lacroix-Andrivet, Preuves à conserver, 111.12, p. 70; Carbonnier, p. 336.)

Addressors of the Evidentiary Language Acts

There are two sides to burden of proof rules: positively, they regulate which party must prove their allegations; negatively, they indicate which party loses the case in a situation where there is not enough foundation for the formation of a judgment.[35] This is part of a communicatory structure that attracts evidentiary language acts from a certain party.[36] The purpose-point at this moment serves as destination as compared to the earlier example, where the purpose-point is the look-out-point of the judge as addressee/addressor. As addressee one takes the position of a purpose-point from which one perceives, interprets and gives sense, and in that instant, when sense is given, one has shifted from being addressee to the language act and is now addressor of the following language act: through linking one has passed a judgment, sometimes a legal judgment.[37] That party is the addressor of the language act and decides what evidentiary language act to present.[38] The evidentiary language act is chosen from the point of view of the allegations in need of verification.[39]

The fact-finding system as a communicatory structure consists of rules allowing and disallowing the linking of a certain language act onto another.[40] Burden of proof rules are a structure that expresses the expectation that a language act (a claim regarding a right or a legal consequence or an allegation regarding a fact with legal relevance) be followed by a particular language act (evidence – whether the linking is immediate or through the extension of other links[41]) and that they both have the same addressor. To both language acts the instances of addressor and addressee remain; the linking does not include a shift of the positions of addressor and addressee instances. When the burden of proof rests on the party whose allegations are the object of a particular means of evidence there is a direct link between the party's allegations and the evidence. When the evidence rests on the opponent, the object of proof of the allegation is transferred into its negation and it is that negation (of the allegation) that must be supported with evidence. The situation

35 35:6 CJP; Prop. 2004/05:131, p. 13; *see also* Prop. 1942:5, p. 515; SOU 1938:44, p. 383. The parties' burden to present evidence limits the court's power to investigate the matter in Swedish cases amenable to out-of-court settlement, as was noted in RH 2009:50. NJA 2004 s. 874; NJA 2006 s. 520 *re* the relation between 35:6 CJP and 35:7 CJP (commented by Lindell, Civilprocessen, p. 263). *See also* Ekelöf, IV, pp. 34 ff; Heuman, Lars. *Bevisbörda och beviskrav i tvistemål.* 1st ed., Norstedts Juridik, 2005; 9 CPC; Carbonnier, p. 336; Aynès, Vuitton, Chapitre 2; Lagarde, Xavier. *Réflexion critique sur le droit de la preuve.* L.G.D.J., 1994, p. 104.

36 Lyotard, pts. 111, 184.

37 Lyotard, pts. 195, 196.

38 Cf., however, Lyotard, p. 11 *Prétexte*, pts. 90, 151, 188.

39 Lyotard, pts. 30, 31, 33, 36, 39, 41.

40 Lyotard, pt. 40.

41 As discussed in Chapter 5.

therefore results in or is based on a presumption: the positive allegations are true until the opposite is proven. When the burden of proof rests on a party the Roman law motto *da mihi factum, dabo tibi ius* (give me the facts, and I'll give you the law) is followed. When, on the other hand, the judge has investigative powers the motto may be supplemented with – "*da mihi factum*, or I'll seek it myself – thereafter, *dabo tibi ius*." In Swedish cases amenable to out-of-court settlement the Roman law motto is complete as such and can benefit from no supplementation. The situation may be resembled to a child with a lump of coins in his hand laying the coins on the counter in a sweetshop asking: "What can I get for this?"

They who contribute with material on their own initiative take this initiative for a reason, and this reason is an idea and a standpoint. Even if the standpoint is merely "I'd like to know more," this is so because it follows an assessment of the state of the material at that moment. Wanting to know more is a standpoint that there may be more, which is not yet known – and that this unknown material may potentially contribute to the investigation and the understanding of the case. It is therefore a statement that what is presented may be "incomplete" and that more information may alter the picture of the already known information.[42] Whether the judge has taken a stance in the final – legal – judgment or not, it follows that a judgment has been made regarding the state of the investigation. This means that the introduction of more information on the part of the judges is always a statement regarding the robustness of the material thus far introduced.[43] Accordingly, at that point, the judge does *not* think that what they see is all there is. It also means that the value of the different pieces of evidence has been temporarily assessed. As the judge seeks information the judge is both the addressor and the addressee of that specific information, that specific language act. From the perspective of that new information, the rest of the material will be seen and given a sense. When more information is introduced on the initiative of the judge, this may alter the understanding of material previously introduced by the parties in their making themselves heard. The message that the parties are attempting to put forward is impacted by the judge's own "message." This means also that the judge's spatio-temporal commonality – that is the geographically and historically relative common knowledge and idiom to which the judge has access[44] – will be given influence not only as interpretative context for the assessment of the totality of the language acts that

42 Boman, Robert. *Om åberopande och åberopsbörda i dispositiva tvistemål*. P.A. Norstedt & Söners Förlag, 1964. This reasoning is found also in NJA 1982 s. 175 I and II.

43 In Swedish law, 'robustness' is a concept used primarily in criminal proceedings. The concept is however also relevant in cases not amenable to out-of-court settlement, *see* for such cases: Kaldal, Anna. *Parallella processer: en rättsvetenskaplig studie av riskbedömningar i vårdnads- och LVU-mål*. Jure, 2010, Dissertation, pp. 205 ff.

44 Chapter 3.

the parties have presented, but will in itself be directing the contribution of ostensive language acts on the basis of which the case is to be determined.

The Medical Case Book – the Court as Addressor

Whereas the negative side of the burden of proof rules implies that the party who does not meet the standard of proof loses the case,[45] in certain types of cases the court has the responsibility[46] or freedom[47] to ascertain that the case is satisfactorily investigated. The reality of the case is a complex of ostensive, nominative or descriptive language acts[48] which may be sorted under (share the same sense as) a complex legal fact.[49] When the court therefore adds material to the case, new language acts will be added, the senses of which will be contributing to the determination of the case. If the court would have investigative powers in one jurisdiction, whereas in another the same type of case would belong to a different regime, the reality of the case would be determined on diverse material, a diverse collection of facts, in both courts.

This may be illustrated with the example of a torts case from the Swedish Supreme Court where the plaintiff sought damages for decreased working ability due to a brain injury resulting from a car accident.[50] The medical expertise assessed that the plaintiff's attitude towards rehabilitation indicated that he was suffering from a brain injury which could not have resulted from the relatively mild car collision in question. Instead, they concluded that other harm caused to the plaintiff (he was a former prisoner of Auschwitz) was more likely to have caused the decrease in brain function. The court however reasoned in a more binary fashion: whereas before the accident the plaintiff could work, after it, he could not, and so the accident was deemed the cause of the decreased working ability. Therefore, the causal link between the defendant's actions and the plaintiff's bodily harm was the deciding factor. In short, one may say that the medical expertise made a medical assessment of the causality, whereas the court made a legal assessment of the same.[51] This case may be seen as an example of the collision of different

45 Ekelöf, IV, p. 79.
46 Swedish cases not amenable to out-of-court settlement, 36:5 CJP, 17:3 CJP (e contrario).
47 French cases within the *régime libre*, where the object of proof is a *fait juridique* as opposed to an *acte juridique*. (1100–1100-2 CC)
48 Lyotard, pts., 81, 82.
49 Ekelöf, P. O. et al. *Rättegång I*. 9th ed., Norstedts Juridik, 2016, p. 49; Nordh, Robert. "35:5 rättegångsbalken. En rättsfråga om vad?" *Svensk juristtidning*, 1994, p. 82.
50 NJA 1969 s. 311.
51 *Re* the interpretation of this case, see Wahlberg, Lena. *Legal Questions and Scientific Answers: Ontological Differences and Epistemic Gaps in the Assessment of Causal Relations*. Lund University, 2010. Dissertation.

human practices,[52] the human practice of law took the upper hand and imposed itself on the human practice of medicine.[53]

A similar case may occur in a diagonal situation, where the expert evidence is found on the territory of another Member State than that of the forum. Because evidence has both a legal and a non-legal side it points to a cognitive referent belonging to law's environment; in this case cognitive human practices.[54] In the following will be studied the effects on the evidence in a situation where the procedural law of one jurisdiction restricts the case material to that submitted by the parties, whereas in the other jurisdiction the court does have investigative powers. Let us imagine that a Swedish national is in a car accident while visiting France. He was examined directly after the accident at a French hospital, before driving back to Sweden. In Sweden, he was examined again, by a Swedish doctor. Let us imagine that in the torts case that follows the Swedish driver claims medical damages from the French driver. The case is tried in France.[55] As this is a case concerning an accident the object of proof is a legal fact (*fait juridique*[56]) and therefore the evidence is free.[57] Under the principle of evidentiary liberty (and so only regarding legal facts) the French judge may take investigative measures.[58] The judge may also "invite" the parties to explain their claims and allegations when they do not appear clearly.[59] The parties are required to cooperate with the judge in the investigations by submitting the evidence requested.[60] All facts that are relevant for the solution of the case may be the issue for preparatory investigations[61] at any stage

52 Chapter 3.
53 Lyotard, pt. 183.
54 Lyotard, pt. 50.
55 Articles 4.1 and 7.1 Regulation (EU) No 1215/2012 of the European Parliament and of the Council of 12 December 2012 on jurisdiction and the recognition and enforcement of judgments in civil and commercial matters (recast), OJ L 351, 20.12.2012, p. 1 (Brussels I) both assign jurisdiction to the French courts. (Kadner Graziano, Thomas. *Cross-border Traffic Accidents in the EU – The Potential Impact of Driverless Cars.* Directorate-General for Internal Policies, PE 571.362, 2016, p. 18.)
56 1100–2 CC; Halperin, Jean-Louis. "La preuve judiciaire et la liberté du juge." *Communications,* vol. 84, no. 1, 2009, pp. 21–32; Cornu, Gérard. "Fait juridique." *Vocabularie juridique*, 9th ed. Quadrige PUF, 2011, p. 444.
57 1358 CC; art. 4 Ordonnance n° 2016–131 du 10 février 2016.
58 10 CPC; Cass. civ. 3e, 10 févr. 2009, n° 07–21.134, NP; Civ. 1e, 24 sept. 2002, n° 00–22.466, *Bill. civ.* I N° 216 p. 167 (both *re* the judge's discretionary power to refuse to investigate a matter (commented in Lacroix-Andrivet, Jean-Paul. "Mesures d'instruction – droit interne." *Droit et pratique de la procédure civile – Droit interne et européen,* edited by Serge Guinchard, 9th ed., (2017/2018). Dalloz, 2016, 342.11, p. 1184); *see also* Aynès, Vuitton, p. 85.). Aynès and Vuitton suggest that this implies a possible relief of the burden of proof. (Aynès, Vuitton, p. 82.)
59 8 CPC; Aynès, Vuitton, p. 81.
60 11 CPC.
61 143 CPC; Cass. soc., 3 nov. 2010, n° 09–67.493, NP *re* the relevance and usefulness of the evidence; Cadiet, Loïc, and Emmanuel Jeuland. *Droit judiciaire privé.* 10th ed., Lexis-Nexis, 2017, pp. 469 ss; Aynès, Vuitton, pp. 82, 86; Lacroix-Andrivet, Jean-Paul. "Mesures

of the proceedings as long as the judge does not possess enough elements of proof to adjudicate.[62] This means that from the moment of the submissions to the court until the final judgment has entered into legal force the judge may seek more evidence.[63] The judge may only investigate invoked (alleged) facts.[64] Preparatory investigations must also never be taken to alleviate the burden of proof of the parties,[65] but may be taken when the party on whom lies the burden of proof does not possess enough evidence to support his allegations.[66] This means that the judge may enter new language acts into the chain thus influencing the following language acts, through which the senses of the previous language acts are decided or at least delimited.[67]

In our example, the Swedish party presents evidence in the form of the medical case books from the French as well as the Swedish hospitals in support of their allegations that they have been suffering from a severe whiplash injury due to the accident. The French case book is quite clear in support of this claim. The French judge however uses their powers of investigation.[68] Through the means of a Swedish court, the French court is given access to the physician at the Swedish hospital and requests some clarifications.[69] The

d'instruction – droit interne." *Droit et pratique de la procédure civile – Droit interne et européen,* edited by Serge Guinchard, 9th ed., (2017/2018). Dalloz, 2016, 342.11, p. 1184.

62 144 CPC; Cass. civ. 3e, 11 janv. 1978, 76–12.771, 76–12.772, *Bull. civ.* 3 N. 30 P. 22 (*re* the judge's discretion as to what investigative measure to take), *as commented in* Aynès, Vuitton, pp. 83, 88; Lacroix-Andrivet, Mesures d'instruction, 342.12, p. 1184; *also* Cadiet, Jeuland, p. 469, note 261.

63 Cass. civ. 2e, 8 mai 1980, 78–41.737, Bull. civ. 2 N. 101; Lacroix-Andrivet, Jean-Paul. "Preuves à conserver." *Droit et pratique de la procédure civile – Droit interne et européen,* edited by Serge Guinchard, 9th ed., (2017/2018). Dalloz, 2016, 342.171, p. 1197; Blanc, Emmanuel. *La Preuve judiciaire. Commentaire du Décret du 17 décembre 1973.* Librairie du Journal des notaires et des avocats, 1974, p. 12.

64 Aynès, Vuitton, p. 85.

65 146 CPC; Cass. soc., 23 nov. 2011, n° 10–20.933, NP, Cass. civ. 12, 16 juin 2011, n° 10–17.898, NP, Cass. civ. 1e, 10 mai 1995, n° 93-15.910, *Bull. civ.* I N° 200 p. 143, Cass. civ. 1e, 15 nov. 1989, n° 88–13.548, NP (*re* the relation between the burden of proof in general and 146 CPC), Cass. com., 9 déc. 1997, n° 95–16.777, NP (*re* investigative measures in situations where it is not possible for a party to bring evidence, due to, for example, the means of evidence), Cass. com., 7 mars 1989, n° 87–11.827, NP (*re* the interplay between the burden of proof in specifically 1353 CC and 146 CPC), Cass. civ. 2e, 10 mars 2011, n° 10–11.732, *Bill. civ.* II, n° 65; Aynès, Vuitton, p. 85–86; Cadiet, Jeuland, p. 469.

66 146 CPC; Cass. civ. 1e, 28 mars 2000, n° 98–12.806, *Bull. civ.* I N° 103 p. 69, where no investigative measures were taken due to the fact that no evidence was presented by the plaintiff which could be supported by the investigative measure; commented in Lacroix-Andrivet, Mesures d'instruction, 342.12, p. 1184. *See also* Cass. civ. 1e, 2 mars 2004, n° 02–15.211, *Bull. civ.* I N° 70 p. 56, where the court refused to take investigative measures regarding the mental health of a testator and in turn (explicitly) interpreted the plaintiffs' lack of evidence as an indication of their poor relations with the testator.

67 Lyotard, pt. 142 primarily, but *also* pts. 46, 48.

68 232 CPC; Aynès, Vuitton, p. 146; Cadiet, Jeuland, p. 534.

69 Articles 14, 19 Regulation (EU) 2020/1783 of the European Parliament and of the Council of 25 November 2020 on cooperation between the courts of the Member States in the taking

Swedish doctor happened to know the patient as well as the injuries that he had suffered from before the trip to France. The Swedish doctor did not conclude that the severity of the injury was the result of the accident, but that a former injury was merely worsened by the car accident in France. In light of the Swedish physician's report, the French case book appears less apparent, and thus less convincing to the judge. The French medical case book contains facts, yet these facts must be reassessed when the Swedish physician's report is included in the material.

Had the case been tried in Sweden, the parties would have the burden of proof, and the judges would have limited possibilities to investigate the case and add material to the foundation of the judgment.[70] Anyone who possesses a document that can be presumed to have some value to the examination of a case is obliged to submit such a document to the court upon request.[71] Public documents may be requested by the court to be used as evidence if they do not contain secret information or derive from persons who would not be required to testify.[72] In cases amenable to out-of-court settlement (like this torts case) this should however always be upon request from a party.[73] In the Swedish courts, it would therefore have been easier for the Swedish plaintiff to hide the aspects of reality that did not support their case.

The evidence presented by the plaintiff was in my example changed by the added evidence[74] sought by the court, for additional language acts contribute to the senses which constitute reality. New language acts open up for new senses also of the previous language acts and therefore alter the description

of evidence in civil or commercial matters (taking of evidence) (recast), OJ L 405, 2.12.2020, p. 1; consider also judgment of 6 September 2012, *Lippens*, C-170/11, EU:C:2012:540, para. 33; judgment of 21 February 2013, *ProRail*, C-332/11, EU:C:2013:87, para. 46.

70 17:3 CJP. The judge may guide the parties to clarify their position in matters on which they have not been specific enough. (42:8:2 CJP) In NJA 1987 s. 766 the court was seen to have neglected its responsibility according to this provision. The provision is seen to correlate with the restrictions to the parties' right to alter their claims and allegations at a later stage in the proceedings. (SOU 1986:26, p. 103. *See also* RH 2009:68 (*re* 13:3 CJP); 43:4:2 CJP; NJA 1987 s. 766.) The balance between the prohibition in terms of seeking evidence on the one hand and the prescriptions in terms of substantive guidance seems to be that the court is allowed to ask questions regarding the relevance of the material presented during the preparations and main hearing in the eyes of the party who has expressed them. (SOU 1986:26, pp. 124–125.)

71 The obligation to submit written evidence is on the whole restricted to the same extent as the obligation to testify. (38:2 CJP, Prop. 1942:5, pp. 92, 332–333, 372, 426; SOU 1938:44, pp. 43–44, 412–414; NJA 2011 s. 241; NJA 1982 s. 650; NJA 1998 s. 590; NJA 2001 s. 404; NJA 2014 s. 651; NJA 1992 s. 307; NJA 1998 s. 829; NJA 1988 s. 652; NJA 2002 s. 41; NJA 2000 s. 648; NJA 2012 s. 628; NJA 1995 s. 347; NJA 2012 s. 289; *Re* the connection to 36:6:2 CJP above: NJA 1999 s. 469; NJA 1986 s. 398; Lindell, Civilprocessen, pp. 319, 492–494; Ekelöf, IV, pp. 259–260, 270–272; 38:3 CJP, Lindell, Civilprocessen, p. 496; Ekelöf, IV, pp. 273–275.)

72 38:8 CJP; NJA 1981 s. 982; NJA 1987 s. 742. Lindell, Civilprocessen, p. 496; Ekelöf, IV, p. 273.

73 35:6 CJP.

74 Lyotard, pts. 240, 245; Bennington, pp. 124, 132.

of the object of proof.[75] The language acts that are added by the judge are included in the totality of the material – "all there is"[76] – and the totality in relation to which the details are understood is another. The one impacts the signification of the other; the interpretation of two facts will differ when they are both known as opposed to if only one is known.[77] Therefore, the sense of the French medical case book as evidentiary language act was differently understood when first presented to the court as compared to what senses could be attributed to it as seen in relation to the Swedish doctor's assessment. The French judge acted as addressor of the evidentiary language act and sought as object of proof the plaintiff's right to compensation under an applicable legal rule. They thus "rounded" the plaintiff's allegations. Had the case been tried in Sweden, that would not have been possible, and the evidence that the plaintiff presented would constitute the foundation on which the judge would form their judgment.

It may be argued that the evidence did not change, and this is of course true if evidence is understood as an extra-linguistic permanence.[78] However, evidence is a means; its value in the proceedings does not lie in any possible extra-linguistic property, but in its sense in relation to an object of proof.[79] When the judge has investigative powers, the evidentiary language acts may be connected closer to the legal rule than is the case when the judge relies on the evidence provided by the parties because it is brought in on the initiative of the judge. Therefore, the judge is in a sense both addressor and addressee of those language acts, as well as being the addressor of the legal judgment that is rendered on the basis of those language acts.[80] The judge in the moment of decision, as addressor, has one perspective – stands at the purpose-point. When the judge is address*or* of evidentiary language acts which constitute the foundation of the judgment as well as being addressor of the judgment, the parties are held one step further away from the judgment: and despite their right of contradiction there is a risk their being heard is impaired,[81] because the contradiction is made regarding the language acts that the judge has added, and of which the judge already has, therefore, attributed some sense.

It has been argued in Swedish jurisprudence against the judge's introducing material on their own initiative in cases that are amenable to out-of-court

75 Lyotard, pts. 27, 28, 60.

76 See further Chapter 8 *re* the acronym WYSIATI (what you see is *all there is*) by Kahneman, Daniel. *Thinking Fast and Slow.* MacMillan Publishers, 2015.

77 Lyotard, pts. 46, 118.

78 Lyotard, pt. 50.

79 Chapter 3.

80 Lyotard, pt. 25.

81 Paraphrasing Hamson, C.-J. "La procedure civile en Angleterre et en France." *Revue internationale de droit comparé*, vol. 2, no. 1, 1950, p. 82 ("l'hypothèse anglaise est que le juge, même lettré, ne peut lire; l'hypothèse française semble être que le juge civil, même s'il n'est pas dur d'oreille, a des difficultés à comprende la voix humaine.").

settlement.[82] It is held in this line of argument that the parties may be regularly doing business with each other and to rescue their future relations, and save unnecessary cost, they may agree to limit the scope of the conflict to a specific question.[83] What might happen if the parties have such an agreement, but the case is brought before a French court where the judge has investigative powers in all types of cases where the object of proof is free?[84] If the case is then tried in France, the French courts may initiate an investigation, whereas if the case were tried in Sweden, the parties' agreement to delimit the conflict would, on the basis of restrictions laid on the judges in such a case, be respected.[85] Since what you see is all there is,[86] reality consists of the swarm of the senses before you.[87] Investigative measures may open Pandora's box with possible conflicts which the parties – in view of future good relations – may have agreed better stay closed. In such a case, an agnostic attitude on the part of the court may be what renders the most just judgment.

The Will – Order for Linking the Evidence

The following example presents a succession law conflict which demonstrates that the order in which evidence is linked may determine the outcome of the case. The conflict concerns a Swedish national who spent most of his adult life in France and moves back to Sweden after retirement. While living in France the testator, let's call him Mr Ernest, writes a will regarding the real estate that he owns in France. He wills the estate to his late French wife's daughter Miss Fairfax. The will is established in accordance with article 971 CC, which means that the will of the testator has been dictated to a notary public who has recorded the will in writing in the presence also of a second notary public.[88] Before the will was locked away in the archives, the will was read out aloud for the testator who then signed it.[89] By following this procedure, the document is given the highest degree of evidentiary value: it is an *acte authentique (public)* and as such perfect written proof.[90] Other

82 The strongest opponent to the court's interfering with and contributing to the material in cases amenable to out-of-court settlement may be Boman, in *Om åberopande och åberopsbörda*.

83 For other reasons why a party may wish not to invoke a circumstance, see Boman, 18 ff.

84 In a case tried in the *tribunal de commerce*, the judges have investigative powers. (865 CPC)

85 17:3 CJP.

86 Chapter 8.

87 Lyotard, pt. 82.

88 Aynès, Vuitton, p. 137.

89 972 CC.

90 1369 CC, 1371 CC. A will established in this manner is spoken of as received (971 CC) – perhaps expressing that its signification as evidence is its primary signification – that the intention/will of the testator has been received by the notaries public who have then taken notes for the purpose of evidence in the future.

French forms of wills are *olographe* and *mystique*,[91] and they are of lower evidential value.[92]

Let us now imagine that the Swede also has established a will after having relocated to Sweden.[93] He has done this in accordance with the formality requirements that follow from Swedish succession law, which means that it is a written document, signed before two witnesses, who have been informed that the document is the will of the testator, and who have also signed the document, in close proximity to the testator's signing.[94] The title of the particular document is "Will concerning my movable and immovable property" and the only inheritor mentioned is his niece, Miss Cardew.[95] As the assets of the "Swede" are to be shifted after his passing, Miss Fairfax claims her right to the French real estate with reference to the "French will." The shifting of the property left is to be administered in its entirety in accordance with the law in which the diseased had his habitual residence at the time of death.[96] Since the Swede passed while living is Sweden, Sweden has jurisdiction.[97] If Miss Fairfax cannot present the French will to the Swedish court, it must be transferred to Sweden through the application of the Evidence Regulation.[98]

The first question which arises is perhaps whether the will is evidence at all. According to Swedish law, contracts and wills are seen as either norms

91 969, 970, 976 CC.

92 Aynès, Vuitton, pp. 156, 220–222.

93 In the case from Svea Court of Appeal (Svea hovrätts dom av den 13 december 2016 i mål nr T 8932–15), there were three wills from the same testator. For another Swedish case, *see also* RH 1994:67. For French examples, see Cass. civ. 1e, 13 jan. 2021, 19–16.392; Cass. civ. 1e, 8 juil. 2015, 14–18.875, Bulletin 2016, n° 834, 1re Civ., n° 91.

94 10:1 ÄB; NJA 1994 s. 145; NJA 1994 s. 34 (*re* the evaluation of a written evidence as opposed to subsequent oral testimonial concerning the same object of proof, namely, the presence of the testator at the completion of the formal requirements of the will); RH 1995:145 (*re* formalities of the will), NJA 1994 s. 145 (*re* the proximity between the testator's signing of the will and the witnesses' confirming signing). *Re* other forms of pre-constituted/regulated evidence in Swedish law, see 4:7 JB (*re* acquisition of real estate), NJA 1987 s. 211 (*re* relation between the application for public reorganization of the land and the validity of a real estate purchase contract), NJA 1991 s. 262 (*re* the encompassing of non-invoked circumstances in the foundation of the judgment); 7:3 ÄktB (*re* prenuptial agreements), (new phrasing, through Lag (2019:235) om ändring i äktenskapsbalken, see Prop. 2018/19:50, p. 136), NJA 1997 s. 37 (*re* the parties' freedom to make changes in their prenuptial arrangements); RH 1994:48 (*re* the extent of the parties' freedom to dispose over assets in prenuptial agreements).

95 Cass. civ. 1e, 13 jan. 2021, n° 19–16.392.

96 Article 21 and recital 37 Regulation (EU) No 650/2012 of the European Parliament and of the Council of 4 July 2012 on jurisdiction, applicable law, recognition and enforcement of decisions and acceptance and enforcement of authentic instruments in matters of succession and on the creation of a European Certificate of Succession, OJ L 201, 27.7.2012, p. 107.

97 Article 4 Succession Regulation.

98 Article 12 Evidence Regulation. *Re* the French will's validity in a Swedish court: 3 § Lag (2015:417) om arv i internationella situationer.

or hybrids between norms and evidence.[99] This is because their content is binding on the court, like a legal provision.[100] In Swedish procedural law, the divide between legal rules and facts is strictly followed (in theory and in the extent that it is practically possible).[101] This divide requires a legal provision that can be translated into an if-then schema. Accordingly, the rule is what gives the courts the right and obligation to consider the will a . . . rule. According to such a perception the intent of the testator is a fact.[102] The legal rule when applying a will is the rule that directs the court to the will. The main legal rule is phrased as follows:

> A will is to be given the interpretation that may be assumed to correspond with the will of the testator; and what is prescribed below in §§ 2–9 shall therefore only be complied with insofar as nothing else must be understood as to be following from the disposition with regard to the purpose of the disposition and other circumstances.[103]

From the perspective of the court, this means that the court is to render a judgment where the legal consequence is in accordance with the will/intent of the testator as expressed in the will-document. In the if-then schema this in turn means that if the testator wills something and this is expressed in a will-document, then this is what the judiciary is to make happen. The object of proof is then not only the will of the testator, but the will/intent such as it is expressed in the will-document. The will of the testator is not sufficient as an object of proof. What is not an object of proof in these cases is either the legal provision or the concretion of this, through concrete legal facts, as was said in the previous chapter to be the case when the evidence is regulated. We are here referring to another object of proof, further down the chain.

The object of proof, in Swedish legal theory is the concretion of a criterion as expressed in a provision.[104] As a main rule, these are concretized through the allegations of the parties which then become the object of proof. When there is a will, however, the object of proof is the intent of a deceased person

99 Samuelsson, Joel. *Tolkningslärans gåta*. Iustus, 2011, pp. 171 ff, *similar reasoning already in* Samuelsson, Samuelsson, Joel. *Tolkning och utfyllning*. Iustus, 2008, pp. 445 and 542 ff. For the French context, *see* 1103 CC.

100 Samuelsson, Tolkningslärans gåta, p. 169.

101 NJA 1999 s. 629, *commented by* Samuelsson, Tolkning och utfyllning, pp. 246–256; NJA 1991 s. 152 (where the interpretation of the will is said to be bound by what may be presumed to be the last wish of the testator as well as the wording of the will).

102 Cf. Lyotard, pts. 111–113.

103 11:1 ÄB; Cf. 1188 CC for a similar reasoning in French law *re* regarding the interpretation of contracts.

104 Boman, Robert. "Om mellandom och omröstningar om omständigheter." *Festskrift till Welamson*, edited by Olle Höglund and Lars Welamson, Norstedts, 1987, p. 86; Lindell, Sakfrågor, p. 27; Lindblom, Processens arkitektur, p. 174.

such as it has been expressed in a will. The parties have no autonomy over the central part of a conflict concerning the content of a will. This particular aspect of the will indeed is equivalent to a legal rule. In the procedural schema of linked language acts, this fact nevertheless does not transform it into a legal rule. It does however push the parties' allegations down one link. The linking is: the antecedent of the legal rule, the will of the deceased as expressed in the will-document, and then the parties' allegations of the will of the testator and the will-document. The court is therefore free to determine the content of the will without being restricted to the parties' allegations. A will which is constituted in order to express the last wish of the testator, that is, that which is binding on the court, must be seen as evidence in the sense that the Evidence Regulation is applicable (in its hybridity).[105] The French reasoning that legal acts (*actes juridiques*)[106] are performed with the intent of creating a legal effect, why evidence of them may therefore be pre-constituted and the act and the evidence therefore coincide in one (language) act, must reasonably be applicable (*mutatis mutandis*) also in the case of Swedish wills. The Swedish court is therefore confronted with two wills, the wordings of which are arguably incompatible. As one is subsequent to the other, according to Swedish caselaw, the latter may be seen as a correction of the first, or the expression of a changing of the testator's will, that is, the last will is that expressed in the last documentation of an intent.[107] Such an interpretation would imply that the Swedish will substitutes the French will.[108] Such a conclusion must follow from a proper investigation as to the real intent of the testator,[109] but in our case there is no other evidence that contributes to the determination of the last wish of the deceased.[110] Miss Fairfax would in this reasoning not be assigned the French property; it would go to Miss Cardew. The Swedish court would find that since Mr Ernest drew up his French will, he had "clearly changed his mind."

Let us now turn the example around and imagine that the assets of the Swede are to be shifted in France.[111] In France the same case might have been administered differently. The French will, being an *acte authentique* (and as

105 As noted, the Evidence Regulation lacks a definition of 'evidence.' In her Opinion of 18 July 2007, *Tedesco*, C-175/06, EU:C:2007:451, para. 17 and 68, the Advocate General, argued in favor of an extensive interpretation of the notion. Chapter 4.

106 P. 72, n. 58.

107 RH 1994:67; Lind, Göran, and Gösta Walin. *Ärvdabalken Del I, En kommentar Del I (1–17 kap.) Arv och testamente*. 7th ed., JUNO, 2021.

108 Cf. French law: 1035 CC which requires an expressed wish to replace the former will with the latter. (Cass. civ. 1e, 8 juil. 2015, 14–18.875, Bulletin 2016, n° 834, 1re Civ., n° 91.)

109 11:1 ÄB; NJA 2001 s. 865; Silfverberg, Christer. "Arvs- och gåvoskatt." *Skattenytt*, 2002, pp. 319–322.

110 Cf. RH 1994:67, where the former will was generally expressed whereas the latter was more specific. The two wills were read as compatible. Our example is the opposite to this.

111 Making necessary changes in the example for it to be in accordance with the Succession Regulation.

such a perfect proof), is held to either be reliable or false.[112] When there are several formats to choose from to establish a binding will, the form itself may be seen to carry meaning. The evidentiary language act consists of an addressor and an addressee, a referent and a sense, and the document itself is preferably understood as an addressor or taking the place of the addressor in the evidentiary language act.[113] The information content is given a sense, in turn, in relation, primarily, to the addressor – that is the document. The form of the document therefore plays a role in the interpretation of the content. The form is attributed sense. This sense was not noted in the Swedish court, according to my aforementioned reasoning.

The second aspect to the *acte authentique* is that it is evidence of the *entirety* of the legal act that it concerns in the sense that no evidence may be brought to alter its content; evidence regarding its interpretation may however be presented.[114] An *acte authentique* cannot be contested without questioning its validity.[115] The clarity of its intelligible content[116] is supposedly ascertained by the notary public.[117] In our example there is no ambiguity in the content of the document itself: it is possible to identify both the beneficiary and the property and neither party alleges that the will is false.[118] Moreover, in the French judge's perspective, the French will is perfect proof, which means that only evidence of the same category is accepted to question the evidence.[119] It is nevertheless possible to supplement the evidence with other evidence, in particular regarding its interpretation. (It is also possible to question the *validity* of perfect proof, in which case it is held to be false or not meet the formality requirements.[120]) The correct interpretation can be proven through any means, but its place in the hierarchy is statutory. It is likely that the French court would prefer the interpretation that the clear will of the higher hierarchical value is compatible with the latter will,[121] the form of which does not correspond to any of the prescribed forms for a valid will in the Code civil.[122]

If it is to retain its status in accordance with French law, the Swedish will must take the position of auxiliary evidence, in the sense that it is seen to be brought as evidence regarding the interpretation of the French. As the French

112 1369, 1371 CC.

113 PP. 26 ss.

114 1188–1192 CC concerning the interpretation of contracts.

115 1371 CC; Aynès, Vuitton, pp. 156 ff., 166 ff.

116 1365 CC.

117 Aynès, Vuitton, pp. 133.

118 It is not on this point therefore that the differend occurs, since there is agreement.

119 1359 CC.

120 Aynès, Vuitton, p. 156.

121 Cass. civ. 1e, 8 juil. 2015, 14–18.875, Bulletin 2016, n° 834, 1re Civ., n° 91, where the question was raised whether two wills (first a *testament authentique,* then a *testament olographe*) should be seen as cumulative.

122 Cass. civ. 1e, 12 mai 2010, n° 09–11.133, Bulletin 2010, I, n° 111 is an example of how an *acte authentique* may also be used as an act of interpretation.

will does not express the last intent of the testator it is possible to read the Swedish will in relation to – and thus as supplementary to – the French will.[123] Accordingly, if the case is tried in France, the Swedish will serves as evidence of the French will – specifically, auxiliary, regarding the interpretation of the writing. Alternatively, it could possibly be understood as a *commencement de preuve*[124] regarding some other part of the estate that is not seen to be covered by the French will. If, as I would expect, the French will would, in a French court, retain its hierarchical status, and the Swedish will would be seen as auxiliary or *commencement de preuve*, the French estate would be admitted to Miss Fairfax, and the remainder of the left property admitted to Miss Cardew.

The linking scheme in Sweden according to the reasoning presented here would be: purpose-point/object of proof/reality: last wishes – (to be determined on the basis of the) wording of the Swedish will. The French will would find no place in it. In France, the linking would, according to my argument, be: purpose-point/object of proof/reality: last wishes – rules regarding the format of wills – from here the linking would split into two: that which regards the French will (the first to be given signification and sense) and that which regards the Swedish will (in second place). The object of proof is as noted, in both cases, the last wishes of the deceased; the reality that is to be detected from the evidence is the reality of the deceased's last wishes.[125] The difference of the two outcomes may be explained by the communicatory structural linking of the wills. Whether Mr Ernest had changed his mind or not is assessed depending on the applicable communicatory structure of civil procedural fact-finding.

Professional Secrecy – Obstructed Investigations

The last example here presented of how the communicatory structure regiments the language acts which may be introduced in the material for the determination of the case concerns divergent rules regarding professional secrecy.[126] As noted in Chapter 2, the evidence serves two purposes: to let the parties be heard and to give the court knowledge of the case. In this chapter, procedural rules that regiment how the parties may be heard and how the court may receive the knowledge have been studied comparatively. In the case of professional secrecy, one finds a collision between rules that regulate a profession which may serve expert knowledge to the court and the parties' right to be heard, as their right to present *their* case to the court. In both

123 Cass. civ. 1e, 8 juil. 2015, 14–18.875, Bulletin 2016, n° 834, 1re Civ., n° 91.

124 1362 CC; Aynès, Vuitton pp. 254 s.

125 Lyotard, pts. 3–5, 10, 28–29, 37, 47, 50, 54, 60,–61, 82–83.

126 Article 16.1 Evidence Regulation allows for the requested court to refuse to execute a request for the examination of a person who is prohibited from giving evidence under national law.

French and Swedish civil procedure there are rules delimiting the possibility and obligation to present evidence. For example, the obligation of a witness to testify may be delimited due to the relation to the party, including specific professional relations.[127] The party's obligation to present evidence of a specific form may be restricted due to the family relations between contracting parties.[128]

In Swedish civil procedure, the court and the parties are prohibited from asking questions regarding matters covered by professional confidentiality.[129] The provision is thus directed towards the parties and their representatives, and the court must apply the provision of its own motion.[130] The right not to answer implies a connection to the 'duty of truth' following the rendering of the oath, which implies a connection to the criminal offense of perjury.[131] It is also possible for a witness to lawfully refuse to leave information about trade secrets or private matters covered by rules on secrecy, unless there is a particular reason to require the witness to leave the information.[132] The obligation to testify[133] is however not impacted as such; instead the person in whose interest the professional confidentiality is erected may give his

127 36:16 CJP; 205, 259 CPC; Aynès, Vuitton, p. 278.

128 36:3 CJP; Prop. 1942:5, pp. 87, 424, 508, 519; SOU 1938:44, p. 390; NJA 2007 s. 874 (criminal law case, commented by Bylander, Eric. "Part närstående vittne – Handtag, famntag, klapp eller kyss?" *Juridisk Tidskrift*, no. 3, 2007/08, p. 660); Lindell, Civilprocessen, pp. 72, 465, 473–476, 529; Ekelöf, IV, pp. 230–231. *Re* French doctrine of *impossibilité morale*: Cass. civ. 1e, 5 janv. 1999, N° 97–10.379, Non publié; Aynès, Vuitton, p. 268.

129 36:5 CJP; Prop. 2004/05:131, pp. 154 ff; Prop. 1942:5, pp. 87, 428, (*see also* pp. 431, 432, 435 *re* the role of expert witnesses in the courts of appeal, not covered in this study); SOU 1938:44, pp. 391–394; NJA 2015 s. 631, RÅ 2001:67; NJA 1990 s. 537; NJA 2010 s. 122, RÅ 2000:58; NJA 1986 s. 470; NJA 1987 s. 724; Olivecrona, Karl. "Frågeförbud beträffande försvarare." *Svensk juristtidning*, 1947, p. 357; Lindell, Civilprocessen, pp. 72, 465, 472, 487, 496, 529.

130 Fitger et al. "Rättegångsbalken." *Kommentaren till 36:5*, JUNO, 2020.

131 36:6 CJP establishes a right for the witness not to answer a question asked to him if the answer would reveal a criminal or dishonorable act committed by himself or a close relation. (Prop. 1942:5, pp. 87, 424–426; Chapter 15 BrB.) The following cases concern mainly that connection: NJA 2001 s. 183; NJA 1982 s. 836; NJA 2007 s. 624; NJA 1985 s. 774. Cases concerning bankruptcy matters: NJA 2001 s. 563; NJA 1991 s. 123; NJA 2005 s. 407. *Re* the connection to the obligation to submit written evidence in accordance with 38:2 CJP: NJA 1992 s. 307; NJA 1995 s. 347; NJA 2012 s. 289; RH 1997:109; Lindell, Civilprocessen, pp. 465, 475–476, 487, 498, 529; Ekelöf, IV, pp. 232–235.

132 36:6:2 CJP. For references to preparatory works, see this note above *re* 36:6 CJP in general; caselaw: NJA 1999 s. 469; NJA 1986 s. 398; RH 2016:1; Lindell, Civilprocessen, pp. 465, 475–477.

133 36:7 CJP, Prop. 2004/05:131, pp. 87, 154–157; NJA 2006 s. 188; RH 1995:53; Ekelöf, IV, 240; Lindell, Civilprocessen, pp. 266–267 (*re* sanctions for a witness' absence). Anyone may be heard as a witness. (36:1 CJP; Prop. 1942:5, pp. 86, 515; SOU 1938:44, p. 389; Lindell, Civilprocessen, pp. 72, 472; Ekelöf, IV, pp. 222–230.) Persons under the age of 15, or mentally ill persons, may testify should the court decide so (36:4 CJP; Prop. 1990/91:194, p. 10; Prop. 1942:5, pp. 87, 331, 371; SOU 1938:44, pp. 391–394; Lindell, Civilprocessen, p. 472).

permission that the question be put forward.[134] In a Swedish case from 1987, the question regarding the extent of professional confidentiality of a physician was raised.[135] The case in substance concerned the validity of a will, which was questioned on the basis of the mental health of the testator. The Swedish Supreme Court balanced the patient's right of integrity that is protected by medical confidentiality rules, as well as criminal law defamation rules, against the parties' interest to have access to evidence in their cause. The court stated that although medical confidentiality does continue to apply after the patient's death, it does not apply to the same extent as while the patient is still alive. The physician could therefore be heard on the matters in question.

French civil procedure also contains rules regarding medical confidentiality in respect of patient privacy.[136] For example, the *Cour de Cassation* has clarified that plaintiffs cannot request that the medical experts, called by themselves, be present at the medical examination of the testator, ordered by the court, in order to assess that person's mental health.[137] In another case, the *Cour de Cassation* clarified that the parties do not have a right in accordance with the principle that both sides must be heard[138] to directly access the medical files that have been established by the court medical expert. Instead, the parties may appoint their own medical expert who would be allowed access to the files.[139] The court expert is, in these cases, the only person who is allowed to investigate and assess directly the mental state of the patient. Their assessment can only be questioned on the basis of the medical case book thus established and only by another medical expert (although this expert may be appointed by the parties).[140]

Although French and Swedish civil procedure both involve rules that restrict the access to the evidence that may expose intimate knowledge about a patient, their regulations differ. Both in Sweden and in France the medical profession is protected in regards of the patient's trust in his or her doctor. In Swedish civil procedure, the patient's personal integrity is protected by rules according to which the doctor is not obliged to answer a question that puts their patient's integrity at peril.[141] This means that the cross-examination – central to the Swedish procedural fact-finding[142] – is restricted and that certain language acts cannot enter the case material. A party may call their doctor, but the doctor will only be required to give the information that the patient

134 10:1, 12:2 Offentlighets- och sekretesslag (2009:400).

135 NJA 1987 s. 724.

136 Aynès, Vuitton, pp. 22 ff, 111 ff; Leclerc, Olivier. *Le Juge et l'expert: Contribution à l'étude des rapports entre le droit et la science*. L.G.D.J., 2005, p. 319 ff.

137 Cass. civ. 1e, 25 avr. 1989, n° 87–19.253, *Bull. civ.* I N° 169, p. 111; Leclerc, p. 319.

138 16 CPC.

139 Cass. civ. 1e, 8 déc. 1987, n° 85–15.444, *Bull.* N° 337, p. 242; Leclerc, p. 319.

140 Leclerc, p. 290.

141 36:5:2 CJP.

142 36:17 CJP; NJA 2006 s. 520.

himself has allowed the doctor to reveal. The lack of balance that this causes between the parties must be compensated for through the free assessment of the doctor's account according to the general rules for assessing evidence.[143]

In French civil procedure there is no cross-examination.[144] Hearings may be held with different witnesses in order to establish counter-facts, but the expert is not exposed to any cross-examination.[145] Instead, as the aforementioned cases show, the court expert investigates the object that or the patient who requires investigation and passes on the necessary information to the court.[146] It is even possible for the court to decide that the court expert render their statement without full insight of the parties and thus without a full possibility for the parties to contradict the statement.[147]

This means that both legal orders delimit access to information that infringes on the patient's integrity. It is possible to state here that the regulations differ; it is, however, not obvious that these differences have cross-border implications that are relevant under this section: namely, whether the rules regarding restrictions to hear witnesses of certain professions constitute a delimitation to the party's equality of arms and right to be heard when evidence is taken from one jurisdiction to another.[148] In the Swedish courts the parties may call a physician and allow that person to only reveal certain details, with the effect that the opponent is inhibited to perform a proper cross-examination with the physician and thus may be hindered to expose evidentiary language acts in their interest. On the other hand, in a French court, the judge may have full access to the physician's statement, whereas the opponent receives the information from the court. This means that the judge determines what is relevant information for the opponent, and thus delimits the opponents' possibility to find and expose evidentiary language acts in their interest. Both such situations would cause a differend and a wrong[149] but neither are apparently altered by cross-border taking of evidence.

If the case is tried in one Member State whereas the rules regarding professional secrecy regulating the practice of the professional witness originate from another Member State, the cross-border implications may depend on the national rules of professional secrecy. One can imagine a situation where the French judge has investigative powers to request an expert report regarding the Swedish party's health,[150] but the Swedish physician contacted by the

143 35:1 CJP, Prop. 1942:5, pp. 84, 515.

144 *Re* oral hearing of a witness in French civil procedure, 204–231 CPC; Lacroix-Andrivet, Mesures d'instruction, 342.150 ff, p. 1194 ff. 204 CPC prescribes that hearings with witnesses are carried out by the judge.

145 214 CPC; Aynès, Vuitton, pp. 278 ff, 311.

146 250, 257, 282, 283 CPC; Lacroix-Andrivet, Mesures d'instruction, 342.213–342.241, pp. 1202–1203; 342.281–342.281, pp. 1209–1210.

147 Leclerc, pp. 319–320.

148 Article 6 ECHR.

149 Lyotard, p. xi.

150 249, 256, 263 CPC in conjunction with a Article 16 Evidence Regulation.

French court may refuse to testify on grounds of professional secrecy.[151] The sought-after evidentiary language acts would not be included in the material and would not contribute to the reality of the case.[152]

Conclusion

The comparative study undertaken in this chapter has shown that rules concerning who may take the position of addressor and thus contribute to the case material with evidentiary language acts, such as rules regarding burden of proof and the court's investigative measures, have an impact on the sense of the language acts presented by other addressors. From the perspective of the parties, it means that their being heard in the sense that their possibility of presenting the case as they see it, is impacted by the invitation of other human practices through the investigative powers of the court. These rules are found to differ between the two legal orders compared with the consequence that the evidence presented by the parties is given different sense in the two legal orders. It has also been found that non-chronological structures of evidence rules, where one piece of evidence is placed in the position of object of proof in relation to another, impact the sense that evidence is given. Differences between the legal orders compared are also found when comparing such rules. This means, from a party perspective, that the evidence they present will not be heard in the same manner in both judiciaries.

The two links of the legal judgment, connecting two heterogenous human practices, namely, the normative and the descriptive, subvert all attempts to create an area with a single sense of justice. This connection hinges on both the national procedural laws and the legal environment, that is, the evidence's habitat with the rootage of the senses that are attributed to language acts in the environment where they "come along" and from which the law is to receive knowledge of the case, from which senses are collected in the aim to construct the case. If one were to reason that the national procedural orders should be harmonized[153] to eliminate the structural obstructions to justice, one would nevertheless still face the void of the unknown, foreign extra-legal environment of the cross-border evidence. This point will be discussed in the following chapter.

151 25:1 Offentlighets-och sekretesslag (2009:400).

152 Lyotard, pts. 82, 88.

153 European Law Institute, European Law. & UNIDROIT. *ELI-Unidroit Model European Rules of Civil Procedure: From Transnational Principles to European Rules of Civil Procedure*. OUP, 2021. For an account of the content and development of procedural autonomy: Fartunova-Michel, Maria. *La preuve dans le droit de l'Union européenne*. Bruylant, 2013, Chapters 1 and 2. For a thorough examination of the concept: Krans, Bart, and Anna Nylund, editors. *Procedural Autonomy Across Europe*. Intersentia, 2020. For a discussion on the importance of cultural aspects of procedural law, *see* Andersson, Torbjörn. *Harmonization and Mutual Recognition: How to Handle Mutual Distrust, Enforcement Agency Practice in Europe*. British Institute of International and Comparative Law, 2005, p. 399 s.

Bibliography

Andersson, Torbjörn. *Harmonization and Mutual Recognition: How to Handle Mutual Distrust, Enforcement Agency Practice in Europe*. British Institute of International and Comparative Law, 2005.

Aynès, Augustin, and Xavier Vuitton. *Droit de la preuve, Principes et mise en œuvre processuelle*. 2nd ed., LexisNexis, 2017.

Bennington, Geoffrey. *Lyotard: Writing the Event*. Manchester UP and Columbia UP, 1988.

Bentham, Jeremy. *Rationale of Judicial Evidence: Specially Applied to English Practice*. Vol. V. Hunt and Clarke, 1827.

Bentham, Jeremy. *Rationale of Judicial Evidence*. Edited by J. S. Mill, Vol. I, Hunt and Clarke, 1827.

Boman, Robert. *Om åberopande och åberopsbörda i dispositiva tvistemål*. P.A. Norstedt & Söners Förlag, 1964.

Boman, Robert. "Om mellandom och omröstningar om omständigheter." *Festskrift till Welamson*, edited by Olle Höglund and Lars Welamson, Norstedts, 1987.

Bylander, Eric. "Part närstående vittne – Handtag, famntag, klapp eller kyss?" *Juridisk Tidskrift*, no. 3, 2007/08.

Cadiet, Loïc, and Emmanuel Jeuland. *Droit judiciaire privé*. 10th ed., LexisNexis, 2017.

Carbonnier, Jean. *Droit Civil*. Vol. I, 1st ed., Quadrige PUF, 2004.

Cornu, Gérard. "Fait juridique." *Vocabularie juridique*, 9th ed. Quadrige PUF, 2011.

Douzinas, Costas, and Ronnie Warrington. "'A Well-Founded Fear of Justice': Law and Ethics in Postmodernity." *Law and Critique*, vol. II, no. 2, 1991, pp. 115–147.

Edelstam, Henrik. *Sakkunnigbeviset*. Uppsala, 1991. Dissertation.

Ekelöf, P. O. "My Thoughts on Evidentiary Value." *Evidentiary Value: Philosophical, Judicial, and Psychological Aspects of a Theory*, edited by Peter Gärdenfors et al., Gleerups, 1983.

Ekelöf, P. O. et al. *Rättegång IV*. 7th ed., Norstedts Juridik, 2009.

Ekelöf, P. O. et al. *Rättegång I*. 9th ed., Norstedts Juridik, 2016.

European Law Institute, European Law & UNIDROIT. *ELI-Unidroit Model European Rules of Civil Procedure: From Transnational Principles to European Rules of Civil Procedure*. OUP, 2021.

Fartunova-Michel, Maria. *La preuve dans le droit de l'Union européenne*. Bruylant, 2013.

Fitger et al. "Rättegångsbalken." *Kommentaren till 36:5*. JUNO, 2020. Accessed 01 Oct. 2020.

Fitger et al. "Rättegångsbalken." *Kommentaren till 38 kap*. Om skriftligt bevis, Inledning, JUNO, 2020. Accessed 01 Oct. 2020.

Fitger et al. "Rättegångsbalken." *Kommentaren till 38 kap*. JUNO, 2020. Accessed 01 Oct. 2020.

Goodwin, Jean. "Wigmore's Chart Method." *Informal Logic*, vol. 20, no. 3, 2000.

Halperin, Jean-Louis. "La preuve judiciaire et la liberté du juge." *Communications*, vol. 84, no. 1, 2009, pp. 21–32.

Hamson, C.-J. "La procedure civile en Angleterre et en France." *Revue internationale de droit comparé*, vol. 2, no. 1, 1950.

Heuman, Lars. *Bevisbörda och beviskrav i tvistemål*. 1st ed. Norstedts Juridik, 2005.

Kahneman, Daniel. *Thinking Fast and Slow*. MacMillan Publishers, 2015.

Kaldal, Anna. *Parallella processer: en rättsvetenskaplig studie av riskbedömningar i vårdnads- och LVU-mål*. Jure, 2010. Dissertation.

Krans, Bart, and Anna Nylund, editors. *Procedural Autonomy Across Europe*. Intersentia, 2020.

Lacroix-Andrivet, Jean-Paul. "Mesures d'instruction – droit interne." *Droit et pratique de la procédure civile – Droit interne et européen*, edited by Serge Guinchard, 9th ed., (2017/2018). Dalloz, 2016.

Lacroix-Andrivet, Jean-Paul. "Preuves à conserver." *Droit et pratique de la procédure civile – Droit interne et européen*, edited by Serge Guinchard, 9th ed., (2017/2018). Dalloz, 2016.

Lagarde, Xavier. *Réflexion critique sur le droit de la preuve*. L.G.D.J., 1994.

Leclerc, Olivier. *Le Juge et l'expert: Contribution à l'étude des rapports entre le droit et la science*. L.G.D.J., 2005.

Lind, Göran, and Gösta Walin. *Ärvdabalken Del I, En kommentar Del I (1–17 kap.) Arv och testamente*, 7th ed., JUNO, 2021.

Lindblom, P. H. "Processens arkitektur." *Vänbok till Torleif Bylund*, edited by Torbjörn Andersson and Bengt Lindell, Iustus, 2003, pp. 171–260.

Lindell, Bengt. *Sakfrågor och rättsfrågor: en studie av gränser, skillnader och förhållanden mellan faktum och rätt*. Iustus, 1987.

Lindell, Bengt. *Civilprocessen*. 3rd ed. Uppsala and Iustus, 2012.

Lyotard, Jean-François. *The Differend – Phrases in Dispute*. Translated by Georges Van Den Abbeele, University of Minnesota Press, 1988.

Malpas, Simon. *Jean-François Lyotard*. Routledge, 2003.

Nordh, Robert. "35:5 rättegångsbalken. En rättsfråga om vad?" *Svensk juristtidning*, 1994, pp. 81–93.

Nordh, Robert. *Bevisrätt C, Bevisvärdering*. Iustus, 2013.

Olivecrona, Karl. "Frågeförbud beträffande försvarare." *Svensk juristtidning*, 1947, pp. 357–359.

Samuelsson, Joel. *Tolkning och utfyllning*. Iustus, 2008.

Samuelsson, Joel. *Tolkningslärans gåta*. Iustus, 2011.

Sawyer, Dylan. *Lyotard, Literature and the Trauma of the Differend*. Palgrave Macmillan, 2014.

Schum, David. "A Science of Evidence: Contributions from Law and Probability." *Law, Probability and Risk*, vol. 8, 2009, pp. 197–231.

Silfverberg, Christer. "Arvs- och gåvoskatt." *Skattenytt*, 2002, pp. 319–322.

Wahlberg, Lena. *Legal Questions and Scientific Answers: Ontological Differences and Epistemic Gaps in the Assessment of Causal Relations*. Lund University, 2010. Dissertation.

Wigmore, John H. *The Principles of Judicial Proof*. Little, Brown, and Co., 1913.

Wigmore, John H. "Problem of Proof." *Illinois Law Review*, vol. 8, no. 2, 1913–1914, pp. 77–103.

Woodward, Ashley. "Testimony and the Affect-Phrase." *Rereading Jean-François Lyotard*, edited by Heidi Bickis and Rob Shields, Ashgate, 2013.

Chapter 7

The Bald King, the Graphologist, the Social Worker and the Acupuncturist

Evidence as the Link Between the Normative and the Cognitive

Introduction

Whether evidence is presented by the parties in the aim of convincing the judge that the allegations are true or – in the case where evidence is sought by the court, in the aim of convincing the judge what is true[1] – in order that substantive law may be correctly applied,[2] evidence is intended to point out reality, which may convince the judge of the truth-value[3] of the allegations, that there is a correlation between the allegations and reality,[4] i.e., that the allegations are true.[5] In the chain of language acts, the evidence is positioned between the allegations and the reality which the evidence is pointing out, and connects them in a link on the instance of the sense. Lyotard illustrates how linking may be done onto any of the instances but both his explanation as to how the phrase universe is composed and his illustration of how linking is done onto the referend, the addressor or the addressee instances seem to require that the instance of the sense is occupied first. I understand this to mean that whatever instance the linking is done onto, the sense is always also involved. This also follows from the position that the sense is given by the human practice and its purpose-point. As noted in the previous chapters, in different civil procedural communicatory structures the *actual factum probandum*, that is, the immediate purpose-point of the evidentiary language act, varies, as well as what language acts may be immediately linked to this *factum probandum*.

1 Chapter 5.

2 Chapters 2 and 3.

3 Frege, Gottlob. "On Sense and Nominatum." *The Philosophy of Language*, edited by A. P. Martinich, translated by Herbert Feigl, 2nd ed., OUP, 1990.

4 Tarski, Alfred. "The Semantic Conception of Truth and the Foundations of Semantics." *The Philosophy of Language*, edited by A. P. Martinich, 2nd ed., OUP, 1990, p. 49; Russell, Bertrand. "On Denoting." *The Philosophy of Language*, edited by A. P. Martinich, 2nd ed., OUP, 1990, p. 205.

5 Lyotard, Jean-François. *The Differend – Phrases in Dispute*. Translated by Georges Van Den Abbeele, University of Minnesota Press, 1988/Lyotard, Jean-François. *Le Différend*. Éditions de minuit. 1983, pt. 61.

DOI: 10.4324/9781003495383-7

Language acts follow grammatical rules for their formation, pertaining to the communicatory structures.[6] As an ostensive language act the presentation of evidence in a judicial procedure may also be understood as a descriptive/cognitive language act, namely, one that alleges that the evidence presented *is*, for example, a picture which is in itself a case of, for example, hate speech, as was held in the matter of Little Sweetheart. This is again a major strength of Lyotard's theory of the phrase: the distinction between different language acts is only momentary. This chapter will continue the study of the chain. In the previous chapter, it was asked how the civil procedural communicatory structure impacts the sense of the evidence by sifting out what is impertinent or inconsistent.[7] In this chapter, it will be asked, what extra-legal human practices may serve as source of knowledge for the law and how this determines the sense as well as relevance of the evidentiary language act.

Heard or Silenced in the Idiom of the Court

As was noted in the Medical Case Book example the communicatory structure determines the linking, and thus delimits the totality of the case material. For example, in Swedish cases amenable to out-of-court settlement, only the parties may contribute with evidence to determine the specificities of the case, and in French cases under the *régime légal*, like in the Swedish cases where evidence is regulated, prescribed, pre-constituted evidence is necessary.[8] No matter what communicatory structure, however, linking seems to take place onto the instance of the sense of the language act. Just like the other instances, the sense is not determined "before the event"[9] – that is, before the language act takes place. The language act has no predetermined sense, it does not "come along"[10] with its instances already occupied. Instead, the sense is given[11] to the language act (1) by the human practice into which it is adopted, and is determined in the language act that follows (2), that is connected to the language act (1) which is thus given a sense. This may cause a conflict between different understandings and interpretations of language acts (namely, a differend[12]), as the case of Little Sweetheart illustrates. Arts, critical race theory, pedagogics and yet others competed[13] in the determination of what sense to attribute to the picture.

6 Lyotard, pts. 78, 185.
7 Lyotard, pt. 40.
8 Chapters 5 and 6.
9 Lyotard, pt. 131.
10 Lyotard, pt. 184.
11 Not as a permanence! Cf. Lyotard, pts. 50, 56 etc.
12 Lyotard, pts. 40, 92, 93, 183, 184, 188, 201.
13 Lyotard, pt. 234; Bennington, Geoffrey. *Lyotard: Writing the Event*. Manchester UP and Columbia UP, 1988, p. 143; *see also* Derrida, Jacques. "Force de loi: le Fondement mystique de l'autorité." *Cardozo Law Review*, vol. 11, nos. 5–6, Jul/Aug. 1990, p. 967.

To support the allegation that Little Sweetheart was a case of hate speech, critical race theory would have had to win the competition; to acquit the accused, pedagogics would have needed to win. This is not to say that these categorizations are stable even within a human practice as a field of knowledge – there may have been representatives of pedagogics who also held that Little Sweetheart was a case of hate speech. This is only intended as an illustration of how different human practices serve as standard, with their banks of knowledge and idioms, for the interpretation of what is said and done, in short, what takes place. In the case of Little Sweetheart, the ultimate winning human practice – law – (ultimate because the case was tried legally, and the legal truth established in a legal judgment is a stable type of truth, for *ne bis in idem*) focused on the criterion of 'criminal intent' and avoided as such the determination of the picture. With this decision, the argument about the sense of Little Sweetheart was silenced, neither one nor the other were able to make their case. By finding that not all criteria of the legal rule were fulfilled in the case, law has the capacity to silence all parties.

Let us study this passage. For this purpose, the Little Sweetheart case will be transcribed[14] into a torts case based on a defamation case adjudicated by the Swedish Chancellor of Justice in 2007.[15] That case concerned a caricature of the prophet Muhammed pictured as a dog.[16] The case was not considered to be of the severity of a crime. Like the Little Sweetheart case it was handled as a freedom of speech/hate speech case, and not a matter of slander. Unlike the Little Sweetheart case, there was no disagreement regarding the sense of the caricature. In our transcription, the picture of Little Sweetheart is consequently presented as evidence in a torts case. Now, what is the court to make of it? The party who presents the picture as evidence attributes to it the sense of an insult, with the intention to mock persons who are seen as resembling the picture. For this to be possible to interpret as mockery, the mass of knowledge and idiom of other human practices than law are necessary. The history of slavery contains knowledge (mass of language acts) which has been attributed the sense of mockery (to stay within the phrasing of the law of defamation), insult, offense to pictures sharing similarities with Little Sweetheart. This mass of knowledge consisting of a mass of language acts constitutes a context and foundation for the interpretation of the picture. Some of these language acts will also be imagined to be presented in the case, as auxiliary facts. Some of them

14 Lyotard, pts. 30, 79, 237.

15 Decision of the Chancellor of Justice of 2007.09.20, Dnr 6010-07-30, 6119-07-30, 6164-07-30, 6220-07-30 and 6339-07-30.

16 Similar expressions have been judged to be slander in accordance with the Swedish criminal act, *see for example* RH 2011:5; NJA 2004 s. 331; RH 2021:4; NJA 1989 s. 374.

will not be mentioned, but merely alluded to, taken for granted as *a priori*.[17] These *a priori* language acts will serve the function of the commonplace generalizations, common knowledge, common sense[18] – expressed in ordinary language,[19] the common idiom, referred to here as pertaining to the human practice of spatio-temporal commonality, and as such they tacitly serve as inferential mud and glue.[20]

As those who were offended by Little Sweetheart were reminded of centuries of slavery, tyranny, oppression and mockery, they made the inference that Little Sweetheart was another example of the same, and on that basis, they made the inference that the picture was an expression of contempt, and as such it was an expression of racial hatred. Inferences are senses attached to language acts, given by a human practice, recognized by its idiom. Several human practices competed in attributing sense to Little Sweetheart. The defendant in such a torts case would present alternative interpretations of the picture, supporting this interpretation with other auxiliary facts, pertaining to other human practices (toddler pedagogics perhaps). Both parties would present evidentiary language acts that they would argue to be supporting their sense of the picture, because of the knowledge and idiom of the human practice, the mass of language acts that constitute the human practice and the senses that are recovered therein.[21]

This chapter focusses on the issue of what may serve as a source of knowledge in the first place. This involves the question of what an area of expertise may be and what this expertise finds to be relevant. As was noted in the traffic accident case in Chapter 6, the medical expert and the judge did not agree on the question of causality, they made judgments in accordance with different human practices and so they gave relevance to different purpose-points. In this chapter it will be found that the question of relevance does not only depend on the determinant human practice such as law or medicine, nor only on the communicatory structure of judicial fact-finding, but also on what is here referred to as the idiom of the ordinary language, namely that which pertains to a spatio-temporal commonality. Lyotard stresses that to be heard the sense of the language act must be found expressible in the idiom of the court.[22] If one cannot be heard, there is a differend – and a wrong.[23]

17 Lyotard, pt. 97.
18 Chapter 3.
19 Lyotard, pts. 30, 91, 97, 108, 146.
20 Lyotard, pts. 12, 21, 23, 44, 201, 237, 251. *See also* pts. 160, 219, 234, 235 *re* the relation between idiom, narrative and myth.
21 Cf. Lyotard, pt. 78.
22 Lyotard, for example, pts. 12, 37 and 176.
23 Lyotard, p. xi, pts. 13, 42.

Expert Cognitive Language Acts

In Swedish law, experts[24] are characterized by the object of proof that they are called to inform the court about.[25] Unlike common knowledge of facts (such as Paris being the capital of France) and 'commonplace generalizations,'[26] the knowledge that the expert may contribute is of course not commonplace, but *expert* knowledge. Expert generalizations "require specific studies of medicinal, technical or other form."[27] A distinction is made between generalizations and facts in particular as regards the expert. Singular events that may require evidence are facts. A witness may be called because they have seen the specific event of the case. That witness cannot be replaced by anyone else. An expert is called, however, because of their general – albeit expert – knowledge. They can therefore in principle be exchanged for any other expert in the field.[28] Their main function in the proceeding is to share their knowledge and assessment of certain matters of fact.[29] It is also possible that an expert witnesses a specific event and because of their expertise is particularly apt to render their account of the event. In these situations, it is unclear whether the rules regarding witnesses or those regarding the experts are to apply.[30]

The expertise may be called by the court or by the parties.[31] It is more common that the experts are called by the parties.[32] It is likely also in those situations that the expert may act as both a witness and an expert. For example, if a patient has visited a physician and been diagnosed, they may want to call the physician to render a statement in court in support of their claims for compensation.[33] The court only has the power to initiate the consultation of an expert in cases not amenable to out-of-court settlement,[34] that is, in the cases where the court is responsible for the facts of the case to be thoroughly examined in order for the court judgment to be correct both in matters of fact and in matters of law. The expert may only be called by the court if it is

24 *Re* the terminology, see Edelstam, Henrik. *Sakkunnigbeviset*. Uppsala, 1991, p. 21. Dissertation.
25 Edelstam discusses three alternative criteria that could distinguish the expert from other witnesses, *see* Edelstam, p. 210.
26 35:2 CJP, Chap 40 CJP; Edelstam, p. 547; *also* note **11**; *see also* Lindell, Bengt. *Notorietet och kontradiktion*. Iustus, 2007 *re* the term in connection with 35:2 CJP, section 4.3.
27 Hassler, Åke. *Svensk civilprocessrätt*. Nord. bokh., 1963, p. 407 (the translation from Swedish is my own); Edelstam, p. 116. For a discussion of the distinction between the two forms of generalizations, see Edelstam, pp. 116–118.
28 Edelstam, p. 188.
29 Ekelöf, P. O. et al. *Rättegång IV*. 7th ed., Norstedts Juridik, 2009, p. 282.
30 Edelstam, pp. 204–206.
31 40:1, 40:19 CJP; SOU 1938:44, pp. 424–425; NJA 1985 s. 634; Ekelöf, IV, p. 286.
32 Ekelöf, IV, p. 294.
33 Ekelöf, IV, p. 293.
34 35:6 CJP; Prop. 2004/05:131, p. 151; Ekelöf, IV, p. 287.

deemed necessary,[35] which means that the expert may only be called to support the court in matters of the expertise, which in turn means matters not known by the common man.[36] The expert opinion is a means of helping the court in its autonomous[37] evaluation of the evidence and is as such not an independent means of evidence. Another way of expressing the dependence of the expert opinion is that it is a means of evidence one or more links away from the ultimate object of proof[38] in a chain of evidence and is therefore not a means of evidence which can be directly applied to a legal fact.

In the examples that follow the aim is to illustrate the lack of commonality between what may be perceived as neutral and objective cognitive language acts. It will be argued, here, that the spatio-temporal commonality imposes itself on other human practices and determines what is and what is not a cognitive human practice, from which law may "borrow" its foundations, to legally qualify and deliver correct legal judgments.

The Recruitment Process – What Is an Extra-Legal Source of Knowledge for the Legal Matter?

In a labor law case, the legal question may be whether a person was discriminated against in an employment procedure. In case AD 47/2008 a woman claimed to have been subject to wrongful discrimination on grounds of ethnicity.[39] She was unsuccessful in the recruitment process for the position of receptionist at the company due to an alleged lack of satisfactory language skills. The recruitment process included an aptitude test.[40]

Let us now imagine that in this case the applicant were a person with habitual residence in Sweden, whereas the employer were situated in France. Parties in employment contracts with cross-border aspects may choose

35 40:1 CJP; Prop. 1942:5, pp. 408, 421–422; SOU 1938:44, p. 420; Lindell, Bengt. *Civilprocessen*. Iustus, 3rd ed., Uppsala 2012, pp. 498–499; Ekelöf, IV, pp. 281, 283, 285, 288.

36 Edelstam, p. 239.

37 35:1 CJP; Terré, François. *Droit civil, Les Obligations*. Dalloz, Paris, 2005, p. 163.

38 Wigmore, John H. *Treatise on the System of Evidence in Trials at Common Law: Including the Statutes and Judicial Decisions of All Jurisdictions of the United States*. Little, Brown, and Co., 1904, § 267; *see also* Ekelöf, IV, p. 22; Lindblom, P. H. "Processens arkitektur." *Vänbok till Torleif Bylund*, Edited by Torbjörn Andersson and Bengt Lindell, Iustus, 2003, pp. 202–203.

39 The case was tried under the now abolished law Lag (SFS 1999:130) om åtgärder mot diskriminering i arbetslivet på grund av etnisk tillhörighet, religion eller annan trosuppfattning, replaced with diskrimineringslagen (SFS 2008:567). *See also, for example* AD 11/2018, AD 19/2014 (The case was tried on the basis of diskrimineringslagen (SFS 2008:567), föräldraledighetslagen (SFS 1995:584) and Directive 2006/54/EC of the European Parliament and of the Council of 5 July 2006 on the implementation of the principle of equal opportunities and equal treatment of men and women in matters of employment and occupation (recast), OJ L 204, 26.7.2006, p. 23–36. *Also*, for an example of a French case *re* discrimination on the basis of sex, see Cass. soc., 30 sept. 2015, n° 14–25.736, NP).

40 AD 47/2008, *see also* AD 19/2014.

jurisdiction.[41] Let us imagine that the case is tried in Sweden. The employer opposes the accusation and explains that the applicant dropped out of an ordinary recruitment process and that no illegitimate regard was paid. Unlike what is common in Sweden, in France it is somewhat customary for a recruitment firm to use a graphology test as a step in the recruitment process in order to determine whether the applicant's personality is suitable for the job.[42] Until recently, these tests seem to have been considered unproblematic forms for selecting between different employment applicants in France.[43] It has also been reported that the graphologists themselves consider their service to be not only scientific, but a particularly French artform.[44]

To the Swedish reader, this is likely a clear case where the court may reject evidence as "obviously without any effect" – much like a crystal ball.[45] This means that in a cross-border situation where a labor contract is concluded

41 Articles 19 and 21 Regulation (EU) No 1215/2012 of the European Parliament and of the Council of 12 December 2012 on jurisdiction and the recognition and enforcement of judgments in civil and commercial matters (recast), OJ L 351, 20.12.2012, p. 1. The parties may choose the applicable substantive law. (Article 8 Regulation (EC) No 593/2008 of the European Parliament and of the Council of 17 June 2008 on the law applicable to contractual obligations, OJ L 177, 4.7.2008, p. 6.)

42 Balicco, Christian. "L'utilisation de la graphologie dans le recrutement de cadres au sein des cabinets conseils." *L'orientation scolaire et professionnelle*, vol. 31, no. 2, 2002; Marchal, Emmanuelle. "Graphologie et entreprises: histoire et controverses." *Sociologies pratiques*, vol. 10, no. 1, 2005, pp. 57–76. *See also, Accord portant sur l'égalité professionnelle entre les femmes et les hommes*, 03/06/2019, T05119001312, Date de publication sur Légifrance: 23/07/2019.

43 For examples of the use of graphology in recruitment procedures, *see* CA. adm. de Marseille, 4e, 22 fév. 2011, n° 08MA00020, NP; *see also* Cass. crim., 18 avr. 1991, n° 91–80.657, NP, where it is stated that a circular letter from the Chancellery, dated 17 Dec. 1969 stresses the importance to distinguish between the expertise of graphology and that of handwriting analysis reminding that graphology is the study of correlations between a person's handwriting and their character, or their moral or physical state, whereas expertise in handwriting analysis aims at establishing whether a handwritten text or signature were written by a particular person.

44 Balicco, p. 10. Maybe the following is worth considering here: "Chaque époque a une prédilection pour un mode de prevue. Le Moyen Âge chrétien avait une préférence pour l'ordalie et le serment. L'Ancien Régime a développé l'écrit et l'aveu qui impliquait la torture. Notre époque a une prédilection pour l'expertise." (Jeuland, Emmanuel. "Expertise." *Dictionnaire de la Justice*, edited by Loïc Cadiet, PUF, 2004.)

45 35:7 p 3 CJP through the application of 3:7 LRA. The courts' mandate to disallow evidence is regulated in 35:7 CJP; Prop. 2004/05:131, pp. 13 and 156–158; Prop. 1942:5, p. 85; SOU 1938:44, p. 383; NJA 2006 s. 520; NJA 1990 s. 286; RH 1994:11; RH 2019:27 (*re* the disallowing of evidence in support of an uncontested fact). The situations listed in 35:7 CJP may be divided into two categories. The first three grounds concern situations where the evidence lacks relevance in the case. The last two grounds concern a lack of proportionality between the effort to achieve the evidence and the benefit of the evidence. The third ground for refusing evidence is when the evidence "clearly" has no evidentiary value, or because of the lack of relation between the evidence and the object of proof, or both. (Westberg, Peter. *Anskaffning av bevisning i dispositiva tvistemål*. Norstedts Juridik, 2010, p. 623.) Such an assessment may come across as quite clear – the examples in the Swedish

on the basis of a graphology test as part of a recruitment process, in the one jurisdiction the test may serve as a relevant evidentiary fact whereas in the other it would likely be perceived as nonsensical and lacking all value in the proceedings. The employer who wishes to support their claim that there was no discrimination involved in the employment procedure might struggle to make themselves heard through the means of such a test as evidence.[46] However, not only does the French employer want to submit the graphology test that is part of the recruitment process in this imagined scenario, but the French employer also wishes to present the opinion of a psychologist specialized in graphology, in support of the interpretation of the test according to which it is clear that the Swedish applicant was indeed less suitable for the job than her competitor. In France the graphologist opinion could be submitted on the written documents.[47] In contrast, because of the main rule prohibiting affidavits in Swedish courts,[48] if the employer wishes to put forward the opinion of the graphologist, the expert would need to be called to speak orally before the court and be interrogated by both parties' representatives.[49] Such an interrogation incurs costs.[50] In this situation the court would again be able to reject the witness testimonial as evidence "obviously" without value.[51]

The graphology test situation presents a collision on more than one level between the two legal orders' understanding of what constitutes a fact. Firstly, the employer might struggle to have the evidence accepted in a Swedish court. Truth as a correlation between a proposition and reality requires that there is a statement,[52] so for the result of the test to be true it must be seen as a statement, that is, a descriptive language act.[53] But as seen by Swedish legal eyes, the test result is given a value that can be neither true nor false, just like the statement regarding the baldness of the King of France.[54] If it can be neither true nor false, it cannot be a fact. On the basis of the graphology test it would not be possible, according to Swedish law and the common

textbooks include such things as the presentation of a crystal ball. (Westberg, Anskaffning av bevisning, pp. 624–625.)

46 Article 6 ECHR; Lyotard, p. xi.

47 200, 201, 205 CPC; Cadiet, Loïc, and Emmanuel Jeuland. *Droit judiciaire privé*. 10th ed., LexisNexis, 2017, p. 529.

48 Prop. 2004/05:131, pp. 166–167; Prop. 1942:5, pp. 86, 324; SOU 1938:44, p. 387; NJA 2012 s. 269; NJA 2019 N 1; NJA 2018 s. 301; NJA 2016 s. 1195; Lindell, Civilprocessen, pp. 488–491.

49 36:1, 36:16 CJP, Prop. 1942:5, pp. 86, 515; SOU 1938:44, p. 389; Lindell, Civilprocessen, pp. 72, 472; Ekelöf, IV, pp. 222–230.

50 Evidence could be taken through telecommunications in accordance with article 12.4 Evidence Regulation, incurring less cost.

51 35:7 p. 3 CJP.

52 Frege, On Sense and Nominatum.

53 Lyotard, pt. 77.

54 Russell, p. 205.

knowledge, common sense and common language of the spatio-temporal commonality, to conclude whether a person is suitable for a position or not. The graphology test cannot be given a sense that the tested person is or is not suitable for the job. The test is not, therefore, seen as pointing to a reality:[55] it has no deictic function;[56] it does not "pinpoint a world."[57]

The situations in which a court or a party may wish to dismiss evidence on the basis that it may not give any indication of an in itself relevant object of proof may be several. Types of evidence that one might want to dismiss from the Swedish side, on the basis of the "crystal ball exception," could for example be expert evidence in the fields of homeopathy and osteopathy. These are fields of knowledge whose practice is covered by tax funding in some of the Member States and one may on that basis argue that they enjoy public recognition.[58] I would argue that on the basis of Swedish spatio-temporal commonality, the evidentiary value of the graphology test would be attributed the sense of nonsense. Should a party submit a piece of evidence that is estimated as so low this may risk decreasing the credibility/reliability of the rest of that party's plea. In such a case that party has not been heard in the sense of having been understood. This would in my opinion be a real risk should a graphology test be submitted by the employer in support of the argument that the recruitment procedure was legitimate and non-discriminatory. Should the case be tried in France, the hearing of the judges would – paraphrasing Professor Hamson – possibly be less impaired, compared to that of the Swedish judges.[59]

If on the other hand, the matter were tried in a French court, the plaintiff applicant might struggle to prove the discrimination. The evidentiary regime in this case would in France be that of evidentiary freedom.[60] The French judge assesses the evidence autonomously[61] and adjudicates on the basis of their *intime conviction*. Their *intime conviction* is the conclusion they reach regarding the matters of fact after considering the evidence presented. It is a standard of proof; if the judges are not convinced, they lack foundation for the legal judgment. It corresponds (but is not identical) to the Swedish freedom of appreciation.[62] Unless the Swedish party request a second

55 Lyotard, pt. 82.

56 Lyotard, primarily, pts. 50, 51, 61, 67, 72, 81, 121.

57 Lyotard, pt. 82.

58 For a similar and more developed reasoning, *see re* the lists of experts at the service of the French courts and the legitimating and normalizing effects, Leclerc, Olivier. *Le Juge et l'expert: Contribution à l'étude des rapports entre le droit et la science*. L.G.D.J., 2005, pp. 199 ss.

59 Hamson, C.-J. "La procedure civile en Angleterre et en France." *Revue internationale de droit comparé*, vol. 2, no. 1, 1950, p. 77–83.

60 Cass. soc., 27 mars 2001, n° 98–44.666, Bull. 2001, V, n° 108.

61 Terré, p. 163.

62 *Re intime conviction*, see Tournier, Clara. *L'intime conviction du juge de jugement*. ANRT, 2003. Lille thèses; Normand, Jacques. *Le juge et le litige*. L.G.D.J., 1965, pp. 305, 327, 353

opinion, the French court might base the judgment on the graphologist opinion (supporting the interpretation of the test results) and conclude that there was no illegitimate discrimination. The graphology test may be seen to present a fact; the graphologist would assert that it was known to be true. In sum, in a French court one means of evidence may be seen as presenting a fact which would give the court a foundation for a judgment, while the same means in a Swedish court may be seen as presenting no fact at all and thus serve as *no* foundation of the legal judgment. As the graphology test example illustrates, the mere presentation of the test may impact the assessment of a party's case to the extent that the evidence has the opposite effect in one court as compared to another. And this is in the application of the same substantive law rule, in the protection of the same EU regulated right.

The Child Custody Case – What Extra-Legal Matters Matter Legally?

The following example is of a cross-border custody case where a court expertise is used to support the judgment. The conflict of the following example concerns a family consisting of a French parent, a Swedish parent and a child. The family has lived in France for the first eight out of the child's eight and a half years, at which point they have moved to Sweden. After six months in Sweden, the French parent wants the child to reside with them in France, whereas the Swedish parent wants the child to reside in Sweden. At the time of the custody proceedings, the family resides in Sweden and the Swedish courts therefore have jurisdiction,[63] and it will consequently be imagined that the case is tried in Sweden. Both French and Swedish substantive law require that the court decide the matter on the basis of what they assess will be in the best interest of the child.[64] The 'best interest of the child' is a matter of international law, and recognized in the UN Convention on the Rights of the Child of 1989 signed by both France and Sweden in 1990. It will be seen to serve as ultimate object of proof, and thus as purpose-point, in this example, since both countries in theory have the same legal criteria to establish the custody matter.[65] This is therefore what is at stake in the case, whether the conflict is tried in Sweden or in France.

ff; Blanc, Emmanuel. *La Preuve judiciaire. Commentaire du Décret du 17 décembre 1973*, Librairie du Journal des notaires et des avocats, 1974, p. 19.

63 Article 8 Brussels II.

64 UN Commission on Human Rights. *Convention on the Rights of the Child.* 7 Mar. 1990, E/CN.4/RES/1990/74, https://www.ohchr.org/en/instruments-mechanisms/instruments/convention-rights-child; 6:2a FB; 337, 371–4, 373–2-1 CC; Cass. civ. 1e, 13 juil. 2017, 16–24.084, Publié au bulletin; Kaldal, Anna. *Parallella processer: en rättsvetenskaplig studie av riskbedömningar i vårdnads- och LVU-mål.* Jure, 2010. Dissertation. For example, p. 77. *See also* Grahn-Farley, Maria. *Barnkonventionen: en kommentar*, Studentlitteratur, 2019.

65 The fact that this is not the case in practice is a matter that falls outside of the scope of this project. If, however, it had fallen within the scope of this study, the difference in content of

If the case is administered in a Swedish court, as we assume here, it categorizes as *not amenable to out-of-court settlement.*[66] The parents' possible agreement in a particular matter is accordingly not binding on the court in this type of case.[67] In both Sweden and France, the evidence is free in child custody cases. Some exceptions aside,[68] the parties may present anything they consider to be relevant for the foundation of the judgment, while on the other hand, the judges are free to consider all facts that they regard to be relevant for the correct outcome of the case and to freely attribute the evidence with value.[69] There is in that regard no restriction as to the amount or type of language acts that may be included in the foundation for the judgment raised by the communicatory structure of civil procedure.

The categorization of the matter also means that the court is responsible to investigate the matter to the point that it finds the circumstances clarified and the foundation for the judgment robust.[70] The judge may – and is to a certain extent obliged to – investigate the case: the judge must ascertain that the foundation is robust and must investigate relevant questions if they are unclear.[71] Both legal orders recognize that 'the best interest of the child' is a legal term and that it is for the judge to decide what is in the best interest of the specific child. Both legal orders also include rules allowing the court to investigate the matter through the assistance of an expert in child health and/or child psychology. In Sweden this person is a social services official,[72] and

---

a legal rule in different countries despite the fact that it is a rule of international law, merely goes in line with the argument I am putting forward.

66 6:19 FB; 17:3 CJP; Cegrell Karlander, Isa. *Officialprincipen i migrationsprocessen: Domstolens utredningsansvar.* Uppsala, 2021, p. 49. Dissertation.

67 Cf. 6:17a FB, 6:17b FB.

68 35:7 CJP (commented in relation to the Recruitment Process example, in this chapter); *Re* French law: 9 CPC stipulates that each party must prove in accordance with the law the necessary facts in support of his claims. (Civ. 1e, 26 sept. 2012, n° 11–10.960, *Bull. civ.* I, N° 189; Bolard, Georges. "La Matière du procès et le principe du dispositif." *Droit et pratique de la procédure civile – Droit interne et européen*, edited by Serge Guinchard, 9th ed., (2017/2018). Dalloz, 2016, 221.91, p. 860.) As an example, the grounds for a divorce summons may be proven by any means (259 CC) so long as they are not an offence to the right to privacy. (Aynès, Augustin, and Xavier Vuitton. *Droit de la preuve, Principes et mise en œuvre processuelle.* 2nd ed., LexisNexis, 2017, pp. 107 ff.) Any elements entered into the case material acquired by illicit means will be excluded from the file (259–2 CC, L110–3 Code de commerce, L123–23 Code de commerce).

69 P. 44, n. 83. *Re* French law: 1358 CC; The object of proof is a *fait juridique,* p. 90.

70 42:6 CJP; 6:19 FB; Kaldal, p. 205; Ekelöf, IV, pp. 187–189; Cegrell Karlander, p. 113.

71 36:5 CJP states that in cases not amenable to out-of-court settlement the court may gather evidence on its own initiative. (Prop. 2004/05:131, p. 13.) In 43:4:2 CJP it is prescribed that the court is to ascertain that the case is investigated to the extent that it is necessary. In the preparatory works, it is explained how the rule relating to the main hearing correlates to that in 42:8:2 CJP. (Prop. 1986/87:89, pp. 216–217; NJA 2018 s. 1062, MÖD 2017:24; NJA 2014 s. 212 (*re* the relation between 42:2:2 CJP and 43:4:2 CJP); NJA 1990 s. 617; NJA 1987 s. 766; RH 1995:38; NJA 2004 s. 561; NJA 1987 s. 450.)

72 40:1 CJP; Prop. 1942:5, pp. 408, 421–422; SOU 1938:44, p. 420; Lindell, Civilprocessen, pp. 498–499; Ekelöf, IV, pp. 281, 283, 285, 288.

in France the person is publicly accredited and listed at the court.[73] The court expert makes their report available in writing.[74] The report shall include the requested opinion as well as the foundations on which this opinion has been reached.[75] The French rule prescribes that the investigation concern the family situation and the parents' capacity to assume their parental responsibilities.[76] The Swedish rule merely prescribes that the court is responsible to ascertain the questions regarding the custody, residence and relations, and that the social services may be given a commission to carry out an investigation.[77] These are fairly loosely phrased regulations regarding the content of the investigations. It is possible that the lack of detail is due to the fact that the expert is expected to be competent to assess what information is relevant in such matters, that is, that the purpose of the investigation makes it unnecessary.

This far, the proceedings are similar and the differences between the communicatory structures seem to have little impact on the evidentiary language acts. This study is however in search of differends, that which does not come to the surface.[78] The barrier which is found here, therefore, is that which concerns the spatio-temporal commonality.[79] This is the mass of language acts that constitute the soil on which we live our lives;[80] it is the part of the infinity of the inflation of senses[81] that is not questioned but taken for granted. It is part of the sun rising in the morning – and it is also part of what is considered a normal consumption of wine weekly. Although the Nordic countries have increased their wine consumption since the 1990s, they are still a bit below the average in the EU.[82]

73 373–2-12 CC; 1072 CPC regarding the court's power to request an investigation, article 1 Décret 2009–285 du 12 mars 2009 relatif aux enquêteurs sociaux et à la tarification des enquêtes sociales en matière civile regarding the list of persons competent to investigate on behalf of the court the social conditions of the child and the family. *See also* Cadiet, Jeuland, p. 534.

74 40:7:1 RB; 6:19 FB; 1072 subsection 3 CPC; 200, 201, 205 CPC.

75 40:7:3 RB; 6:19 FB; 1072 subsection 4 CPC.

76 1072 CPC.

77 6:19 FB.

78 Lyotard. p. xi.

79 Geertz, Clifford. "Common Sense as a Cultural System." *The Antioch Review*, vol. 67, no. 4, Geertz at Antioch (Fall 2009), pp. 770–790; *See also*, Lévy-Bruhl, Henri. *La Preuve judiciaire*. Essai de sociologie juridique, Marcel Rivière, 1963; Edelstam, pp. 109–116, 547; Lindell, Notorietet.

80 Gane, Nicholas. *Max Weber and Postmodern Theory: Rationalization Versus Re-enchantment*. Palgrave Macmillan, 2002, p. 92; Gualandi, Alberto. *Lyotard*. 2nd ed., Les Belles Lettres, 2004, p. 76; the always-already, Lyotard, pt. 160; de Man, Paul. "The Epistemology of Metaphor." *Critical Inquiry*, vol. 5, no. 1, 1978, pp. 13–30.

81 Lyotard, pts. 75–77.

82 OECD. *Preventing Harmful Alcohol Use*, OECD Health Policy Studies, OECD Publishing, 2021, https://doi.org/10.1787/6e4b4ffb-en. "Wine consumed in pure alcohol, litres per capita, age 15+." WHO Regional Office for Europe, Copenhagen, Denmark, https://gateway.euro.who.int/en/indicators/hfa_428-3052-wine-consumed-in-pure-alcohol-litres-per-capita-age-15plus/#id=20008&fullGraph=true. Accessed 4 Dec. 2024.

What is in the best interest of the child is a matter which has been found to be culturally, politically and ideologically determined.[83] A study on the Danish social services' investigations regarding interventions for children found that the assessments are made, not based on "real assessments of risk" but in relation to what is perceived as a "good childhood." These investigations assess "whether the home is neat and tidy, and whether there is any abuse of alcohol or drugs, instead of investigating concrete harm of the child, the child's own experience or specific circumstances in the home that increase the risk for the child."[84] Let us therefore imagine that the French parent drinks a bottle of wine per day: a glass or two for lunch, half a bottle for dinner, another glass in their reading-chair when the child has gone to sleep. In both France and Sweden, it might be seen as less than ideal, but if the French court would see it as irrelevant information, because for example, the French parent copes with their job, pays their rent and other bills, spends quality and quantity time with the child, and has good relations to their own parents, who also live in the neighborhood and play an active role in the child's life, the Swedish court may find the mere alcohol consumption as an aggravating circumstance which is not affected by the paying of the rent etc. The French expert may omit the information regarding the wine consumption from the report because it is not given a sense of relevance, whereas the Swedish expert might have. The circumstance is thus hidden in the French report, whereas it may have been expressed in the motivations of the Swedish report.

Contrariwise, the same may of course take place if the case were tried in a French court. Let us imagine that the Swedish parent regularly works night shifts and the relations with their own parents are non-existent. The child then must spend many nights at a night-time childcare because, one could argue, the relations between the Swedish parent and the child's grandparents are poor. Swedish law raises no safeguards for the protection of the relationship between a child and their grandparents, but the French Code civil establishes this to be a relation that is a right of the child, within the concept of 'the best interest of the child.'[85] The reasons and counter-reasons[86] to determine the best interest of the child and the most stable family environment would – were they presented to the courts – consist in two contrasting situations. The components of the scenario would be a comparatively large wine consumption, good contact with the grandparents, being able to sleep at home at night on the one hand, and on the other hand, a smaller wine consumption, no contact with the grandparents, sleeping at a night-time

83 Kaldal, pp. 74–76.

84 Kaldal, p. 107 with reference to Egelund, Tine. *Beskyttelse af barndommen. Socialforvaltningers risikovurdering og indgreb*. Lund, 1997, p. 109. Dissertation. (The translations are my own.)

85 371-4 CC; Hilt, Patrice, and Frédérique Granet-Lambrechts. *Droit de la Famille*. 6th ed., Ebook Pdf and PUG, 2018, p. 190.

86 Key, Ellen. *Folkbildningsarbetet särskilt med hänsyn till skönhetssinnets odling*. K. W. Appelbergs boktryckeri, 1906, p. 15; Chapter 3.

childcare regularly. How the courts would weigh this is a matter of law, not of fact; but how the experts weigh this (and may perhaps not even be aware of it, so spatio-temporally commonsensical is it perceived to be) is a matter of evidence and thus of fact.

Thus far we have not considered the differences in communicatory structure between the two legal orders compared. These differences become relevant from the moment of the reception of the expert report. In Sweden, after the written report has been submitted, the expert will be called to the main hearing and be exposed to a cross-examination.[87] Unlike the situation when the parties have called an expert witness,[88] when the expert is appointed by the court, it is the court that initiates the interrogation.[89] The parties are however allowed to directly ask the expert questions after the initiating questions of the court.[90] In France, on the contrary, as noted earlier, there is no cross-examination taking place in civil procedure.[91] The parties in the French court do possess a right to request a second opinion, but they may not in direct communication with the expert request an elaboration on a certain point or hear the expert with the possible effect that certain points be questioned.[92] The French expert may, according to the Evidence Regulation, deny such participation in the proceeding.[93] In contrast, the Swedish expert cannot, following Swedish law, deny participation.[94]

This opens to a new set of questions. Should the Swedish court allow the hearing of the Swedish expert without also hearing the French? Or would this unbalance the equality of arms? It may be worth considering the possibility to give clear instructions with specific questions to the investigating expert.[95] Research shows that Swedish courts rarely use this possibility.[96] Such questions may possibly contribute to more comparable reports in a cross-border case. But spatio-temporal commonality contains knowledge and reasoning which are tacit, of which we cannot be fully aware – partially because it is shared in the local community and therefore perceived as

87 40:8 CJP; RH 2000:39; RH 1998:98; 35:19 CJP.
88 40:19 CJP.
89 40:10 CJP.
90 40:10 CJP.
91 Herzog, Peter E., and Martha Weser. *Civil Procedure in France.* Springer, 2014, p. 76. *See also*, p. 102, n. 144.
92 373-2-12 subsection 2 CC.
93 Article 16.1 Regulation (EU) 2020/1783 of the European Parliament and of the Council of 25 November 2020 on cooperation between the courts of the Member States in the taking of evidence in civil or commercial matters (taking of evidence) (recast), OJ L 405, 2.12.2020, p. 1. (Evidence Regulation) It is understood here that as French civil procedure does not entail a format for cross-examinations, it is likely not possible that cross-examinations be administered in France, by the assistance of a French court or central authority. (Article 14 Evidence Regulation.)
94 36:1 CJP; Wennergren, Bertil. "Om vittnesplikten." *Svensk juristtidning*, 1998, p. 42.
95 6:19:3 FB.
96 SOU 2005:43, p. 728; Kaldal, s. 264.

"common sense." How could judges or legal representatives identify the differences in spatio-temporal commonality that may impact the expert's assessment to thus cover all possible aspects of relevance to determine which living arrangement out of two is in the best interest of the child? These questions remain unanswered. There is no escaping that perspective and so judgment, of a child expert concerning what is good for the specific child in each case, is included in the judge's foundation for the legal judgment without the judge nor the parties being fully aware of the details.[97] As expert perspective is invited by the judge it is not necessarily in line with what the parties want to say and what they want to be heard by the judges. It is a language act where the parties are neither addressors nor addressees; instead, the judge, as instigator of the report, is in a sense the addressor of the report as well as being its addressee: the judge stands at the purpose-point both as instigator and as recipient. The possibility for the parties to nuance and contradict the report is in these situations limited.[98]

Conclusion

The comparative study illustrates the importance of the spatio-temporal commonality as sieve for what is and what is not a relevant source of knowledge in the determination of the case. It is found that there are differences in what is perceived as a source of knowledge for the court and thus a relevant extra-legal human practice to point to in support of one's claims and in the aim of being heard. In both examples investigated in this chapter, language acts were found connected to the evidence that may have been hidden to the adjudicating court. It was concluded that these language acts would likely not have been attributed the same sense and relevance by the legal orders compared. In these examples it is primarily the party against whom the evidence is presented that the hidden senses cause a silencing: without knowing what information is hidden in the evidence it is not possible to use one's right to contradict. In the previous chapters, differends have been found to occur where the frame of the conflict differs in the legal orders compared in such a way that the object of proof alters and what the party may wish to express for that reason becomes irrelevant. Differends were also found where language acts are sorted in such a manner that the senses possible to attribute to them differs depending on the order in which they are included. In this chapter, the interplay between expert human practices, spatio-temporal commonality and law was studied. In each example, irresolvable differends were found when evidence is taken from the jurisdiction of one Member State to another. In the following chapter, the differends found in the comparative chapters will be studied at depth.

97 Kaldal, pp. 205–206; Cegrell Karlander, pp. 55–56.
98 Lindell, Notorietet.

Bibliography

Aynès, Augustin, and Xavier Vuitton. *Droit de la preuve, Principes et mise en œuvre processuelle*. 2nd ed., LexisNexis, 2017.
Balicco, Christian. "L'utilisation de la graphologie dans le recrutement de cadres au sein des cabinets conseils." *L'orientation scolaire et professionnelle*, vol. 31, no. 2, 2002.
Bennington, Geoffrey. *Lyotard: Writing the Event*. Manchester UP and Columbia UP, 1988.
Blanc, Emmanuel. *La Preuve judiciaire. Commentaire du Décret du 17 décembre 1973*. Librairie du Journal des notaires et des avocats, 1974.
Bolard, Georges. "La Matière du procès et le principe du dispositif." *Droit et pratique de la procédure civile – Droit interne et européen*, edited by Serge Guinchard, 9th ed., (2017/2018). Dalloz, 2016.
Cadiet, Loïc, and Emmanuel Jeuland. *Droit judiciaire privé*. 10th ed., LexisNexis, 2017.
Cegrell Karlander, Isa. *Officialprincipen i migrationsprocessen: Domstolens utredningsansvar*. Uppsala, 2021. Dissertation.
de Man, Paul. "The Epistemology of Metaphor." *Critical Inquiry*, vol. 5, no. 1, 1978, pp. 13–30.
Derrida, Jacques. "Force de loi: le Fondement mystique de l'autorité." *Cardozo Law Review*, vol. 11, nos. 5–6, Jul/Aug. 1990.
Edelstam, Henrik. *Sakkunnigbeviset*. Uppsala, 1991. Dissertation.
Egelund, Tine. *Beskyttelse af barndommen. Socialforvaltningers risikovurdering og indgreb*. Lund, 1997. Dissertation.
Ekelöf, P. O. et al. *Rättegång IV*. 7th ed., Norstedts Juridik, 2009.
Frege, Gottlob. "On Sense and Nominatum." *The Philosophy of Language*, edited by A. P. Martinich, translated by Herbert Feigl, 2nd ed., OUP, 1990.
Gane, Nicholas. *Max Weber and Postmodern Theory: Rationalization Versus Re-enchantment*. Palgrave Macmillan, 2002.
Geertz, Clifford. "Common Sense as a Cultural System." *The Antioch Review*, vol. 67, no. 4, Geertz at Antioch (Fall 2009), pp. 770–790.
Grahn-Farley, Maria. *Barnkonventionen: en kommentar*. Studentlitteratur, 2019.
Gualandi, Alberto. *Lyotard*. 2nd ed. Les Belles Lettres, 2004.
Hamson, C.-J. "La procedure civile en Angleterre et en France." *Revue internationale de droit comparé*, vol. 2, no. 1, 1950, p. 77–83.
Hassler, Åke. *Svensk civilprocessrätt*. Nord. bokh., 1963.
Herzog, Peter E., and Martha Weser. *Civil Procedure in France*. Springer, 2014.
Hilt, Patrice, and Frédérique Granet-Lambrechts. *Droit de la Famille*, 6th ed., Ebook Pdf. PUG, 2018.
Jeuland, Emmanuel. "Expertise." *Dictionnaire de la Justice*, edited by Loïc Cadiet, PUF, 2004.
Kaldal, Anna. *Parallella processer: en rättsvetenskaplig studie av riskbedömningar i vårdnads- och LVU-mål*. Jure, 2010. Dissertation.
Key, Ellen. *Folkbildningsarbetet särskilt med hänsyn till skönhetssinnets odling*. K. W. Appelbergs boktryckeri, 1906, http://runeberg.org/folkbildn/0027.html. Accessed 18 Sep. 2021.
Leclerc, Olivier. *Le Juge et l'expert: Contribution à l'étude des rapports entre le droit et la science*. L.G.D.J., 2005.
Lévy-Bruhl, Henri. *La Preuve judiciaire*. Essai de sociologie juridique. Marcel Rivière, 1963.
Lindblom, P. H. "Processens arkitektur." *Vänbok till Torleif Bylund*, edited by Torbjörn Andersson and Bengt Lindell, Iustus, 2003.
Lindell, Bengt. *Notorietet och kontradiktion*. Iustus, 2007.

Lindell, Bengt. *Civilprocessen*. 3rd ed. Uppsala and Iustus, 2012.
Lyotard, Jean-François. *The Differend – Phrases in Dispute*. Translated by Georges Van Den Abbeele, University of Minnesota Press, 1988.
Marchal, Emmanuelle. "Graphologie et entreprises: histoire et controverses." *Sociologies pratiques*, vol. 10, no. 1, 2005, pp. 57–76.
Normand, Jacques. *Le juge et le litige*. L.G.D.J., 1965.
Russell, Bertrand. "On Denoting." *The Philosophy of Language*, edited by A. P. Martinich, 2nd ed., OUP, 1990.
Tarski, Alfred. "The Semantic Conception of Truth and the Foundations of Semantics." *The Philosophy of Language*, edited by A. P. Martinich, 2nd ed., OUP, 1990.
Terré, François. *Droit civil, Les Obligations*. Dalloz, Paris, 2005.
Tournier, Clara. *L'intime conviction du juge de jugement*. ANRT, 2003. Lille thèses.
Wennergren, Bertil. "Om vittnesplikten." *Svensk juristtidning*, 1998, pp. 40–44.
Westberg, Peter. *Anskaffning av bevisning i dispositiva tvistemål*. Norstedts Juridik, 2010.
Wigmore, John H. *Treatise on the System of Evidence in Trials at Common Law: Including the Statutes and Judicial Decisions of All Jurisdictions of the United States*. Little, Brown, and Co., 1904.

Chapter 8

Differends in Cross-Border Evidence

Introduction

In this book I present juridical justice as approximative. I do this on the basis of the differends I have found with cross-border evidence. I hold that the cross-border travel of the evidence aggravates a situation which is already there in domestic cases with no cross-border aspect. I will now first put the evidence in relation to the judgment of the case, and thereafter discuss the differends that I have found in the comparative study. In the following chapter I will present how approximative justice may be an approach that allows for differences in perception between citizens of Europe[1] as parties, as well as respect the differences between worldviews in the EU, without imposing a common sense of justice neither for the judiciaries nor for the citizens. In short, I will suggest a sense of justice "that does not put an end to disputes and differences, that is continually in search for its rules and its laws rather than presupposing and simply applying them to each case."[2]

To Prove and the Collection of Senses

Evidence is a means to establish the truth about a contested fact;[3] the truth is a matter of correlation between a cognitive language act and reality. Reality is here understood as consisting of an unlimited number of human practices, all of which with their own perspective on life. As describes Lyotard: "Reality: a swarm of senses [sets] upon a field pinpointed by a world. It is able to be signified, to be shown, and to be named, all three. The emphasis is sometimes put on one of these, sometimes on another."[4] Reality, therefore, is not

1 Chapter 1.
2 Carroll, David. "Rephrasing the Political with Kant and Lyotard: From Aesthetic to Political Judgments." *Diacritics*, vol. 14, no. 3, 1984, Special Issue on the Work of Jean-François Lyotard, p. 75.
3 35:7 CJP, 6 and 9 CPC; Villenave. *Des Jurés et de la conviction intime*. Malassis, 1796.
4 Lyotard, Jean-François. *The Differend – Phrases in Dispute*. Translated by Georges Van Den Abbeele, University of Minnesota Press, 1988/Lyotard, Jean-François. *Le Différend*. Éditions

DOI: 10.4324/9781003495383-8

one, but varying, depending on perspective, that is, the purpose-point of the human practice prevailing at each given moment, as well as on the different senses that are attached to the descriptive/cognitive language acts which are connected to the purpose-point through the sharing of senses. This means that reality is

> a complex of possible senses. . . . The correct sense of a [language act] cannot be determined by a reference to reality, since the referent itself does not fix sense and reality itself is defined as the complex of competing senses attached to a referent.[5]

Lévy-Bruhl means that to succeed in proving is to reach the conviction of the judge.[6] For Lyotard, to succeed in proving is to have reached an agreement with another person regarding the properties of the object of proof and its shared sense(s) with the purpose-point.[7] Lyotard further means that to establish the reality of a referent, the addressor and the addressee must both agree on the sense of a referent,[8] which arguably means that the addressor has convinced the addressee. When the judge agrees with a party regarding the sense of evidence presented, namely, that it has the sense of an alleged fact, that evidence will contribute to the establishment of that alleged fact. The collection of senses which are thus accepted will constitute the case as what is legally qualified.[9] Only that which the judge can give sense (i.e., only what makes sense to the judge, or has any meaning to the judge) can be seen as relevant to the judge – or seen at all.

The case, as that which is legally qualified by the judge, consists of the sense that the judge is capable of perceiving. Daniel Kahneman teaches us that human minds make judgments on the basis of what is before them as if that information were all the relevant information there could be. This process of constructing an understanding of a situation on the basis of the knowledge one has, is referred to as a rule given the acronym WYSIATI: What You See Is All There Is. People thus base their judgments on the facts that they have access to *as if* those were the only existing facts – as if what

de minuit. 1983, pt. 82 (the translation is slightly adjusted, here); *and further* Lyotard, page 131, Kant, Immanuel. *Kritik av omdömeskraften*. Translated by Sven-Olov Wallenstein, Thales, 2003. (Kant, Critique of Judgment), 10; s*ee also* Günther, Gotthard. "Life as Poly-contexturality." *Wirklichkeit und Reflexion*, edited by H. Fahrenbach (Hrsg.), Festschrift für Walter Schulz, 1973, pp. 187–210.

5 Woodward, Ashley. "Jean-François Lyotard (1924–1998)." *Internet Encyclopedia of Philosophy*, http://www.iep.utm.edu/lyotard/. Accessed 2 Sep. 2021.

6 Lévy-Bruhl, Henri. *La Preuve judiciaire*. Essai de sociologie juridique, Marcel Rivière, 1963, p. 21.

7 Lyotard, pt. 76.

8 Lyotard, pt. 28, *also* pt. 147 *re* conviction as a stake (purpose-point).

9 P. 29, n. 101.

we know of is the totality of the relevant facts.[10] But as Kahneman points out, this way of behaving is risky, as every new piece of information may change entirely the understanding of "what there is."[11] When the decision must be made and the horizon is thus blocked, the reality of the case is a "wysiati-reality" – a limited reality consisting of the swarm of senses that the judge can perceive.[12]

The evidentiary language act is an ostensive language act with deictics pointing out the reality of the singular case by connecting to the purpose-points set out by the law.[13] The extra-legal reality consists of a muddle of human practices all competing[14] to give sense to the evidentiary language act. Evidence is a sense which is given to ostensive or descriptive language acts, and from many such descriptive language acts is formed a wysiati-reality. The comparative study explores the evidence's road[15] from a muddled reality of a multitude of human practices[16] (whose purpose-points determine the relevance – and therefore the sense – of the language acts that take place), to the swarm of senses which will constitute the reality of the case.[17]

If the conditions for attributing sense to a particular piece of evidence differ between the two legal orders compared, it is held that the evidence is not the same at take-off and landing: it therefore gives rise to a *differend.* The comparative study seeks differends that may arise because of divergent purpose-points, communicatory structures and human practices as three stages of the fact-finding process. It has been found that there are three types of barriers for the message of the parties to get through to the judges that are of particular import in cross-border cases. One hinderance found is the purpose-point from which the material is perceived, as presented by the applicable (primarily substantive) law. The wysiati-reality is seen by the judge as one holistic reality,[18] but it itself, as a whole, impacts the sense and import that may be attributed to each language act of the material.[19] Another barrier consists of the cultural pre-understandings that rest in the spatio-temporal commonality which imposes itself on the case specific material before reaching the wysiati-reality, and thus attributes and adds senses to the case specific material. This causes differends at the level of human practices.[20] The third barrier consists of the shape of the proceeding as such and its allowing or

10 Kahneman, Daniel. *Thinking Fast and Slow.* MacMillan Publishers, 2015.
11 *Re* 'swarm of senses,' Lyotard, pt. 82.
12 Lyotard, pt. 82.
13 Chapters 3 and 5.
14 Lyotard, pt. 234.
15 Cf. Lyotard, pt. 78.
16 Chapter 3.
17 Lyotard, pt. 82.
18 Cf. epistemic probability, Kolflaath, Eivind. "Bevisbedømmelse: sannsynlighet eller fortellinger?" *Jussens Venner,* vol. 39, no. 5–6, Mars 2005, pp. 279–304.
19 NJA 1986 s. 175; Lyotard, pts. 60, 82, 131.
20 Lyotard, for example, pt. 40.

disallowing certain language acts in the foundation for the legal judgment and is what is here referred to as the communicatory structure.[21] This causes differends at the level of communicatory structures.[22]

In the comparative study I have elaborated six examples of situations where the treatment of the evidence differs in the two legal orders compared with such effect that the determination of the case would differ had the same case been tried in both jurisdictions. The proceedings hinder senses which would come through in the proceeding of the other legal order. The evidence is not a neutral conveyor of facts, as it speaks differently to different jurisdictions and different judges.

Differends at the Level of Communicatory Structure

To present evidence constitutes one example of linking language acts together. Verification[23] must be done in accordance with the rules that are applicable to the specific human practice.[24] Those rules have here been referred to as communicatory structures.[25] Included in the communicatory structure are rules regarding what language acts may be included (rules of admissibility), and who may be addressor of an evidentiary language act. This means that rules may restrict who may say something and contribute to the totality of the language acts that constitute the foundation of the judgment,[26] but also who may initially decide what is and what is not relevant, as in what extra-legal language acts are also legal, as in relevant for the legal human practice, and for the legal judgment.

Differends at the level of communicatory structure are found in the examples in Chapters 5 and 6. Two examples will be mentioned here. The Car Purchase Contract case is an illustration that the object of proof alters when the evidence is regulated. When the contract is valid only once it has been taken down in written form, what constitutes object of proof and what constitutes proof is different compared to when the contract takes place and is valid

21 Lyotard, pt. 185.

22 Lyotard, pt. 40.

23 Lyotard speaks more of validation than verification; 'validation' is a more general term and suitable for a genre of discourse (validation can be a genre of discourse, but not a human practice, as it lacks the specific field of knowledge and function which are attributed to the human practice). Lyotard, pts. 41, 178 ff. *Consider also,* "Validation consists in showing cases of provisional nonfalsification." (Lyotard, 90; Woodward, Ashley. "Testimony and the Affect-Phrase." *Rereading Jean-François Lyotard,* edited by Heidi Bickis and Rob Shields, Ashgate, 2013, p. 176.)

24 Lyotard, 76, and also, comparatively, p. 118 (Kant 2).

25 Lyotard, page 10, Thèse; Fritzman, J. M., "Overcoming Capitalism." *Lyotard, Just Education*, edited by Pradeep Ajit Dhillon and Stanley Paul, Routledge, 2000, p. 74.

26 Wronged is that person who may not speak, or that perspective that may not be spoken of. (Lyotard, pts. 6–8; Sawyer, Dylan. *Lyotard, Literature and the Trauma of the Differend.* Palgrave Macmillian, 2014, p. 65.)

already at the point in time when an agreement has been reached between the parties. The two alternatives open to different horizons.[27] It also illustrates that the expressions of agreement depend on the spatio-temporal commonality: when two persons whose behavior and preconceptions are in reference to different spatio-temporal commonalities it may be uncertain whether the concluding of a contract may be said to have taken place at all. There are two incommensurable objects of proof, with equal validity. To give one prevalence over the other would be a case of a differend.

The second example to mention here concerns the forms and assessments of two possibly mutually exclusive wills. One is written within a regime of evidentiary freedom where formality requirements regarding legal acts are scarce. The system lacks a hierarchical structure for different forms of pre-constituted evidence. The other is written within a regime of regulated evidence with such a hierarchy. Within this hierarchy, the will of the example has the highest value. The competition between these wills rests on the communicatory structures which are incommensurable, and the conflict therefore insoluble. This is also an example of a differend at the level of the communicatory structure.[28]

Differends at the Level of Purpose-Point

The purpose-point of the legal judgment as decision is the conflict between the parties' claims in the case.[29] The legal judgment, however, is the connection of two language acts, where the one validates the other.[30] The validation of the claims is done by reference to another language act.[31] Which type of language act this is and from where the judge may take it differs in the different civil procedural fact-finding systems compared. It was found in Chapter 5 that the purpose-point of the evidence varies between different forms of civil procedure. Three different types of purpose-points were found in the two legal orders compared: one specific to each legal order, and one which the two share. In the French *régime libre* and the Swedish cases not amenable to out-of-court settlement the purpose-point of the evidence is the law rule which the court has found to be applicable, or finds to be applicable at some point in the process. In the French *régime légal*, and the same is true regarding the Swedish exceptions, on the other hand, the purpose-point of the evidence is the legal rule which prescribes a certain means of evidence. The direct aim of the evidence is therefore to show that it is – shares the sense

27 Derrida, Jacques. "Force de loi: le Fondement mystique de l'autorité." *Cardozo Law Review*, vol. 11, nos. 5–6, Jul/Aug. 1990, p. 966.
28 Lyotard, pt. 40.
29 Chapter 5.
30 Lyotard, pts. 31, 41, 184.
31 Lyotard, pts. 41, 45, 86.

of – the referent of the evidentiary law rule.[32] In Swedish cases amenable to out-of-court settlement, the purpose-point of the evidence is the allegations. It is in relation to them that the court must give the evidence a sense. This sense can be found to correspond to the allegations or not. In the *régime légal* the linking of language acts ends with the claims of the plaintiff. The claims are thus a language act to which the plaintiff is the addressor, and the adjudicating judge is the ultimate addressee.[33] To this is connected a substantive law rule. This rule is chosen by the adjudicating judge, and therefore the adjudicating judge is themselves both addressor and addressee to this rule.[34]

To this rule is connected first, an allegation, and thereafter an evidentiary law rule, prescribing what type of means of evidence is needed for validating the descriptive language act of the allegation and thus making it possible for the judge to render the legal judgment. The validation of the allegation is done, not by an ostensive language act but by a prescriptive.[35] It is in turn the prescriptive (or normative) evidentiary law rule which is validated by an ostensive, which is the language act that in cases where the evidence is free points to the extra-legal,[36] as it belongs to another human practice before the human practice of law grabs hold of it.[37] But there is no link when the evidence is regulated in terms of means and value,[38] no language act, which

32 Chapter 5.

33 Lyotard, pt. 240 illustrates the shifting of the roles of the addressor/addressee. The judge is the ultimate addressor of the judicial proceeding, as they render the legal judgment.

34 When focusing on legal fact-finding and legal judging, it seems reasonable and pragmatic (as well as coherent with the linking scheme here used for analysis) to understand the judge as the addressee of a legal rule. It is of course also possible to understand us all, subjects of the law, as the addressees of legal rules, *see for example,* Lyotard, pt. 176; Goyal, Reena. "Serving Justice through Authorship: A Phenomenological Approach to the Authority of Law." *University of Toronto Faculty of Law Review*, vol. 62, no. 1, 2004, p. 41.

35 Lyotard, pt. 64; paraphrasing Luhmann, the closure is doubly normative. ("We pass over all the problems arising with the application of this concept to social systems in general and to the system of society in particular. What matters here is how the legal system distinguishes self-reference and other-reference. At the level of those operations which attribute legal validity, this happens through the distinction between normative and cognitive expectations. *The system operates under normative closure and cognitive openness.* It identifies itself with the function of keeping to normative expectations, if necessary counterfactually, but is, vis-à-vis the environment, prepared to learn." Luhmann, Niklas. "Legal Argumentation: An Analysis of its Form." *Modern Law Review,* vol. 58, no. 3, May 1995, p. 296 (*italics added*).)

36 What is in law perceived as the matters of fact and the relevant-to-law but yet external to it (it is extra-legal but not non-legal). King, Michael, and Chris Thornhill. *Niklas Luhmann's Theory of Politics and Law*. Springer, 2003, pp. 55–56 *re* relevance; *see also* Lyotard, pt. 50.

37 Lyotard, pts. 180–181.

38 Evidence is given value when it is given sense, in accordance with the scheme described in Lyotard, pt. 28. With evidentiary value is also meant, in evidentiary probability theories, reliability of the evidence, i.e., the likelihood that the evidence occurs when the object of proof occurs, or that the object of proof is the cause of the evidence, i.e., in both cases, the likelihood of correlation between the two. This likelihood is suggested to be calculated on the basis of normality, that is commonplace generalizations and common knowledge, which are

establishes the legal facts, that is, what facts are legally relevant. Instead, there is an establishment that an evidentiary language act shares the sense of an evidentiary law rule. This establishment is made by the adjudicating judge.[39]

Whilst it is the judge who ultimately decides the senses of the language acts and which language acts may contribute to the reality of the case, the parties presenting evidence will have already signified something with the evidence and allegations that they present.[40] Like a magnet, the purpose-point pulls the senses of the language acts towards itself. The perspective of the purpose-point is where the language act is "going" (and thus the senses that it will be given is determined in relation to this purpose-point) whereas it, as it "comes along" is a response to what has previously come along. As such, it gave senses to previous language acts, and its signification may be said to have been just that. The language act therefore has no sense "in the present"[41] but is always relative to the past and the future – linked to previous language acts as a response to them; the evidence and the allegations that the parties present are given senses within an extra-legal idiom,[42] as responses to language acts which preceded.

In the *régime libre* and the cases not amenable to out-of-court settlement, the parties are addressors of the claims, and the judge is the addressee. The referent of the claim is the legal consequence that the party wishes to take place. The claim may be said to be a prescriptive language act.[43] To the claim is connected a legal rule, a normative or prescriptive language act to which the judge is both addressor and addressee.[44] (This is what makes the judge the judge.) A judge also assesses the evidence and is thus the addressee of the evidentiary language acts.[45] The assessment of the evidence is a matter of giving the evidence a sense which composes a reality which is assessed to have legal relevance.[46] The parties and judges may all contribute with evidence, that is, the judges and the parties bring in the language acts with the senses of which the judges thereafter construct a reality which may or may not be legally relevant. The fact that the judges themselves may contribute to the construction of this reality makes it more likely that this reality is found legally relevant; it is unlikely that the judges bring in material which they find irrelevant, that is,

culturally conditioned and of which, more importantly, there is no empirically established knowledge; 35:2 CJP; Comp. Lindell, Bengt. *Notorietet och kontradiktion*. Iustus, 2007.

39 In some cases, this establishment follows after it has been made also by the preparatory judge. (780–797 CPC)

40 Lyotard, pt. 28.

41 Lyotard, pt. 88; *see also* Derrida, pp. 961, 963.

42 Lyotard, pts. 50, 51, 60, 61.

43 Lyotard, pt. 240, *as well as* pp. 118–119 (Kant 2).

44 The substantive law rule is not seen here as part of the communicatory structure, only procedural rules regarding the fact-finding and the administration of evidence are.

45 Lyotard, pt. 240.

46 Lyotard, pts. 28, 61–67, 180, 181, 184, 188.

non-legal.[47] However, as the ultimate end of the chain is the legal judgment which is made in relation to, and therefore restricted by, the parties' claims, the senses of the evidentiary language acts will be tested in relation to the claims of both the plaintiff and the defendant. This is the ultimate (canonical[48]) language act, and that which will direct the senses of all the language act as they are included in the material.[49]

If the purpose-points vary between different legal orders regarding the same extra-legal conflict – the same pre-procedural reality – the ultimate object of proof varies, and the entire construction of the wysiati-reality may alter. As the example of the Car Purchase Contract case illustrates,[50] there is an important difference between proving a binding agreement of which no written evidence was made, but any evidence is admissible because of the purpose-point of the evidence and one where evidence is regulated. In the former, it is indeed the binding agreement that is primarily at stake; in the latter, it is the senses that may be attributed to the content of the written (if it is not the reliability itself, in which case it is the sense of the form that is in question).

Differends at the Level of Human Practices

Another type of differend is found in the assessment of relevance, namely, that between human practices.[51] Lyotard holds that one does not prove the existence of something but the sense of something.[52] If the contested allegation is that a child is better off with their French parent, what needs proving is that the situation with the French parent presents properties, that is, consists of circumstances, which together are attributed a more beneficial sense than the totality of properties presented by the situation with the child's Swedish parent (both situations as imagined in the future).[53] The circumstances that the situation presents, the properties, senses, of that situation. The reality which needs proving consequently consists of a swarm of senses.[54]

47 King, Michael, and Chris Thornhill. *Niklas Luhmann's Theory of Politics and Law*. Springer, 2003, pp. 55–56, *re* relevance.

48 Lyotard, *for example*, pts. 186, 210, 212, where Lyotard describes the purpose-point as a canonical language act, phrased as a question.

49 Lyotard, pts. 28, 61–67, 180, 181, 184, 188.

50 Chapter 5.

51 Lyotard, pt. 40.

52 Lyotard, pt. 76: "One does not prove something, one proves that a thing presents a signified property."

53 Was there a person whose name was Shakespeare, who was born and raised in Stratford-upon-Avon, who was married to a woman called Anne Hathaway, and who wrote a great number of theatrical plays some of which were performed on the stage of the Globe theater, which he was a joint owner of? These descriptions are all senses. "Who was Shakespeare?" is not a question regarding his inner essence, his being, his intimate person. It is a question which asks for senses. Did a person who presented those senses exist? (Roland Emmerich's film *Anonymous* of 2011.)

54 Lyotard, pt. 82.

The allegations are cognitive language acts, which means they may be true or false.[55] They are verified by language acts which are designators of reality (such as here, there, now, then), designating "their object as an extra-linguistic permanence, as a 'given,'" a *datum*, a posited fact.[56] The evidentiary language act is a language act which aims at pointing out the signification of the allegation, namely, the binding contract between the parties that is the sense and signification of the paper-contract.[57] The sense of the ostensive phrase is to point to a thing, which "presents the signified property."[58] This is therefore one point where it is likely that the party and the judge in a case – a cross-border case in particular – miscommunicate: the two may disagree on what is signified (there is a case of a differend).[59]

In the example of the Recruitment Process the employer may have had no intention of discriminating against the applicant. The process may have been developed by a person specialized in behavioral sciences and human resources, perhaps external to the employer. Without the graphology test there might however have been no basis for the choice of the successful applicant at the expense of the unsuccessful. The use of such tests varies and so does the assessment of them. What sense should be attributed to them? The exclusion of the test for lack of relevance would deny the employer a right to be heard; the senses that they attribute the graphology test would not be included in the swarm of senses lighting up the field[60] and contribute to the wysiati-reality[61] that the judge would constitute of the case and that would be legally qualified by the judge.[62] It is therefore an example of a differend, here in a collision between the spatio-temporal human practice in the environment of one legal order and the spatio-temporal human practice in the environment of another.[63]

Another example of a differend because of different attribution of relevance to factual circumstances is found in the Child Custody case. That case raises the possibility that the spatio-temporal commonality attributes different senses to factual circumstances with the consequence that expertise pertaining to different spatio-temporal commonalities does not express itself on that matter: it is not relevant to the human practice of the expertise in that spatio-temporal commonality. The judge would in a domestic case share

55 Frege, Gottlob. "On Sense and Nominatum." *The Philosophy of Language*, edited by A. P. Martinich, translated by Herbert Feigl, 2nd ed., OUP, 1990.

56 Lyotard, pts. 50, 61; Woodward, Testimony and the Affect-Phrase, p. 175; *see also* Legrand, Pierre. "Paradoxically, Derrida: For a Comparative Legal Studies." *Cardozo Law Review*, vol. 27, no. 2, Nov. 2005, pp. 631–718.

57 Lyotard, pt. 76.

58 Lyotard, pt. 76.

59 Lyotard, pt. 13.

60 Lyotard, pt. 82.

61 With wysiati-reality is here meant the reality that is seen through the swarm of senses that light up a field; Lyotard, pt. 82.

62 Lyotard, pt. 88.

63 Lyotard, pt. 9.

the perception of relevance with the expertise – not because of the expert knowledge but because of the spatio-temporal commonality. This may also be commented from the perspective of the human practice of the expertise: the two situations illustrated in the Child Custody case may be differently assessed by one and the same court expert. If the court of the forum chooses to take the evidence directly on the territory both of its own jurisdiction and that of the requested Member State, it is possible that two locally normal family situations would be assessed as one being less normal than the other, and therefore less beneficial for the child.

Under the circumstances illustrated in the cases of the comparative study it is not reasonable to expect that neither the judge nor the parties and their legal representatives look into the horizon of the cross-border evidence and see what miscommunication may have been. The horizon is blocked by the heterogeneity of communicatory structures and human practices. The bifurcation of the possibilities of senses attributable to the language acts presented, presupposed and ignored is endless. Nevertheless, the obligation to listen is not less because the hearing is impaired.[64]

Conclusion

Several sources of miscommunication have been found in the comparative study to be involved when evidence is taken across borders. Both substantive law and procedural law shape the evidence: both the purpose-point of the evidence as the actual object of proof and the communicatory structure as the form of civil procedural fact-finding shape the evidentiary language act by restricting what sense and signification it may be attributed, and what inference may therefore be made. It was also found that the regulatory environment[65] of spatio-temporal commonality restricts what human practices may serve as sources of knowledge in the formation of the legal judgment. Moreover, it was found that the evidentiary language act may be linked to cognitive language acts which are not presented but nevertheless form part of the collection of senses on which the reality of the case is determined and which may have been omitted as impertinent or irrelevant had they been expressed.

This means that the cross-border evidence is an unreliable source of information for the judge, and an equally unreliable means for the parties to be heard.[66] As means to establish the truth of the case, it does not serve its

64 P. 93, n. 81.

65 Joerges, Christian. "The Challenges of Europeanization in the Realm of Private Law: A Plea for a New Legal Discipline." *Duke Journal of Comparative & International Law,* vol. 14, no. 2, Summer 2004, pp. 149–196.

66 Chapter 2, *also* Lyotard, pt. 7.

purpose as the reality of the case cannot be what is "pre-procedural"[67] but the swarm of senses that the court has "collected" – by attributing sense to the evidentiary language acts that have been presented after the sifting of the communicatory structure and the spatio-temporal commonality in accordance with the perspective of the purpose-point.[68] If evidence therefore as source of knowledge is unreliable, there cannot be a correct judgment in the sense of hitting the bull's eye. There are simply too many bull's eyes per dart.

Bibliography

Carroll, David. "Rephrasing the Political with Kant and Lyotard: From Aesthetic to Political Judgments." *Diacritics*, vol. 14, no. 3, 1984, Special Issue on the Work of Jean-François Lyotard, pp. 74–88.

Derrida, Jacques. "Force de loi: le Fondement mystique de l'autorité." *Cardozo Law Review*, vol. 11, nos. 5–6, Jul/Aug. 1990.

Ekelöf, P. O. "Review of Sakfrågor och rättsfrågor. Akademisk avhandling. Bengt Lindell. Uppsala 1987." *Svensk juristtidning*, 1988, pp. 23–39.

Ekelöf, P. O. "Bevisvärdemodellen kontra bevistemamodellen." *Svensk juristtidning*, 1989, pp. 23–39.

Frege, Gottlob. "On Sense and Nominatum." *The Philosophy of Language*, edited by A. P. Martinich, translated by Herbert Feigl, 2nd ed., OUP, 1990.

Fritzman, J. M. "Overcoming Capitalism." *Lyotard, Just Education*, edited by Pradeep Ajit Dhillon and Stanley Paul, Routledge, 2000.

Goyal, Reena. "Serving Justice through Authorship: A Phenomenological Approach to the Authority of Law." *University of Toronto Faculty of Law Review*, vol. 62, no. 1, 2004.

Günther, Gotthard. "Life as Polycontexturality." *Wirklichkeit und Reflexion*, edited by H. Fahrenbach, Festschrift für Walter Schulz, 1973, pp. 187–210.

Joerges, Christian. "The Challenges of Europeanization in the Realm of Private Law: A Plea for a New Legal Discipline." *Duke Journal of Comparative & International Law*, vol. 14, no. 2, Summer 2004, pp. 149–196.

Kahneman, Daniel. *Thinking Fast and Slow*. MacMillan Publishers, 2015.

Kant, Immanuel. *Kritik av omdömeskraften*. Translated by Sven-Olov Wallenstein, Thales, 2003 (Kant, Critique of Judgment).

King, Michael, and Chris Thornhill. *Niklas Luhmann's Theory of Politics and Law*. Springer, 2003.

Kolflaath, Eivind. "Bevisbedømmelse: sannsynlighet eller fortellinger?" *Jussens Venner*, vol. 39, no. 5–6, Mars 2005, pp. 279–304.

Legrand, Pierre. "Paradoxically, Derrida: For a Comparative Legal Studies." *Cardozo Law Review*, vol. 27, no. 2, Nov. 2005, pp. 631–718.

Lévy-Bruhl, Henri. *La Preuve judiciaire*. Essai de sociologie juridique. Marcel Rivière, 1963.

Lindell, Bengt. *Notorietet och kontradiktion*. Iustus, 2007.

Luhmann, Niklas. "Legal Argumentation: An Analysis of Its Form." *Modern Law Review*, vol. 58, no. 3, May 1995.

67 Ekelöf, P.O. "Review of Sakfrågor och rättsfrågor. Akademisk avhandling. Bengt Lindell. Uppsala 1987." *Svensk juristtidning*, 1988, p. 23; Ekelöf, P. O. "Bevisvärdemodellen kontra bevistemamodellen." *Svensk juristtidning*, 1989, p. 26.

68 Chapter 2.

Lyotard, Jean-François. *The Differend – Phrases in Dispute*. Translated by Georges Van Den Abbeele, University of Minnesota Press, 1988.
Sawyer, Dylan. *Lyotard, Literature and the Trauma of the Differend*. Palgrave Macmillan, 2014.
Villenave. *Des Jurés et de la conviction intime*. Malassis, 1796.
Woodward, Ashley. "Testimony and the Affect-Phrase." *Rereading Jean-François Lyotard*, edited by Heidi Bickis and Rob Shields, Ashgate, 2013.
Woodward, Ashley. "Jean-François Lyotard (1924–1998)." *Internet Encyclopedia of Philosophy*, http://www.iep.utm.edu/lyotard/. Accessed 2 Sep. 2021.

Chapter 9

Approximative Justice

Do No Harm

As mentioned in Chapter 2, whereas both Lyotard and Derrida detect impasses for the just judgment, both also offer a way out of the paralysis. Approximative justice is a suggestion how to move forward so as not to be stuck in a position of conflict and injustice, differends and wrongs. Whereas both Lyotard and Derrida seem to agree that justice must be found in responsibility, approximative justice is an attempt to bring this closer to the practice of law, to the practice of rendering just legal judgments. Before I develop the idea of approximative justice the underlying understanding of justice as responsibility in Lyotard and Derrida will be further laid out.

Lyotard distinguishes between the damage and the wrong:[1] a wrong is what takes place when the damage caused cannot be proven.[2] This is the implication because what takes place can be interpreted in a number of ways, and the interpretation that is not made is not linked upon and is therefore not expressed or recognized – it is therefore wronged.[3] And because the linking possibilities following from the pertinent communicatory structure are limited, what *could have* been said in the prevalent idiom, i.e., that of the court, still does not come forward, but is deported to silence.[4] The wrong is therefore inevitable.[5] Only a slice of reality may constitute the case and this is as mentioned the wysiati-reality of the judge. This means that not only is the correct judgment as objectively correct not possible, it is also impossible not to cause a new wrong when rendering a judgment.

1 Carroll translates 'wrong' into 'injustice.' (Carroll, David. "Rephrasing the Political with Kant and Lyotard: From Aesthetic to Political Judgments." *Diacritics*, vol. 14, no. 3, 1984, Special Issue on the Work of Jean-François Lyotard, pp. 74–88.) *See also* Douzinas, Costas, and Ronnie Warrington. " 'A Well-Founded Fear of Justice': Law and Ethics in Postmodernity." *Law and Critique*, vol. II, no. 2, 1991, pp. 115–147.

2 Lyotard, Jean-François. *The Differend – Phrases in Dispute*. Translated by Georges Van Den Abbeele, University of Minnesota Press, 1988/Lyotard, Jean-François. *Le Différend*. Éditions de minuit. 1983, p. xi, pt. 7.

3 Lyotard, p. xi.

4 Lyotard, pt. 13.

5 Lyotard, pt. 92.

DOI: 10.4324/9781003495383-9

Wrongs are not only done to people, but also human practices and language acts may be wronged.[6] This is paradoxically where we might find the source not to wrong the parties nor the public. Lyotard discusses the effect of human practices to hide or expose differends. He emphasizes the deliberative and the narrative human practices in that regard.[7] I will return to the narrative in relation to symphonic justice and discuss the deliberative in relation to watercolor justice. This chapter argues that the indeterminacy of facts makes all legal judgment an artistic act, where the circumstances are understood, and thus determined approximatively, like a watercolor painting presenting an impression, rather than a construction of pixels in a digital creation. With approximative justice, I am hoping to find a possibility to avoid doing wrong to people by passing – despite passing – inevitably incorrect legal judgments.[8]

The Responsibility of the Open-Hearted Address

Acknowledging the perilous abyss[9] between one language act and the next, Lyotard's theory of justice puts the emphasis on the "responsibility to thought" requiring that the silent feeling of a wrong be listened to.[10] "One's responsibility before thought consists . . . in detecting differends and in finding the (impossible) idiom for phrasing them."[11] Despite the charge of anthropomorphism[12] there is responsibility on the part of the addressee toward the occurrence, the language act itself: "To judge that one ought to do this thing because that thing has already been prescribed is to defy the occurrence and the addressee's responsibility before it."[13] The leap from one language act to the next whereby the first is given its meaning, is an act that demands responsibility of the addressee. The imposition of one human practice on the language act, thereby silencing all other human practices, raises with Lyotard the demand on the addressee that they listen to the silence so as not to perpetuate the wrong – or at least to alleviate the pain.[14]

6 Lyotard, p. xii, pts. 196, primarily, but *also* 93, 151, 236.
7 Lyotard, pts. 210, 219, primarily.
8 "Theories are descriptions of determinate states of affairs while the ethical response is indeterminate, something to be done rather than something said." (Douzinas, Warrington, p. 123.)
9 Lyotard, pp. 123, 130 ff., pts., 178, 180, 207, 217.
10 Lyotard, pt. 236.
11 Lyotard, pt. 202.
12 Lyotard, pt. 91.
13 Lyotard, pt. 234.
14 Lyotard, pt. 236.

Whereas Lyotard's mission with *The Differend* is to save the honor of thinking,[15] Derrida pinpoints the Kierkegaardian moment of madness.[16] Derrida reasons that however mad[17] or mystical[18] the foundation for the judgment may seem, the judge must render a judgment. Connecting again to Lyotard's archipelago, navigating – concatenating – is endless; it is only within the framework of a particular human practice that an activity may come to an end but once that end has been reached a new link will carry the concatenation forward towards a new purpose-point. With Derrida, the anxiety of the continuous navigation and the interruption of suspense that therefore likewise continuously must take place, lays a heavy burden of responsibility on the judge.[19] The judge must overcome their anxiety and grasp the rudder and steer – because as much as a judgment is a decision which halts, it only interrupts the moment of suspense, the moment of uncertainty of that last linking.

To avoid a dejected approach to justice Derrida suggests a "double movement"[20] out of the tension between law and norm on the one hand and freedom and responsibility on the other.[21] The tension may therefore be said to lay between the limitlessness and the limits. I understand this movement to again consist in a consideration of both past and future.[22] Responsibility is limitless,[23] and as such connected to the conscience and the self;[24] it is personal.[25] Derrida notes that responsibility is both *to* the other (as a response perhaps, but nevertheless excessive,[26] without delimitation,[27] and therefore not restricted to calculation and reciprocity,[28] mutuality, debit and credit) and *before* what may be summarized as the institutions: "an agency authorized to

15 Lyotard, p. 10 (Problème).
16 Derrida, Jacques. "Force de loi: le Fondement mystique de l'autorité." *Cardozo Law Review*, vol. 11, nos. 5–6, Jul/Aug. 1990, p. 968.
17 Derrida, p. 967.
18 Derrida, pp. 936 ss., 1023.
19 Derrida, Jacques. "Politics of Friendship." *American Imago*, FALL 1993, vol. 50, no. 3, Love (FALL 1993), pp. 378–380; Gasché, Rodolphe. *Inventions of Difference: on Jacques Derrida*. Harvard UP, 1994, p. 227.
20 Derrida, p. 953–954; Poché, Fred. *Penser avec Derrida: Comprendre la déconstruction*. Chronique sociale, 2007, p. 103.
21 Derrida, p. 944.
22 Peterson, Keith. "Derrida's Responsibility." *Journal of the British Society for Phenomenology*, vol. 28, no. 3, Oct. 1997, pp. 287–303.
23 Derrida, p. 952; Peterson, p. 288; Poché, p. 103.
24 Derrida, p. 954.
25 Derrida, p. 955, Derrida, Jacques. "In Human Language, Fraternity." *Politics of Friendship*, Verso, 2005, p. 229.
26 Gehring, Petra. "The Jurisprudence of the 'Force of Law'." *Derrida and Law*, edited by Pierre Legrand, Ashgate, 2009, p. 128.
27 Derrida, In human language, p. 251; Cisney, Vernon, W. *Deleuze and Derrida. Difference and the Power of the Negative*. Edinburgh UP, 2018, p. 260.
28 Derrida, p. 956. *Also*, Gehring, p. 130.

represent the other legitimately, in the institutional form of a moral, juridical, political community."[29] At the same time responsibility is *towards* the limits of the history, memory, tradition[30] – the history of ideas, the common sense as handed over from generation to generation,[31] the norm, legality,[32] legitimacy.[33] It is an unlimited responsibility with the task "to remember history, origine and the sense: consequently the limits of the concepts of justice, law and right . . . which have been imposed and sedimented."[34] It is, in other words, a responsibility toward the spatio-temporal commonality.[35]

The ultimate addressee in the judicial proceeding is the judge, who renders the legal judgment by which the proceedings are ended. But all members of society carry a responsibility because if it shall indeed be just, as Lyotard claims, that the people govern the language acts ("if it is true that 'the people' is the totality of addressors, addressees, and referents"[36]) then we are all responsible for how we understand what comes before us – and what judgments we make thereupon. The move out of the freeze comes at a cost. It demands that we all grasp the rudder and steer our own judgment. It requires internal dialogue, introspection and meditation. Like Lyotard, Derrida also concludes that the openness toward the other is what justice requires. This involves the addressing of one's self toward the other, the person who is being judged, or whose situation is under judgment.[37] And *this* is possible.[38]

The abyss, the gap, is a crack in the tapestry of knowledge which forces us to give up the obsession of bull's-eye correctness or demands that we keep exploring. It is not all hopeless. As Leonard Cohen teaches us, "there is a crack in everything, that's where the light gets in." Can this crack of light allow for us to see each other both as other *and* beyond otherness? In the following I will discuss how juridical justice may avoid being tyrannical by approximating the facts of the case, the parties to one another, the case to the environment.

Watercolor Justice – Approaching the Parties

Justice presupposes being heard as well as being allowed to contradict.[39] Being heard may occur when the addressor and the addressee share the same idiom and therefore attribute the same sense to the language act; only when

29 Derrida, In human language, p. 252.
30 Gehring, p. 128.
31 Derrida, pp. 953–954; Peterson, p. 288.
32 Derrida, pp. 952–954.
33 Derrida, p. 952; Derrida, Politics of Friendship, p. 380.
34 Poché, p. 103. (My translation) *Also*, Cochran, Patricia. *Common Sense and Legal Judgment, Community Knowledge, Political Power, and Rhetorical Practice*. McGill-Queen's UP, 2017, pp. 88 and 91; Chapter 3.
35 Chapter 3.
36 Lyotard, pt. 229.
37 Derrida, p. 923.
38 Derrida, pp. 946–949.
39 Lyotard, pts. 12, 13, *also* pts. 35, 42; article 6 ECHR.

the sense of the language act can also be expressed/recovered in the idiom of the judge can the addressor be heard.[40] Being heard is therefore something that may happen, and when it happens, it is because the interlocutors' senses coincide.[41] Being heard consequently means being understood.

A positive understanding of evidence holds that through inferences made on the basis of evidence – as means and as fact – the truth about the contested fact is to be established.[42] A perception in line therewith is that evidence as means points to the reality of a "pre-procedural state." This manner of understanding the role of evidence in judicial procedure presents evidence as something which is sent to the judge as a passive receiver. The judge will accordingly accept the message, or reject it as irrelevant or unreliable,[43] but *as it is*.[44] In this traditional[45] understanding of evidence, the evidence as a means is an object or a person who conveys another object, namely, the message about a fact, an evidentiary fact, (primarily) from a party to the judge.[46] This presupposes that the party and the judge have access to the same human practice, that they share an idiom in which the referent (the object of proof) "can be signified" – what the party wishes to talk about can be expressed.[47]

In the positive perception the object and the message may be understood as referent and sense, and external to the interlocutors. In Lyotard's theory, however, these four instances form one unity – a universe.[48] Their interrelations are given by the winning human practice.[49] The evidence that is presented must be given sense in relation to the object of proof in order that the reality of the referent be established.[50] When the object of proof is the party's allegation, in order to prove it, it must be able to be signified also in the idiom of the judge.[51]

40 Lyotard, pts. 13, 78.
41 Lyotard, pts. 12, 37.
42 Villenave. *Des Jurés et de la conviction intime*. Malassis, 1796.
43 35:7 CJP.
44 Cf. Lyotard, pt. 23.
45 Lyotard would likely say 'modern' as he perceives of modernity and postmodernity as two lines of thought that go side by side, not one epoch succeeded by another. Gane, Nicholas. *Max Weber and Postmodern Theory: Rationalization Versus Re-enchantment*. Palgrave Macmillan, 2002, p. 95. (In that perception, 'traditional' would be non-sensical here, and 'modern' more appropriate.)
46 Article 6 ECHR.
47 Lyotard, pts. 28, 82.
48 Lyotard, pt. 4; Bennington, Geoffrey. *Lyotard: Writing the Event*. Manchester UP and Columbia UP, 1988, pp. 125 ff.
49 Lyotard, pts. 181, 186.
50 One must signify something before it may be shown; Lyotard, pts. 28, 131, 234, i.e., Signification *before* Bedeutung. Cf. Frege, Gottlob. "On Sense and Nominatum." *The Philosophy of Language*, edited by A. P. Martinich, translated by Herbert Feigl, 2nd ed., OUP, 1990, p. 190).
51 Lyotard, pts. 37, 176.

Reality is understood as a swarm of senses, but can the senses be recovered[52] in the idiom of the judge or does the judge subsume another reality than that of the parties? Whereas un-sifted reality consists of a swarm of senses[53] sorted in different human practices, the reality of the case consists only of senses relevant in relation to the winning of the purpose-point and pertinent, in relation to the language acts to which they refer,[54] in the idiom of the court.[55] As the material has been collected and the sense of each language act is determined it will be found that the case consists of the collection of senses that have been attributed to the language acts.[56] This swarm of senses[57] is what will constitute the reality of the case and be qualified legally. The reality of the case will thus be restricted to the case material, as what is presented will be perceived as the totality of the reality.[58]

Consequently, Lyotard writes, reality is a matter for the future,[59] that is, it is established on the basis of the language acts presented – on the basis of their senses, as a result of the competition between the human practices. It is not a matter of *knowledge* of the pre-procedural state; the "what happened" is determined after it happened.[60] We also find this line of thinking with Boman, who comments that "the court's primary task is not to establish '*wie es eigentlich gewesen ist*'"[61] but to inform the parties what they are to do in their specific situation. He continues: "Of course the judgments should be correct, but it is enough that they are correct in the sense that the material of the proceedings has been correctly assessed."[62] This expresses the idea that the aim should be that the correctness of the legal judgment is relative to the case material. In cross-border evidence cases, the correct assessment of the case requires a more thorough investigation as to the possible idioms which may be applied for the expression of the evidentiary language acts in order that the party in relation to whom such evidence is presented, also feels heard.[63]

52 Lyotard, pt. 78.
53 Lyotard, pt. 82.
54 Lyotard, pt. 40.
55 Lyotard, pt. 78.
56 Chapter 3.
57 Lyotard, pt. 82.
58 Kahneman, Daniel. *Thinking Fast and Slow.* MacMillan Publishers, 2015.
59 Lyotard, pt. 88.
60 Lyotard, pts. 131, 186.
61 Boman, Robert. *Om åberopande och åberopsbörda i dispositiva tvistemål.* P.A. Norstedt & Söners Förlag, 1964, p. 26. (*Re* "the nineteenth-century objectivist school of historiography" and historical relativism, *see also* Twining, William. *Rethinking Evidence: Exploratory Essays.* 2nd ed., Cambridge UP, 2006, pp. 106 ss.)
62 Boman, p. 27.
63 Lyotard, Jean-François. "The Affect-Phrase." *The Lyotard Reader and Guide*, edited by Keith Crome and James Williams, Edinburgh UP, 2006, pp. 104–10. Supplement to The Differend, 2000; Woodward, Ashley. "Testimony and the Affect-Phrase." *Rereading Jean-François Lyotard*, edited by Heidi Bickis and Rob Shields, Ashgate, 2013; Bamford, Kiff. "A Late Performance: Intimate Distance (Yingmei Duan)." *Rereading Jean-François Lyotard*, edited by Heidi

Hearing thus presupposes a community between the parties and the judge, in sharing the same idiom. Cross-border proceedings are situations where "the language common to the court and the other party"[64] is not also necessarily common to the "foreign" party.[65] As the comparative study shows, this may cause the sense attributed to the evidence by the party not to come through (be expressed,[66] recovered,[67] signified[68]), wherefore differends occur, and the senses of that party are silenced. This puts at risk access to justice, for example by disturbing the equality of arms.[69] Access to justice as a juridical doctrine is possible only when both parties speak the same idiom as the court. Heterogeneity between communicatory structures and sources of knowledge, as well as between the idioms of the parties and the court (the foreign party in particular[70]), demands of the judge, in order to be responsible, to find a way to cope with the lack of knowledge, perhaps even accept an agnostic approach[71] and try to listen beyond understanding. When there is silence, on the other hand, there is a responsibility of the judge to listen to that silence by seeking the senses that are not immediately perceived.[72] An unavoidable failure in the translation process causes a reduction to silence and constitutes an impasse to justice.[73]

The judge must therefore address themselves toward the parties and try to understand what is said in the light of why it is said, and in the light of the preconceptions that are built in the words and expressions used. As Derrida explains, to address something or someone is to turn straight towards the person or the issue with rectitude and establish "a direct line of communication."[74] This turning oneself toward the case, parties and matters of fact, upright, honestly, with humility and face forward[75] turned towards the parties, the case – otherness[76] – is what I refer to as an open-hearted address. It is suggested here that focus must lay on the approximation so as to find an acceptance with the parties regarding the circumstances and

Bickis and Rob Shields, Ashgate, 2013, p. 85; Ingram, David. "The Kantianism of Arendt and Lyotard." *Judging Lyotard*, edited by Benjamin Andrew, Routledge, 1992, p. 135.

64 Lyotard, pt. 37.

65 Lyotard, pt. 42.

66 Lyotard, pt. 37.

67 Lyotard, pt. 78.

68 Lyotard, pts. 12, 111.

69 Article 6 ECHR.

70 Lyotard, pt. 78.

71 Cf. Fox's first of three blocks to spontaneity, as in Ramshaw, Sara. "Jamming the Law: Improvisational Theatre and the Spontaneity of Judgment." *Law Text Culture*, vol. 14, no. 1, 2010, p. 139.

72 Lyotard, pt. 236; Carroll, p. 85.

73 Lyotard, pt. 13.

74 Derrida, pp. 944, 947.

75 Derrida, p. 958.

76 Derrida, p. 970.

their senses and significations. To restrain the wrong resulting from a judgment at the level of the communicatory structure, the judge may approach the parties with an open curiosity and postpone the judgment[77] until they have done their best not only to take the evidence and hear the parties, but also to try to see behind, question one's presuppositions, seek a sensation of awe – a sensation where one's senses are opened to the unexpected and by the unexpected.[78]

To be just would be to reflect on one's own preconceptions,[79] be aware of the singularity of one's "own"[80] idiom – a singularity that operates in all judgments. To assume this responsibility it may be worthwhile seeking inspiration in a pedagogy which uses art as a method, and as described by Agnes Nobel: "activate several of our organs of knowledge."[81] How do we do this? An illustration of a legal argument may inspire. Despite the scenario being fictitious, it is all too realistic.[82] When a little black girl in Mississippi, USA, is violently raped and hanged (but survives) by a gang of white young men her father foresees how the rapists will be acquitted by the racist jury. In despair he shoots and kills them. In his closing argument, the father's white lawyer depicts in detail the rape and hanging of the girl to argue that the father was under such strong emotional stress that it caused him temporary insanity. After the detailed account the lawyer asks the jury to imagine that the girl was white. With this he reveals the hidden racist prejudices among the jurors. They were all strongly moved by the narration of the black girl being so horribly violently treated, but in this story the common racism in the area would have allowed them to regard the lives of black people of less worth than those of white people. That was part of their commonality. When instructed to imagine the girl to be white, they were asked to identify with the black girl and her father – something they were not expected to have done

77 Cf. Derrida, p. 966.

78 Zajonc, Arthur. *Meditation as Contemplative Inquiry: When Knowing Becomes Love.* Lindisfarne Books, 2009, where the three stages of awe, humility and reverence are suggested to enter at state of meditation.

79 Cochran, p. 136.

80 Which is not necessarily an idiolect. See for example Lyotard, p. 62, pt. 145. *Also,* Derrida, Jacques. *Marx Spöken: Skuldstaten, sorgearbetet och Den nya internationalen.* Translated by Jonas Magnusson, Daidalos, 2003, (Derrida, Specters of Marx), p. 44.

81 Nobel, Agnes. *Educating Through Art.* Floris Books, 1996, p. 232; Cf. Lyotard, p. 130, where Lyotard comments that Kant's understanding of the faculty of judgment does not seem to be a cognitive faculty, in Kant's own sense. *Also,* Lyotard, Jean-François. *Driftworks.* Semiotexte, 1984, p. 82, as in Gane, p. 108, where Lyotard holds that art "lends itself to a politics that attacks all forms of libidinal and institutional repression" and describes a "form of politics which is based on the 'letting go of consciousness'." *See also* Carroll, p. 84; Douzinas, Costas, and Adam Gearey. *Critical Jurisprudence: The Political Philosophy of Justice.* Hart Publishing, 2005, p. 11; Gearey, Adam. *Law and Aesthetics.* Bloomsbury Publishing Plc, 2001, p. 53.

82 The plot is from the film from 1996, directed by John Schumacher, based on the John Grisham novel both with the title *A Time to Kill.*

otherwise. This was a rhetorical move in order to displace the jurors, to so vigorously surprise them as to empty them of their preconceptions and with the force of awe open their hearts.[83] Thus, they were in my interpretation humbled and willing to surrender to the newness of the other, being apparently so similar. (The verdict was in the father's favor.) Awe may force also the judge out of the preconceptions of their spatio-temporal commonality and help them perceive a larger room for maneuver where the humanity of the actors of the proceeding may impact the judgment, maybe even the foundation of the judgment. The just judgment does not take presence,[84] it is not a predetermined end; it's an approach: the approach of the open heart – the open-hearted address.[85]

Hannah Arendt's conception of 'common sense' is that of a 'community sense' which makes it possible for us to enlarge our mentality[86] and "move beyond our private feelings, beliefs and idiosyncrasies."[87] With imagination one may represent to oneself what one "knows about the feelings and beliefs of others."[88] For a judgment to be just despite the impossibility of knowledge and correctness, one must ask that the parties move beyond their own experience of hurt and seek compassion for the opponent's emotions and stance so as to find a way forward, a way out of the freeze. Although approximative justice focusses on the matters of fact, as opposed to the matters of law, it also recognizes that the law shapes – and thus distorts – the facts by regulating the point of their being presented to the court (what is here referred to as the purpose-point) as well as the method for fact-finding. Maybe the holding back of judgment is the most just approach.[89] It means not to let the one human practice of expertise or spatio-temporal commonality determine the language acts of the case – letting the determination be indeterminate. Dare to. One may object that justice as refraining from judgment is no way to go about life; a judgment – legal or other – must always be made in order to proceed.[90] The option is paralysis. Paralysis is petrification, sclerosis, death. But to be just, one may need to refrain from judgment momentarily, and humbly,[91] curiously, maybe even playfully,[92] question one's preconceptions.

83 Zajonc.
84 Derrida, p. 961 ff.
85 Derrida, p. 921.
86 Arendt, Hannah. *Lectures on Kant's Political Philosophy*. University of Chicago Press, 1989, p. 73.
87 Cochran, p. 136.
88 Cochran, p. 136.
89 Derrida, p. 960; Gehring, p. 124.
90 No judgment is, as noted, denial of justice, p. 25, n. 53; p. 36, n. 5.
91 Zajonc.
92 "er ist nur da ganz Mensch, wo er spielt," Schiller, Friedrich. "Über die ästhetische Erziehung des Menschen, in einer Reihe von Briefen, Fünfzehnter Brief." Schillers Sämmtliche Werke, vierter Band, J. G. Cotta'sche Buchhandlung, 1879.

Then to proceed, by navigating the spatio-temporal muddy waters humbly, with one's heart open to the otherness of others, with a widened view.

In wet-on-wet painting, the new layer of paint is added before the previous layer has dried, with the effect that the colors blend. As the medium is watercolors, and the paper is also wet, the colors mix in such a way that it divests the artist of control of detail and edges, and requires they follow the hues that appear. The watery paint on the wet paper lets the colors float out, they become "alive"[93] and as they meet, they "play."[94] The approximative understanding may be likened to that of watercolor art. It demands of both the judge and the parties to trust the approximate, to accept the lack of perfection when the colors blend and perceive the case as beyond the cognitive.[95] The differend involved in civil procedure is the unpronounced of the perception of reality, but consensus does not have to be sought between the parties on the matter of facts,[96] but on the solution of the conflicts as to what is to be done to move forward,[97] the (legal) consequence: "What do we do?" Like a wise *bona mater hortensis*, solving conflict between kindergarten children by moving towards the constructive, instructive, away from the deadlock of conflict. This is a question of the deliberative human practice. Deliberations do not hide differends, but lift the eye towards the future, to be emancipated from the locked situation of a conflict.[98]

Following Lyotard, justice stipulates the right to be heard rather than the right judgment.[99] The just judgment, as faculty and as approach, seeks the wise solution which can help the parties out of the conflict and is nevertheless not haphazard in the eyes of the public. It is therefore not the same solution to many equal cases; the pertinent facts will differ of course; what is presented

93 Frödén, Sara, and Moira von Wright. "The Waldorf Kindergarten." *International Handbook of Early Childhood Education*, edited by M. Fleer and B. van Oers, Springer International Handbooks of Education and Springer Science+Business Media B.V., 2018, pp. 1401–1420.

94 Lim, Boo Yeun. "The Magic of the Brush and the Power of Color. Integrating Theory into Practice of Painting in Early Childhood Settings." *Early Childhood Education Journal*, vol. 32, 2004, pp. 113–119. *Also*, as noted on Wikipedia: "In the medium of watercolors, wet-on-wet painting requires a certain finesse in embracing unpredictability. Highly translucent and prone to accidents, watercolor paint will bloom in unpredictable ways that, depending on the artist's frame of mind, can be a boon or a burden." (Wikipedia contributors. "Wet-on-wet." *Wikipedia, The Free Encyclopedia.* Wikipedia, The Free Encyclopedia.)

95 Lyotard, p. 133.

96 The parties' "little narratives," Lyotard, Jean-François. *The Postmodern Condition: A Report on Knowledge.* Translated by Geoff Bennington and Brian Massumi, Manchester UP, 1984, p. 60.

97 Oppenheimer, Sharifa. *Heaven on Earth: A Handbook for Parents of Young Children.* SteinerBooks, 2006, p. 202.

98 Lyotard, pts. 210–212. *Also*, Gearey, p. 124.

99 Dunn, Allen. "A Tyranny of Justice: The Ethics of Lyotard's Differend." *Boundary 2*, vol. 20, no. 1, Duke UP, 1993.

and accepted and attributed relevance and pertinence[100] will depend on the national procedures as well as the idiom of the ordinary language entailing and transmitting senses, habits, customs, knowledge. The solution may be understood to be *approximately* the same to many *approximately* the same cases. It cannot be a correct application of the substantive law rule; it cannot be a matter of binary syllogism with reference to the past, to a previously constituted rule and its previous application onto previously established cases. This does not mean pure invention – our minds and our responsibility are always bound to the knowledge and reasoning that we are imbued in and "[j]ust as the aesthete must create themselves with the available materials, radical legal argument must make use of existing resources."[101] It must be an approximative understanding of the case, in the sense that the case must be seen to consist, maybe even primarily, of a relationship between parties in which, in its current state, they are not content.[102] They want out of it. To focus on a "pre-procedural state" in such a situation may only cause more wrong. For lack of a perfect understanding of the matters of fact (as one may not be found), we need to introduce (gain?) the capacity to forgive into the understanding of justice. The capacity to forgive, driven by the desire to forget and move on, the desire for something other.[103] For lack of a perfect understanding of the truth, approximative justice would rest on a "subtler account of the truth."[104] For even if one did really wrong the other, and they were in sincere bad faith, moving forward is possible through forgiveness, forgetting and letting go.

Symphonic Justice – Resonating With the Local Commonality

Symphonic justice is the aspect to approximative justice which considers the ordinary public in the sense of the neighbor, "diverse others who form a community"[105] – the person in the street, in your local supermarket, your regional social insurance office – or your local off-licence, Systembolaget, or

100 Cf. Woodward, p. 171, who does not seem to consider the distinction between relevance and pertinence.

101 Gearey, p. 123.

102 The Tedesco case (Opinion of 18 July 2007, *Tedesco*, C-175/06, EU:C:2007:451) consisted of two parties in two different Member States where one accused the other of intellectual property infringement. As far as I can understand, they had had no previous contact with each other, and it may be seen as farfetched to claim that they had a relationship. But either the infringement or the accusation did create a connection between them, and it was not one either of them can be expected to have been content with.

103 Gearey, p. 36.

104 Gearey, Adam. "Tell All the Truth, but Tell It Slant: A Poetics of Truth and Reconciliation." *Journal of Law and Society*, vol. 31, no. 1, Mar. 2004, p. 54.

105 Cochran, p. 133.

Alko.[106] Symphonic justice may be understood as that which safeguards "safe positions,"[107] predictability and legal security in the sense of solid ground.[108] The wording here refers to the perception of an entity despite the many sounds, a perception which is partly due to the impossibility to decipher each sound of which the symphony is composed. It therefore focusses on the receiver (the listener) rather than the composer.[109] As noted in Chapter 3, although there is no foundation for a judgment, there is the throwing of gangplanks onto ships: the imposition of one perspective onto another in the connecting of language acts as links in a chain. In the legal qualification, law imposes itself on all other current perspectives.[110] With approximative justice I seek a less repressive imposition – but an imposition, it will always be.[111]

With appeal to spatio-temporal commonality one may reach the just judgment. Through internal reflection the judge may imagine "what would be required to persuade others in [the] community."[112] One must, however, be weary not to replace "one's prejudices with the prejudices of others" – meaning that the just judgment requires more than mere acceptance of a judgment to pass without notice.[113] A balance must be struck between the personal judgment of the judge and that of the person in the street. The responsibility of the judge to think for themselves cannot be escaped.[114] Whereas watercolor justice is an expression for a blending of the parties' understandings of what the reality of the case is and what the parties wish to see in the future, as the outcome of the antagonistic situation, 'symphonic justice' is an attempt to express the objective side to a just judgment which cannot be correct, but which is pragmatic in relation to the purpose-point of law,[115] held here to be some relative stability, predictability etc.[116] This aspect of the just judgment is the general acceptability of judgments, perhaps as the response to expectations.[117] Symphonic justice is what happens when the judgment encompasses the multiplicity of perspectives, which are not all perceptible (the horizon is blocked, and even if it weren't it's endless[118]) and renders a judgment which

106 The latter two being the monopolies in Sweden and Finland where alcohol may be sold.
107 Vilhelm Lundstedt as in Ekelöf, P. O. et al. *Rättegång I*. 9th ed. Norstedts Juridik, 2016, p. 21.
108 Chapter 3.
109 Walter, Bruno. "Bruckner and Mahler." *Chord and Discord*, vol. 2, no. 9, 1948, p. 41.
110 Lyotard, pts. 181, 184.
111 Lyotard, pts. 184, 199.
112 Cochran, p. 137.
113 Cochran, p. 137.
114 Arendt, Hannah. *Lectures on Kant's Political Philosophy*. University of Chicago Press, 1989, p. 71; Cochran, pp. 137–139.
115 Lyotard, The Postmodern Condition, p. 61.
116 Lundstedt as in Ekelöf, I, p. 21.
117 Luhmann, Niklas. *Law As a Social System*. OUP, 2004, p. 138; *see also*, Lyotard, p. 168.
118 Derrida, and the earlier comparative study in Chapters 4–7.

is perceived as just.[119] As in a symphony, a "complex polyphony,"[120] where the details of the sounds are undecipherable, but if the opus is well done, the composition of the sounds is pleasant to the ear – at least, with a shrug of the shoulders and an uninterested thumbs up, it can pass. As such, the judgment on – and as an arrangement of – the senses of the language acts of the case can be accepted as just. Justice – just-ish.

Lyotard notes that reality is a matter of the future, it is determined after the language act, event, occurrence takes place.[121] Like a bouquet of flowers is a composition of the parts – which considers the parts in relation to each other as well as in relation to the totality in order to be perceived as a bouquet, as an arrangement.[122] Lyotard refers to reality, what pertains to the cognitive human practice – as well as to the ethical, of justice.[123] This book is only concerned with the factual, cognitive, as the concern is with the evidence of the matters of fact.[124] Therefore, even though the gaps between the cognitive, ethical and aesthetical are unbridgeable, the purpose-point, to my understanding, may be a wish, a desire, a point to reach in the future,[125] which imposes itself on the cognitive. Knowledge is therefore subsumed under various purpose-points. The choice of purpose-points, however, is often a matter of ethics. In that regard, this book makes the choice of multiplicity of purpose-points – on the EU level. This is a choice easily made, the differend functions as a constant subversive movement, which maintains life and makes local spatio-temporal commonalities resilient to imposition.[126] Whereas Gramsci's theory gives that the spatio-temporal commonality may protect the order of the "dominant groups,"[127] this conservative effect may be a tool for resistance when a majority of political leaders across the EU wish to impose a new legal order on the citizens of Europe. In that regard, multiplicity is therefore not a choice at all, but an unavoidable circumstance.[128] The choice is rather to accept this as a fact.

As noted by Teubner, law cannot answer all of society's demands for justice, but nevertheless we need a concept of juridical justice that makes it

119 Lyotard, The Postmodern Condition, p. 80.
120 Walter.
121 Lyotard, pt. 88.
122 Note 119 with reference to Schenker, p. 5. *See*, for a similar simile, Gearey, Tell All the Truth, p. 45.
123 Lyotard, pt. 181.
124 Lindell, Bengt. *Sakfrågor och rättsfrågor: en studie av gränser, skillnader och förhållanden mellan faktum och rätt*. Iustus, 1987.
125 Gearey, pp. 36–37. The purpose-point has been described as a magnet earlier – at this point the magnetic force of desire must be grasped by the judge's open-hearted approximation of the parties' claims, allegations and evidence.
126 Lyotard, pts. 208. 210, 219; Lyotard, The Postmodern Condition, p. 61; Gane, Chapter "Weber, Lyotard and the Aesthetic Sphere."
127 Cochran, p. 131.
128 Lyotard, pt. 92.

possible at all to render judgments that are not tyrannical.[129] Despite bifurcation, heterogeneity and disintegration, and despite the radicality of Lyotard's thought, shattering the mass of knowledge into occurrences put into language, we must make the effort to show reverence for people's right to their communal perceptions, relative as they are – relative as our own are.[130] Therefore, despite the fragmentation and the lack of foundation, there is a need for a consensus regarding justice – in order that people can accept the judgments as just – in order in turn that the judiciary is not tyrannical. There must be some agreement between those who are subjected to the monopoly of force[131] following a legal judgment and those who render the judgments and titles of execution.[132] This is a particularly discernible conundrum of EU law. In this book this communal agreement[133] has been referred to as the spatio-temporal commonality,[134] a human practice of ordinary language[135] (which is the idiom of the court), common knowledge,[136] common sense, culture, habits, *mores* that are in relation to the monopoly of legitimate force[137] in such a way that people accept it as just. We must seek a sense of justice which respects the lack of universal consensus, of a universal rationality, of a universal ethics or aesthetics, in short, one which does not suppress "the multiplicity of local narratives."[138]

This is again, just like watercolor justice, a negative[139] notion of justice – of acceptance as the non-revolt.[140] One is reminded of the answer that Ekelöf gave the audience when asked what he would do if an undemocratic force took over the democratic institutions, including the courts. The question was directed against the 'law as fact' ideology of legal realism which holds a notion of justice as irrelevant to jurisprudence.[141] Ekelöf's answer was that

129 Teubner.

130 Lyotard, pts. 150–200, but perhaps the clearest expression is found in pt. 196. *See also* Gane, p. 95, Chapter "Weber, Lyotard and the Aesthetic Sphere" for a general reading of Lyotard's understanding of local cultures, what I refer to as spatio-temporal commonalities (thus adding the local general knowledge, such as the unruliness of vegetation and heat – or that of cold and darkness, geographically predetermined). *Re* reverence, see Zajonc.

131 Weber, Max. *From Max Weber: Essays in Sociology*. Edited and translated by H. H. Gerth and C. Wright Mills, Routledge, 2014, p. 78; Derrida, pp. 972 ff.

132 3:1, 3:3 UB and 3:2 UB (*re* foreign judgments); Ekelöf, P. O. *Rättegång II*. 8th ed., Norstedts Juridik, 2010, pp. 122, 124; Ekelöf, P. O et al. *Rättegång V*. 7th ed., Norstedts Juridik, 2010, pp. 13, 20, 230, 282.

133 Gane, p. 92.

134 Cf. "prose," Lyotard, pt. 229.

135 Lyotard, pts. 30, 91, 108, 122, 146.

136 Geertz, Clifford. "Common Sense as a Cultural System." *The Antioch Review*, vol. 67, no. 4, Geertz at Antioch (Fall 2009), pp. 770–790.

137 Weber, From Max Weber, p. 78; Derrida, pp. 972 ff.

138 Gane, p. 99.

139 Cf. Cisney.

140 Cf. Lyotard, pt. 256.

141 *Re* Scandinavian legal realism, see Chapter 2.

in such a case he would abandon law and take to arms. Outrage or violence as the guardians of justice, not law.[142] Symphonic justice as a negative notion implies a validation of the judgment in retrospect – a validation rather than a verification.[143] "Validation consists in showing cases of provisional nonfalsification"[144] like a Like on Facebook, a thumbs-up, an OK without any particular enthusiasm. The justness of a judgment is determined by the community – after its rendering and publication. Just like reality is a matter of the future, determined in the following language act,[145] so is justice a matter of the future, determined in the judgment of the community.[146] Justice as open-hearted address and approach can only be successful if the subjects to the judgment and jurisdiction are respectfully treated, recognized in their otherness as well as similarity, taken seriously.

Although there is no foundation for a judgment, with the correlate that there is no turning back to any rule which may be used time and again on new cases, there is nevertheless recurrence in the narrative.[147] Narrative is used to create community[148] (by creating a difference between them and us) by covering the differends, so that they do not appear.[149] Lyotard illustrates how the narrative of the republic constructs a sense of local community and more importantly, legitimacy.[150] This is not the immediate concern of this book. What is sought here is a concept of justice which is negatively perceived, as the avoidance of popular outrage,[151] in reverence of the people as a conglomerate of a mutuality of others.[152] The Swedish procedural rule which delimits the parties' burden of proof as well as the court's need for evidentiary support to determine the case does this by reference to common knowledge.[153] Both Swedish and French law contain presumptions which also impact the burden of proof.[154] These are often examples of what is perceived as normal within the community (by the community of legislators, perhaps, to be exact).[155] In

142 Ekelöf, P. O. "Om rätt och moral." *Process och exekution, Vänbok till Robert Boman*, edited by Per Henrik Lindblom, Iustus, 1990, pp. 71–83.
143 Lyotard, pts. 41, 178 ff.
144 Lyotard, pt. 90; Woodward, p. 176.
145 Lyotard, pt. 88.
146 At least one cannot be just in the present: Derrida, p. 962; Lyotard, pts. 215–220.
147 Lyotard, pt. 219.
148 Lyotard, pt. 155; Lyotard, The Postmodern Condition, p. 62.
149 Lyotard, pts. 220, 230.
150 Lyotard, pts. 155, 200.
151 Ekelöf, Om rätt och moral.
152 "The ideas of eternal recurrence, the will to power and Zarathustra's doctrine of friendship will be taken as a sustained meditation and transformation of the command to love the other as yourself; the new law appearing from the husk of the old." (Gearey, pp. 51–52.)
153 35:2 CJP.
154 For example, 1:1 FB; 312 CC; Quétand-Finet, Claire. *Les Présomptions en droit privé*. IRJS, 2013, pp. 16 s.; Caire, Anne-Blandine. *Relecture du droit des présomptions à la lumière du droit européen des droits de l'homme*. l'Université de Limoges, 2010, Thèse.
155 Lyotard, pp. 125 ff.

a Swedish case from 2013 the court explicitly referred to common knowledge to determine the amount of the damages in a criminal case.[156] The case drew the attention from the media and caused debate in the general public because it was perceived that the court had misunderstood what was common knowledge, and as such it was a wrongful use of the rule.[157] The offense of the criminal act was deemed so much more severe by the media and the general public that the judgment caused protests (and scorn). The judgment was not validated, not given thumbs up: it was unjust.

This is an example of when the court expressly made a reference to what is here referred to as the spatio-temporal commonality. It is possible to imagine that also disregarded common knowledge would lead to a wrongful judgment to the understanding of the local general public. Let us imagine that a traffic accident occurs and that a witness testifies to having seen clearly the course of events. The reliability of the witness will depend on where and when that accident took place: if it was at 3 pm in November in the North of Sweden further circumstances would need investigating to assess the reliability of the witness in a manner that would not be the case if the accident happened at the same location at 3 pm in April. This particularity is self-evident in a place where November intuitively is associated with darkness. It is however likely to escape the judge who associates 3 pm with daytime.[158] As Cochran quotes Gramsci: "One's conception of the world is a response to certain specific problems posed by reality, which are quite specific and 'original' in their immediate relevance."[159] Without the inferential glue of commonplace knowledge, common to a place, no inferences can be made, no senses can be attributed to the evidentiary language acts, but when the wrong commonplace knowledge is applied the judgment is not perceived as just to the local public because there is no local agreement[160] as to the proper understanding of the factual circumstances.

When considering the role of evidence in the formation of a just judgment one must not overlook the role of common knowledge and its relativity to place as well as time. It is not a matter of creating a fictitious narrative of a "we," a people legitimating ourselves to obligating ourselves,[161] but a matter of relation between a locality and the people whose lives are taking place there. Whereas it does not make any sense to carry a machete to a nightclub in Sweden unless one is looking for a fight, there might be a completely different explanation – a different linking between the machete and the nightclub. Tracing the linking one discovers two distinctly diverse terrains: the machete

156 Göta hovrätts dom den 27 december 2012 i mål nr B 3081–12.

157 For example, the comments from the former chief prosecutor Alhem, in an interview with Jenny Stiernstedt, Svenska Dagbladet, 22 October 2013.

158 Chapter 3.

159 Cochran, p. 91.

160 Gane, p. 92.

161 Lyotard, pt. 155; Douzinas, Warrington, pp. 123–124.

carried in Barcelona by a Spanish speaking person whose practice of carrying a machete became a habit when living by the rainforest in a tropical climate as opposed to a machete carried by someone grown up where 3 pm in November is associated with pitch black darkness and nature is itself a painting of still life, *nature morte*.

The chaining of language acts is recognized in general evidence theory. Wigmorean chains of evidence structure evidence in relation to each other in order to assist the judge to get a better overview of the case material.[162] Auxiliary facts are links farther away from the object of proof than are the immediately relevant evidentiary facts, but in every chain each link is equally important. Commonplace generalizations and other common knowledge are however referred to as the inferential glue,[163] that which makes it possible to draw conclusions regarding *a* on the basis of *b*. Evidentiary facts, auxiliary facts or commonplace generalizations and common knowledge are all language acts which are relevant to the human practice of civil procedural fact-finding and contribute with senses that constitute the case. If the language act cannot be given sense within the prevailing human practice, more links are needed for it to "make sense." It is possible that the missing links are not presented, not introduced, not pertinent from the perspective of the current purpose-point, wherefore the language act remains out of sight of the judge. The distance between the language act links that the judge has access to and that which they cannot (yet) understand and give sense means that the language act is imperceptible; it is too distant in the horizon. The chaining is both chronological and ideo-geographical (as well as logical), as it is relative to other language acts in the same perceived space of ideas.

What is depends on what is relevant and what is pertinent. What is relevant and what is pertinent depends on the purpose-point and the communicatory structure. How this is to be understood depends on the prevailing idiom of the court – understood here as its own human practice as it encompasses ordinary language as well as the common sense and common knowledge which is connected to that specific language – be it Swedish, French or English etc.; be it British, US or Caribbean etc.

When the reality of the case cannot be correctly determined because of the multitude of senses possible to attribute to an evidentiary language act, the collection of senses that the judge selects to determine the case,

162 Wigmore, John H. "Problem of Proof." *Illinois Law Review*, vol. 8, no. 2, 1913–1914, pp. 77–103; Schum, David. "A Science of Evidence: Contributions from Law and Probability." *Law, Probability and Risk*, vol. 8, 2009, pp. 197–231.

163 Schum, David. "Inference Networks and their Many Subtle Properties." *Information and Decision Technologies*, vol. 16, 1990, pp. 69–98 as quoted in Goodwin, Jean. "Wigmore's Chart Method." *Informal Logic*, vol. 20, no. 3, 2000; *also*, Anderson, Terence et al. *Analysis of Evidence*. 2nd ed., CUP, 2010, p. 262; Dwyer, Déirdre. *The Judicial Assessment of Expert Evidence*. Cambridge UP, 2008, pp. 60 ff; cf. *also* for a similar reasoning Lindell, Bengt. *Notorietet och kontradiktion*. Iustus, 2007, p. 57.

expressed in the motivation of the legal judgment, needs to harmonize with the local spatio-temporal commonality. The library of the human practice of spatio-temporal commonality may be understood as the municipal library, whereas there are separate libraries for Medicine, Law, Economics etc., at the universities.[164] The municipal library may be said to contain literature from all the other human practices, primarily in the extent that there is a spatio-temporal consensus regarding the content.[165] It holds a symphonic assembly of knowledge – a legal symphonic arrangement of its constitutive parts.[166] In symphonic justice, the perspectives of the multiplicity of human practices is included, but the spatio-temporal commonality and idiom of the court will likely make the legal judgment resonate a bit better with the local.

Bibliography

Anderson, Terence et al. *Analysis of Evidence*. 2nd ed. CUP, 2010.

Arendt, Hannah. *Lectures on Kant's Political Philosophy*. University of Chicago Press, 1989.

Ashley. "Testimony and the Affect-Phrase." *Rereading Jean-François Lyotard*, edited by Heidi Bickis and Rob Shields, Ashgate, 2013.

Bamford, Kiff. "A Late Performance: Intimate Distance (Yingmei Duan)." *Rereading Jean-François Lyotard*, edited by Heidi Bickis and Rob Shields, Ashgate, 2013.

Bennington, Geoffrey. *Lyotard: Writing the Event*. Manchester UP and Columbia UP, 1988.

Boman, Robert. *Om åberopande och åberopsbörda i dispositiva tvistemål*. P.A. Norstedt & Söners Förlag, 1964.

Caire, Anne-Blandine. *Relecture du droit des présomptions à la lumière du droit européen des droits de l'homme*. l'Université de Limoges, 2010. Thèse.

Carroll, David. "Rephrasing the Political with Kant and Lyotard: From Aesthetic to Political Judgments." *Diacritics*, vol. 14, no. 3, 1984, Special Issue on the Work of Jean-François Lyotard, pp. 74–88.

Cisney, Vernon, W. *Deleuze and Derrida. Difference and the Power of the Negative*. Edinburgh UP, 2018.

Cochran, Patricia. *Common Sense and Legal Judgment, Community Knowledge, Political Power, and Rhetorical Practice*. McGill-Queen's UP, 2017.

Derrida, Jacques. "Force de loi: le Fondement mystique de l'autorité." *Cardozo Law Review*, vol. 11, nos. 5–6, Jul./Aug. 1990.

Derrida, Jacques. "Politics of Friendship." *American Imago*, vol. 50, no. 3, LOVE (Fall 1993), pp. 378–380.

Derrida, Jacques. *Marx Spöken: Skuldstaten, sorgearbetet och Den nya internationalen*. Translated by Jonas Magnusson. Daidalos, 2003 (Derrida, Specters of Marx).

Derrida, Jacques. "In Human Language, Fraternity." *Politics of Friendship*. Verso, 2005.

Douzinas, Costas, and Adam Gearey. *Critical Jurisprudence: The Political Philosophy of Justice*. Hart Publishing, 2005.

164 Chapter 3.
165 Lyotard, pt. 229.
166 Walter.

Douzinas, Costas, and Ronnie Warrington. "'A Well-Founded Fear of Justice': Law and Ethics in Postmodernity." *Law and Critique*, vol. II, no. 2, 1991, pp. 115–147.
Dunn, Allen. "A Tyranny of Justice: The Ethics of Lyotard's Differend." *Boundary* 2, vol. 20, no. 1, Duke UP, 1993.
Dwyer, Déirdre. *The Judicial Assessment of Expert Evidence*. Cambridge UP, 2008.
Ekelöf, P. O. "Om rätt och moral." *Process och exekution, Vänbok till Robert Boman*, edited by Per Henrik Lindblom, Iustus, 1990, pp. 71–83.
Ekelöf, P. O. *Rättegång II*. 8th ed., Norstedts Juridik, 2010.
Ekelöf, P. O. et al. *Rättegång V*. 7th ed., Norstedts Juridik, 2010.
Ekelöf, P. O. et al. *Rättegång I*. 9th ed., Norstedts Juridik, 2016.
Frege, Gottlob. "On Sense and Nominatum." *The Philosophy of Language*, edited by A. P. Martinich, translated by Herbert Feigl, 2nd ed., OUP, 1990.
Frödén, Sara, and Moira von Wright. "The Waldorf Kindergarten." *International Handbook of Early Childhood Education*, edited by M. Fleer and B. van Oers, Springer International Handbooks of Education, Springer Science+Business Media B.V., 2018, pp. 1401–1420.
Gane, Nicholas. *Max Weber and Postmodern Theory: Rationalization Versus Re-enchantment*. Palgrave Macmillan, 2002.
Gasché, Rodolphe. *Inventions of Difference: on Jacques Derrida*. Harvard UP, 1994.
Gearey, Adam. *Law and Aesthetics*. Bloomsbury Publishing Plc, 2001.
Gearey, Adam. "Tell All the Truth, but Tell It Slant: A Poetics of Truth and Reconciliation." *Journal of Law and Society*, vol. 31, no. 1, Mar. 2004.
Geertz, Clifford. "Common Sense as a Cultural System." *The Antioch Review*, vol. 67, no. 4, Geertz at Antioch (Fall 2009), pp. 770–790.
Gehring, Petra. "The Jurisprudence of the 'Force of Law'." *Derrida and Law*, edited by Pierre Legrand, Ashgate, 2009.
Goodwin, Jean. "Wigmore's Chart Method." *Informal Logic*, vol. 20, no. 3, 2000.
Ingram, David. "The Kantianism of Arendt and Lyotard." *Judging Lyotard*, edited by Benjamin Andrew, Routledge, 1992.
Kahneman, Daniel. *Thinking Fast and Slow*. MacMillan Publishers, 2015.
Lim, Boo Yeun. "The Magic of the Brush and the Power of Color. Integrating Theory into Practice of Painting in Early Childhood Settings." *Early Childhood Education Journal*, vol. 32, 2004, pp. 113–119.
Lindell, Bengt. *Sakfrågor och rättsfrågor: en studie av gränser, skillnader och förhållanden mellan faktum och rätt*. Iustus, 1987.
Lindell, Bengt. *Notorietet och kontradiktion*. Iustus, 2007.
Luhmann, Niklas. *Law As a Social System*. OUP, 2004.
Lyotard, Jean-François. *Driftworks*. Semiotexte, 1984.
Lyotard, Jean-François. *The Postmodern Condition: A Report on Knowledge*. Translated by Geoff Bennington and Brian Massumi. Manchester UP, 1984.
Lyotard, Jean-François. *The Differend – Phrases in Dispute*. Translated by Georges Van Den Abbeele, University of Minnesota Press, 1988.
Lyotard, Jean-François. "The Affect-Phrase." *The Lyotard Reader and Guide*, edited by Keith Crome and James Williams, Edinburgh UP, 2006, pp. 104–110 (Supplement to the Differend, 2000).
Nobel, Agnes. *Educating Through Art*. Floris Books, 1996.
Oppenheimer, Sharifa. *Heaven on Earth: A Handbook for Parents of Young Children*. SteinerBooks, 2006.
Peterson, Keith. "Derrida's Responsibility." *Journal of the British Society for Phenomenology*, vol. 28, no. 3, Oct. 1997, pp. 287–303.
Poché, Fred. *Penser avec Derrida: Comprendre la déconstruction*. Chronique sociale, 2007.

Quétand-Finet, Claire. *Les Présomptions en droit privé*. IRJS, 2013.
Ramshaw, Sara. "Jamming the Law: Improvisational Theatre and the Spontaneity of Judgment." *Law Text Culture,* vol. 14, no. 1, 2010.
Schiller, Friedrich. "Über die ästhetische Erziehung des Menschen, in einer Reihe von Briefen, Fünfzehnter Brief." *Schillers Sämmtliche Werke, vierter Band,* J. G. Cotta'sche Buchhandlung, 1879, https://www.projekt-gutenberg.org/schiller/aesterz/aesterz3.html. Accessed 8 Dec. 2021
Schum, David. "Inference Networks and their Many Subtle Properties." *Information and Decision Technologies*, vol. 16, 1990, pp. 69–98.
Schum, David. "A Science of Evidence: Contributions from Law and Probability." *Law, Probability and Risk*, vol. 8, 2009, pp. 197–231.
Villenave. *Des Jurés et de la conviction intime.* Malassis, 1796.
Walter, Bruno. "Bruckner and Mahler." *Chord and Discord*, vol. 2, no. 9, 1948, p. 41. The Bruckner Society of America, https://www.uv.es/~calaforr/walter.html. Accessed 31 Mar. 2022.
Weber, Max. *From Max Weber: Essays in Sociology*. Edited and translated by H. H. Gerth and C. Wright Mills. Routledge, 2014.
Wigmore, John H. "Problem of Proof." *Illinois Law Review*, vol. 8, no. 2, 1913–1914, pp. 77–103.
Wikipedia Contributors. "Wet-on-wet." *Wikipedia, The Free Encyclopedia*. 2021, https://en.wikipedia.org/w/index.php?title=Wet-on-wet&oldid=1241702572. Accessed 2 Apr. 2022.
Zajonc, Arthur. *Meditation as Contemplative Inquiry: When Knowing Becomes Love*. Lindisfarne Books, 2009.

Chapter 10

Good Enough Justice[1]

Against a Common Sense of Justice

This thesis emerged from the paradox between the common EU ambition to increase justice in the Area of Freedom, Security and Justice[2] and the Scandinavian legal realist negation of justice as a legal concept and concern. Traces of such a reasoning can still be seen in Swedish jurisprudence; its hegemony has not been replaced.[3] From the perspective of such a tradition, which has during the last century gradually erased the word justice from its vocabulary,[4] the ambition to give the citizens of Europe a common sense of justice comes across as a rather important example of miscommunication between the legislators of the EU. Considering the silence of Swedish jurisprudence in the matter of justice for more than half a century it is not surprising that the Swedish legislator should believe that what was agreed when establishing the Area of Freedom, Security and Justice and the ambitions to increase justice was merely simpler communication for easier access to court[5] – a technical solution to what is perceived as a technical problem. The remedy to this differend, where justice by some is seen as a historically grounded cultural

1 This expression is originally inspired by Luhmann's justice as "adequate complexity in consistent decision-making," Luhmann, Niklas. *Law As a Social System*. OUP, 2004, p. 219.

2 Treaty of Amsterdam amending the Treaty on European Union, the Treaties establishing the European Communities and certain related acts, OJ C 340, 10.11.1997, p. 1.

3 Bjarup, Jes. "Scandinavian Legal Realism." *The Philosophy of Law: An Encyclopedia*, edited by Mark Tebbit, vol. 2, Routledge, 1999; Strang, Johan. "Two Generations of Scandinavian Legal Realism." *RETFÆRD*, årgång 32, no. 1/124, 2009; Ross, Alf. *On Law and Justice*. University of California Press, 1959. Ekelöf raised the matter in a different manner but did not develop a theory of justice adequate for the positivist and realist perceptions prevailing at his time. Worth mentioning is however his "Är den juridiska doktrinen en teknik eller en vetenskap?" (*de lege*, edited by P. H. Lindblom, Iustus, 1991) for its explicit functionalist understanding of law as a means to reach political aims, that is, purpose-points.

4 Chapters 1 and 2.

5 Bull, Thomas. "Rättighetsskyddet i Högsta förvaltningsdomstolen." *Svensk juristtidning*, 2017, pp. 216–244, p. 232; Ekelöf, P. O. "Access to Justice." *Svensk juristtidning*, 1981, pp. 109–120.

DOI: 10.4324/9781003495383-10

commonality[6] and by others as an administrative formality, is sought in this project.

In the overall aim to assess the possibility of juridical justice through the means of cross-border evidence within the framework of judicial cooperation in civil matters in the EU[7] a critical assessment of the EU ambition of a common sense of justice[8] is included. The thesis argues that these aims are infelicitous because they disregard the legal, cognitive and linguistic differences between the Member States. The thesis therefore suggests an understanding of justice which takes these differences into account – a sense of justice which respects the peculiarities of the different legal contexts in which the evidence is interpreted[9] – a sense of justice which does not seek to create harmony through uniformity, but, perhaps, harmony between diverse senses of justice.

Lyotard's theory of knowledge and justice in *The Differend*[10] presents conditions for the creation of knowledge, as an agreement as to the sense of the occurrences as language acts. The comparative study has indeed found that national civil procedural fact-finding as a communicatory structure conditions language acts in such a way that their sense cannot be recovered when evidence is transferred from one legal environment to the other.[11] It was also found that the purpose-points of legal fact-finding as well as the role of extra-legal human practices in such fact-finding differ. From the perspective of the judge in the position of addressee of the case material, it is perhaps the purpose-points and the divergent assessments of what human practices constitute sources of knowledge that pose the most important restrictions on the perception of the collection of senses of language acts which will constitute the case.[12] The administrative use of cross-border evidence in the national judiciaries implies that the national civil procedural fact-finding will be confronted with evidentiary language acts the sense of which, for the legal judgment to be just, should be sifted through the mud of another spatio-temporal commonality. Otherwise, the party who presents the evidence risks not being heard and the sense that the evidence is given in the requesting court will risk not corresponding with the general understanding of the evidence in the legal environment of the requested court. The national judge in a cross-border case is placed in what is here referred to as a 'diagonal' situation.[13]

6 The Stockholm Programme – An open and secure Europe serving and protecting citizens, OJ C 115, 4.5.2010, p. 1.
7 Storskrubb, Eva. *Civil Procedure and EU Law, A Policy Area Uncovered.* OUP, 2008, pp. 9–12.
8 Chapter 1.
9 For a study of the interpretation of facts in French law, see Ivainer, Théodore. *L'Interprétation des faits en droit.* L.G.D.J., 1988.
10 Lyotard, Jean-François. *The Differend – Phrases in Dispute.* Translated by Georges Van Den Abbeele, University of Minnesota Press, 1988/Lyotard, Jean-François. *Le Différend.* Éditions de minuit. 1983.
11 Chapter 6.
12 Lyotard, pt. 82.
13 P. 57, n. 34.

Judicial cooperation in civil matters and international choice of law rules are meant to neutralize the consequences for the parties of the choice of jurisdiction in conflicts where more than one Member State has jurisdiction.[14] As the national courts follow the same rules of EU legislation to assess which court has jurisdiction over a matter and which substantive law to apply to the case the interests in forum shopping are supposedly lower as there is no assumption that the national court of one Member State will favor the substantive law of that same Member State.[15] Bell notes that in the early years of the millennium, English courts considered litigation in a foreign court that would not apply English law despite it being the "proper" law of the contract "a blatant and unacceptable form of forum shopping."[16] Whereas the rules regulating jurisdiction in cross-border cases are shared within the EU, the rules regarding the substantive law – of EU or national origin – are detached from the rules regulating the forum.[17] This set-up follows the international private and procedural law tradition where the procedure takes the form of the law of the forum (*lex fori regit processum*), whereas foreign substantive law may be applied to the matter of the case. Fragmentation is therefore not eradicated with measures of judicial cooperation as national forms of procedure are held relatively intact.[18] Due to international agreements in judicial matters, there is however less of an incentive for the parties to ascertain that the proceedings are held in a particular Member State when the legal system is no longer hermetically closed because of cross-border implications of a case. This undoubtedly opens up more flexible and pragmatic procedures.

14 Cadiet, Loïc et al. *Approaches to Procedural Law: The Pluralism of Methods*. Nomos Verlag, 2017, p. 63; Storskrubb, Civil Procedure, p. 8, note 11 and pp. 135–138; Janssens, Marie-Christine. "Belgium." *Intellectual Property and Private International Law: Comparative Perspectives*, edited by Toshiyuki Kono, Bloomsbury Publishings, 2012, p. 372.

15 For discussions regarding *forum shopping* as a negative phenomenon, see Storskrubb, Civil Procedure, p. 117.

16 Bell, Andrew S. *Forum Shopping and Venue in Transnational Litigation*. OUP, 2003, pp. 18–19.

17 Other than the Regulation (EU) 2020/1783 of the European Parliament and of the Council of 25 November 2020 on cooperation between the courts of the Member States in the taking of evidence in civil or commercial matters (taking of evidence) (recast), OJ L 405, 2.12.2020, p. 1 (Evidence Regulation), see for example articles 19 and 21 Regulation (EU) No 1215/2012 of the European Parliament and of the Council of 12 December 2012 on jurisdiction and the recognition and enforcement of judgments in civil and commercial matters (recast), OJ L 351, 20.12.2012, p. 1 (Brussels I); article 8 Regulation (EC) No 593/2008 of the European Parliament and of the Council of 17 June 2008 on the law applicable to contractual obligations, OJ L 177, 4.7.2008, p. 6. (Rome I); article 25 Council Regulation (EC) No 2201/2003 of 27 November 2003 concerning jurisdiction and the recognition and enforcement of judgments in matrimonial matters and the matters of parental responsibility, repealing Regulation (EC) No 1347/2000, OJ L 338, 23.12.2003, p. 1. (Brussels II)

18 EU law has trickled into also the national procedures as an effect of its supremacy and requirements of effectiveness. This has however not been an expressed ambition, but a secondary effect; *see*, for example, Wallerman, Anna, *Om fakultativa regler: en studie av svensk och unionsrättslig reglering av skönsmässigt beslutsfattande i processrättsliga frågor*. Gothenburg, Iustus, 2015. Dissertation.

In the matter of evidence, without such a cooperation agreement between different states, it is possible to place evidence in a state where the applicable law is more beneficial to one's own case or maybe even hide it there with the help of state sovereignty and jurisdiction rules.[19] The opponent would then be in a less advantageous situation because the applicable substantive law in one state may require evidence that is not accessible because it is found on the territory of another state. With cross-border evidence, however, we find that the evidence is nevertheless stuck – not on foreign territory but in a structural maze. In those situations, the party can still not be heard through the means of evidence and the judge can still not get knowledge.

The direct effect of union law rights means that the rights can be claimed directly in the national courts. Since the *Rewe-Zentralfinanz* case from 1976, the main rule has been that the Member States' national procedural legislations are to be applied to protect these union rights, according to the EU law principle of procedural autonomy.[20] Procedural autonomy is a matter of the subordinate power of the EU and its members,[21] whereas *forum regit processum* concerns the interplay between equals. The principle of *forum regit processum*, however, may perhaps rather be understood as a basic international procedural law rule, simplifying the cooperation between national courts in their judicial activities.[22] From the perspective of international private and procedural law, the statement in the *Rewe* case might not have been seen as much of an invention. With that, the development of the two principles within EU law seems organic, rather than politically or judicially pro-active. When the Court of Justice stated that the national courts are to use their own form of procedure to ascertain the rights and obligations of EU law, it may simply have been a matter of accepting the state of affairs as they were. The Court was, and still is, reduced to refer the effectiveness of

19 Crawford, James. *Brownlie's Principles of Public International Law*. 8th ed., OUP, 2012, p. 456; Storskrubb, Civil Procedure, p. 117.

20 Judgment of 16 December 1976, *Rewe-Zentralfinanz*, 33–76, EU:C:1976:188, para. 6. The following works indicate the flux and reflux of the tide as well as the rather extended period of time during which the existence of procedural autonomy has been questioned: Kakouris, C. M. "Do the Member States Possess Judicial Procedural 'Autonomy'." *Common Market Law Review*, vol. 34, no. 6, 1997, pp. 1389–1412; Bobek, Michal. "Why There Is No Principle of 'Procedural Autonomy' of the Member States." *The European Court of Justice and the Autonomy of the Member States*, edited by Hans-Wolfgang Micklitz and Bruno De Witte, Intersentia, 2012, pp. 305–324; Wallerman, Anna. "Can Two Walk Together, Except They Be Agreed? Preliminary References and (the Erosion of) National Procedural Autonomy in European Law Review." *European Law Review*, vol. 44, no. 2, 2019, pp. 159–177.

21 This seems to correspond to the relation between the states of the USA and its federal jurisdiction, *see* Hill, Alfred. "State Procedural Law in Federal Nondiversity Litigation." *Harvard Law Review*, vol. 69, no. 1, Nov. 1955, pp. 66–117, preceding the Rewe-Zentralfinanz (note 20, above) and Lück (judgment of 4 April 1968, *Lück*, 34–67, EU:C:1968:24) cases of the Court of Justice.

22 For a short resumé of the history of the *lex fori regit processum* rule, see Garnett, Richard Lyndon. *Substance and Procedure in Private International Law*. 1st ed., OUP, 2012, pp. 5–6.

EU law to the national courts, including their forms of procedure. There is a tug of war between state autonomy and harmonization. On the autonomy side are found such ideas as procedural autonomy and national identity[23] and the regimen and traditions of international law, whereas harmonization is connected to functionality, effectiveness, efficiency, cooperation and supra-national legislation.

The stance is, however, contradictory. From one perspective, procedure has no normative value, and may be distinguished from substantive law, whether supra-state, international or domestic. From another perspective, however, both the *lex fori regit processum* rule and the principle of procedural autonomy indicate the opposite position: that procedure is so closely connected to the core of the judicial power, the legitimacy of the human practice of national law that it cannot be transplanted[24] into a foreign legal human practice through its direct application in national courts. This perspective is held by French and Italian law.[25] It is likely that the two principles, as two sides of the same coin, share the same *raison d'être*: both are seen as expressions of state sovereignty, meaning they have more to do with power than culture.[26] In any case, when procedure is perceived as core to the legal order, and cannot be used by a foreign court, it expresses the notion that the form of procedure is a carrier of a sense of justice of that legal order. The impact of procedural concatenation following its communicatory structure on the evidence may explain at least the very important role that the form of judicial procedure has on the rendering of a substantive justice.[27]

The EU aims at a functioning inter-state system governed by a common sense of justice for the benefit of the sense of legal certainty for the citizens of Europe.[28] The wording "tangibility" gives the notion that citizenship is a formal and administrative matter – a tool to use in order to fend for one's rights to move and act in accordance with the four freedoms.[29] One may indeed assimilate a citizen to a voter or a party to a judicial procedure – a

23 4.2 TEU; Cloots, Elke. *National Identity in EU Law*. OUP, 2015.

24 Watson, Alan. *Legal Transplants: An Approach to Comparative Law*. University of Georgia Press, 1993; Legrand, Pierre. "The Impossibility of 'Legal Transplants'." *Maastricht Journal of European and Comparative Law*, vol. 4, no. 2, June 1997, pp. 111–124; Legrand, Pierre. "What 'Legal Transplants'?" *Adapting Legal Cultures*, edited by David Nelken and Johannes Feest, Bloomsbury Publishing, 2001, pp. 55 ff.

25 Garnett, p. 13; Mayer, Pierre. *Droit international privé*. Montchrestien, 1977, pts. 469 ss.

26 Garnett, pp. 13–15; Mayer, Pierre. *Droit international privé*. Montchrestien, 1977, pt. 95.

27 See also, Lindell, Bengt. *Sakfrågor och rättsfrågor: en studie av gränser, skillnader och förhållanden mellan faktum och rätt*. Iustus, 1987, section 3.6.6.

28 For an example of how this is expressed, *see* judgment of the 5 June 2018, *Coman*, C673/16, EU:C:2018:385.

29 'Tangible' is the word used in English, French and Spanish; in German *greifbar* is used, whereas the Swedish version uses *konkret*. (The Stockholm Programme, p. 4. *See also* EU Citizenship Report 2010 – Dismantling the obstacles to EU citizens' rights, Brussels, COM(2010) 603 final of 27 October 2010.)

subject of public authority – and thus distinguish those roles from those of a worker, a parent or a consumer, all charged with comparatively lower levels of administrative legal formality and also filled with non-formal, extra-legal, inter-human valuables. One is reminded of a quote from Toni Morrison, according to which the term 'citizen' is also used to speak of a group with some interrelations as well as some belonging to the place, the location and the most concrete of things, the soil – *la tierra*.[30] In international private and procedural law, the connection to the soil is fundamental for both jurisdiction and choice of law through the institution of habitual residence of either or both of the parties.[31]

A focal point in the development of the judicial cooperation in civil matters at the Tampere meeting was the establishment of the principle of mutual recognition as the cornerstone of judicial cooperation in both civil and criminal matters within the Union.[32] Mutual recognition of legal judgments is a matter for the courts and authorities, that is, the representatives of the Member State. Mutual trust, however, must reasonably be seen as the mental precursor of recognition, and as such, for there to be a democratic solidity and legitimacy behind the recognition such trust must rest among the citizens of Europe. One might have thought that the trust would be connected to the tangibility of the citizenship, and that it would be deemed important that the trust is shared by the citizens themselves. This is however not how it is expressed; trust is seen as necessary for the mutual recognition which is a purely legal-administrative matter, having to do with the enforceability of foreign judgments in the Member State.[33] The Stockholm Programme expressly states that "mutual trust between authorities and services in the different Member States as well as decision-makers is the basis for efficient cooperation in this area."[34] For there to be legitimacy[35] behind the mutual

30 "When I was young, they called us citizens, [. . .] the word was citizen. Now, citizen suggests some relationship with your neighbors, with your block, with your town, with the village." Toni Morrison (From a talk between Toni Morrison and Angela Davies, broadcast in the New York Library Podcast (Library Talks), 1 February 2016.)

31 Articles 15 and 19 Brussels I, and articles 4, 6 and 10 Regulation (EU) No 650/2012 of the European Parliament and of the Council of 4 July 2012 on jurisdiction, applicable law, recognition and enforcement of decisions and acceptance and enforcement of authentic instruments in matters of succession and on the creation of a European Certificate of Succession, OJ L 201, 27.7.2012, p. 107 (Succession Regulation).

32 European Union: Council of the European Union, Presidency Conclusions, Tampere European Council, 15–16 October 1999, 16 October 1999, para. 33, title VI, https://www.europarl.europa.eu/summits/tam_en.htm. Accessed 30 Nov. 2024; Hazelhorst, Monique. *Free Movement of Civil Judgments in the European Union and the Right to a Fair Trial*. Springer, 2017, p. 4.

33 Brussels I.

34 Stockholm Programme, pp. 5–6, 25. *Re* the relation between mutual recognition and mutual trust, see Hazelhorst, p. 27 f.; Storskrubb, Eva. "Mutual Trust and the Dark Horse of Civil Justice." *Cambridge Yearbook of European Legal Studies*, vol. 20, 2018, pp. 179–201; Weller, Matthias. "Mutual Trust: In Search of the Future of European Union Private International Law." *Journal of Private International Law*, vol. 11, no. 1, 2015, pp. 64–102.

35 Chapter 9.

recognition of judicial decisions between the authorities of the different Member States, the citizens of one Member State must trust the judicial authorities of the other. If the court of the forum is one or the other, the evidence may however be given very shifting meanings in different national courts. The mutual trust between the Member States has little relevance if the evidence cannot allow a party to be heard – mutual trust becomes an empty formality (between states). Procedural justice is more than an empty formality.[36]

The comparative study illustrates that the separation between procedural and substantive justice cannot be done. Procedural autonomy and dependance on national courts are not a course of action neither to ascertain the effectiveness of EU law nor to render access to justice since justice is a matter the sense of which is attributed by people, not a product delivered by administration.

Good Enough Justice

If justice is understood as predictability and the legal certainty of safe positions,[37] then substantive law indeed must be given the same effect across the EU. Delegating the application of EU law to the national courts may not only be seen as an efficient use of the existing judicial organizations in place in the Member States, but also as an expression of respect for the national identity[38] that may perhaps be claimed to be found in the form of judicial procedure sometimes seen as part of constitutional law.[39] The cross-border evidence may likewise seem an efficient solution to a concrete problem in cross-border dispute resolution. It however creates a diagonal situation,[40] and the question that must therefore be asked is if there can be diagonal justice. Although the comparative study was carried out by analyzing civil procedural fact-finding in three stages, two main levels of differends were detected: the legal and the non-legal. The legal differends were found as dependent on the communicatory structure of the fact-finding and its purpose-points. The non-legal differends were found in the spatio-temporal commonalities, which are understood as a type of human practice which imposes itself on all the other cognitive human practices before the human practice of law performs its qualification. For the senses of an evidentiary language act to "reach" the "reality of the case" they must first pass the obstacles of the communicatory structure and the competition of the human practices.

In judicial proceedings, for the judgment to be symphonically just, the arbiter of the war between human practices of expert knowledge is the

36 Cf. Schlag, Pierre. " 'Le Hors de texte, c'est moi' – The Politics of Form and the Domestication of Deconstruction." *Derrida and Law*, edited by Pierre Legrand, Ashgate, 2009, p. 135.

37 P. 22, n. 31.

38 4.2 TEU.

39 Aït Ahmed, Lilia. *Principe de cohérence et droit international privé de la famille européen*. Université Panthéon-Sorbonne - Paris I, 2021. Français. NNT : 2021PA01D002, pt. 403; Mayer, pt. 95.

40 Chapter 4.

spatio-temporal commonality of the particular locality at the particular moment in time.[41] It is in the spatio-temporal commonality where the agglutinating effect to socially bond people is found[42] – in the narrative which hides differends. Most attribution of sense to language acts takes place within a spatio-temporal commonality, the space shared by the persons in the street of a restricted community. (An unusual attribution of sense may cause a stir and require an explanation.) There is a recycling, reciting[43] and reaffirmation of the community through the spatio-temporal commonality storing a rich mass of language acts of habits, traditions, common sense and common knowledge like peat in the soil.

The differends do not disappear because of the local social agreement as to the normal understanding of a language act; they are only covered in the mud of local spatio-temporal commonality. Once that human practice has rendered its judgment, is it time for the legal human practice to impose. The muddle of un-sifted reality is obstructed by communicatory structures, purpose-points and the war between human practices. This is what causes differends; the spatio-temporal commonality, like the narrative of the "we,"[44] hides this. What was also found is however another side to the differend: senses which would not be seen as supporting the prevailing purpose-point nevertheless come through as such, because hidden in the mud of spatio-temporal commonality to which the evidence first points, they are presented and taken – but silent. It was found that possible differends are found at each of the compared stages of the road.

The Evidence Regulation is applicable in all civil and commercial matters where evidence is found on the territory of another EU Member State than that of the proceedings. It does not distinguish between cases whether the applicable civil or commercial law is of national or EU origin. It is however worth mentioning here specifically that when the substantive law is of EU origin, its effect in the Member States will depend on the spatio-temporal commonality of the court. A unificatory application of EU law is not possible since the foundation for knowledge is eroded by differends.[45] If, as Lyotard holds,

41 In the aforementioned (Chapter 9) case from Göta Court of Appeal (Göta hovrätts dom den 27 december 2012 i mål nr B 3081–12) the court who mistakenly referred to common knowledge did this also with a reference to the times that are *a-changing*.

42 Chapter 3.

43 *Récit (noun)* is the French original of the English translation into 'narrative,' Lyotard, for example, pts. 159, 160 (*re* the reciprocal and cyclical of the "we"), 182 ("the great narrative of the end of great narratives"), 193, 198, 219, 254, *also* pt. 6, p. 147 (subtitle Declaration of 1789). (However, the original *narrative (noun and adjective)*, for example in pts. 65, 73, 76, 89, 201, 210, 217, 219, 220. Pt. 205 contains a mistranslation from *non normative* to 'non-narrative.')

44 Lyotard, pt. 155.

45 "How could it be otherwise?" (Joerges, Christian. "The Challenges of Europeanization in the Realm of Private Law: A Plea for a New Legal Discipline." *Duke Journal of Comparative & International Law,* vol. 14, no. 2, Summer 2004, p. 160.)

narrative is used to create a sense of community,[46] could one not argue then that there is already a narrative within the EU, namely that of the European tradition and of the market as guarantor of peace and prosperity[47] and that of the citizens of Europe? One could. But it wouldn't be just.[48] It would be monopoly and suppression of diversity in the name of uniformity. It would also be vain.[49] Narrative is a means to create *local* agreement,[50] and I hold that although there is perhaps a certain European commonality, we need to be vigilant and ask whether it is *local enough* to mediate local justice in concrete.

A just judgment is such only if it is perceived as just. It is only perceived as just if it makes sense to the parties and the public.[51] The local variations of common knowledge (local knowledge[52]) constitute a subversive force against a common sense of justice on a European level. The EU's plan to build "bridges between different systems and traditions" is done through myth.[53] The human practice is a semi-fixed context with its specific knowledge and idiom, as a sort of culture.[54] It's not that our judgments are right as in objectively correct because of universal, human faculties of rationality and common sense – it's that we believe they are.[55]

At this point Lyotard's position that responsibility is towards *thinking* is key: because here thinking is required in order to question the conditions, as restraints *and* prerequisites, and to see beyond them, to critically honor thinking, take responsibility and be intellectually honest. The general knowledge and everyday language are understood as constituting a context of a human practice within which people perceive themselves as a "we"[56] – as

46 Lyotard, pts. 155–160.
47 3 and 8 TEU.
48 Lyotard, pts. 224, 228; Barron, Anne. "Lyotard and the Problem of Justice." *Judging Lyotard*, edited by Benjamin Andrew, Routledge, 1992, p. 32.
49 Lyotard, pts. 190, 191. (Speaking of vanity – the parties' wishes expressed in the claims, as expressions of the subject as an agent, would also be "vainly anthropomorphic" (pt. 241, *also* p. 11 Prétexte, pts. 90, 151, 183, 188). But feelings and thinking are not, and it is the feeling of a desire to be heard and not wronged and the thinking of the differends that is at stake here. (Gearey, Adam. *Law and Aesthetics*. Bloomsbury Publishing Plc, 2001, pp. 36–38.)
50 Gane, Nicholas. *Max Weber and Postmodern Theory: Rationalization Versus Re-enchantment*. Palgrave Macmillan, 2002, p. 92.
51 Kant, Immanuel. *Kritik av omdömeskraften*. Translated by Sven-Olov Wallenstein, Thales, 2003. (Kant, Critique of Judgment), § 40.
52 Geertz, Clifford. "Local Knowledge: Fact and Law in Comparative Perspective." *Local Knowledge: Further Essays in Interpretive Anthropology*. Basic Books, 1983.
53 Lyotard, pts. 12, 21, 23, 44, 201, 237, 251. *See also* pts. 160, 219, 234, 235 *re* the relation between idiom, narrative and myth.
54 Lyotard, pt. 260. *Also*, Gramsci as in Cochran, Patricia. *Common Sense and Legal Judgment, Community Knowledge, Political Power, and Rhetorical Practice*. McGill-Queen's UP, 2017, p. 91.
55 Chapters 1 and 9.
56 Lyotard, pts. 155–160.

they share access to the knowledge and language – the common idiom of ordinary language.[57] It will also be seen as central to any possibility of juridical justice. There can be no justice if the case cannot be determined because the judge attaches the wrong sense to a language act presented by the party, through the means of evidence or in another part of their action.

The balance of powers within the EU was clarified at an early stage: once powers have been conferred by the Member States to the Union (Community), Union law takes precedence over national law.[58] Within the areas of law conferred to the Union, state sovereignty and self-governance are consequently subject to EU law.[59] Since the very beginning, it has been established that the aim of this European cooperation is that it become "ever-closer."[60] Since the Lisbon Treaty and the introduction of the ordinary legislative procedure[61] there can be no doubt that the overall ambition is to harmonize and "streamline" the legislation.[62]

The relativity of evidence enforces the disruptions of the role of evidence in the formation of the just legal judgment when evidence is used across state borders. This shines a critical light on the ambitions to increase access to justice within the EU. A possible conclusion, however, is that there may indeed be a common European sense of justice which is non-consensual but approximative, which encompasses an acceptance of the differends and that there can be no just, in the sense of correct, judgment – in particular across judicial borders. The sense that is attributed to language acts is how we make sense of the world, the senses of which are our world; the sense through which the world makes sense to us. Studying evidence in the formation of the legal judgment with Lyotard's theory of knowledge and justice teaches us that uniformity of the senses of justice in Europe is unjust. It also follows from the endlessness of the different human practices and idioms that are connected to them, that justice is impossible.

The judge who does justice to the parties and to the local community which share the idiom of the court cannot be held to do that same justice to all the idioms of the Member States of the EU. I believe the EU must also show the same respect for the multiplicity of idioms entailed in the cooperation for the cooperation to be just. To the extent that there is any justice it is in the local mud of spatio-temporal commonality. The archipelago as a

57 Lyotard, pt. 30.
58 Judgment of 5 February 1963, *Van Gend en Loos*, 26–62, EU:C:1963:1; judgment of 15 July 1964, *Costa v ENEL*, 6–64, EU:C:1964:66.
59 Judgment of 15 July 1964, *Costa v ENEL*, 6–64, EU:C:1964:66.
60 Treaty Establishing the European Community, 25 Mar. 1957, p. 11 (preamble).
61 289 Treaty on European Union, OJ C 202, 7.06.2016, p. 13 (Consolidated).
62 There are still areas where there is room for differences, an obvious example being the application of directives, which means that the interpretation of the directive may vary in terms of its implementation – not, however, in effect: Article 288.3 Treaty on the Functioning of the European Union, OJ C 202, 7.6.2016, p. 47 (Consolidated).

swamp. It is hard to find an honest[63] alternative to accepting the muddle of human practices and purpose-points and plurality of justices.[64] We must keep muddling through.[65] Enthusiasm for the European project as a peace project[66] is not to be brushed aside, but subsuming diversity under one purpose-point is paradoxical in the most literal sense of the word for an organization which has taken the free market as its modus operandi. It seems to also risk overturning the sympathy for the European project.

It is not that the differends are possible to eliminate – on the contrary differends are means of resistance against uniformity impossible to subject – but they cannot be disregarded if there is to be access to any sense of justice in cross-border judicial procedure. Differends occur because the sense of the occurrence is as slippery as the escargots in the film *Pretty Woman*. For the EU, progress may best be found in the pluralism of different perspectives; consensus is monoculture;[67] it is not to strive for.[68] By studying evidence in civil procedural fact-finding as a language act, I have investigated what types of differends may be resulting from cross-border evidence. The conclusion from the comparative study is that there are cases of differends resulting from differences between the legal orders compared at each of the stages of civil procedural fact-finding. This means that cross-border evidence cannot be a means to justice – if with that is meant the correct application of the law to the case. The identity of the case[69] depends on the legislation, both substantive and procedural. The concrete just legal judgment is a correlation between law and fact. However, the concrete just judgment as a correct legal qualification of the correctly established facts can only be approximative.

63 Cf. Lyotard's purpose with *The Differend*: "to find . . . at least how to save the honor of thinking" (p. xii).

64 Lyotard, Jean-François. *The Postmodern Condition: A Report on Knowledge*. Translated by Geoff Bennington and Brian Massumi, Manchester UP, 1984, p. 66; Carroll, David. "Rephrasing the Political with Kant and Lyotard: From Aesthetic to Political Judgments." *Diacritics*, vol. 14, no. 3, 1984, Special Issue on the Work of Jean-François Lyotard, pp. 74–88; Ward, Ian. *Kantianism, Postmodernism and Critical Legal Thought*. Law and Philosophy Library, vol. 31, Kluwer Academic, 1997, p. 68.

65 Everson, Michelle, and Joerges, Christian. "Facticity as Validity: The Misplaced Revolutionary Praxis of European Law." *Research Handbook on Critical Legal Theory*, edited by Christodoulidis, Emilios et al., Edward Elgar Publishing, 2019.

66 Traité instituant la Communauté européenne du charbon et de l'acier, Paris, 18 avril 1951, recital.

67 The work against monoculture is embraced by the EU in agricultural matters as it increases resilience: https://ec.europa.eu/eip/agriculture/en/news/growing-beyond-monoculture (Visited 8 December, 2021). It may be worth considering increasing the resilience of the EU by embracing also legal pluriculture.

68 Lyotard, The Postmodern Condition, p. 82.

69 That which cannot be adjudicated more than once (*ne bis in idem*) and which cannot be altered after the initial stage of the proceedings (13:3 CJP; Ekelöf, P. O. *Processuella grundbegrepp och allmänna processprinciper: några problem inom den allmänna processrättsläran*. P.A. Norstedts & Söners Förlag, 1956, pp. 81, 86 ss.).

Legal justice is relative to law. The correct legal judgment is relative to the spatio-temporal commonality. This consists of the local agreements[70] as to what is relevant and in what sense (i.e., why it is relevant). In order to achieve juridical justice in cross-border cases some other sense of justice must therefore be found. I have suggested that the result of a civil procedural fact-finding should be understood as approximative. I have also suggested that the judge take an approximative approach to address themselves open-heartedly to the parties. An understanding of justice as approximative is not only a possible, but also a sensible approach to judicial justice – particularly in proceedings with cross-border aspects. As such, approximative justice may be seen as a proposal for what a common sense of justice within the EU may be.[71]

Final Words and Saving Clause

In this book, I have taken on to expose that which suffers from not being able to be exposed – "to be put into phrases."[72] Furthermore, I approached this difficult task through an engagement with cases grounded in empirical reality. Whether this was a successful undertaking is not in my place to judge, but it is my responsibility to admit to its weaknesses. The study was in a sense impossible as the differends that remain after the course of the proceedings will not be mentioned in caselaw. They can for that reason not themselves serve as evidence and make visible the object of proof (the differend). Thus, the argument that I put forward is that differends will always undermine any ambition to create a common, correct and predictable sense of justice that people across Europe will all agree is just. Consequently, I have had to make analogies, imagining cases inspired by real caselaw.[73]

Another weakness of this approach is that to a rather large extent it has had to rely on my own experiences. The choice of France, as country for comparison, could have been aleatory – any Member State would have served the purpose. The choice is not by chance, however. I believe that "there are historical, political, social, demographic, and epistemological reasons for"[74] the shape of positive law at a certain time and place, without the consideration of which positive law cannot be properly understood. To find both the legal and the extra-legal differences I have chosen a legal order with stronger Roman law roots than the Swedish. Seeking to make visible the invisible,[75] I have also made the choice on the basis that it be a country that I am familiar

70 Gane, p. 92.

71 Towards an Area of Freedom, Security and Justice, Brussels, COM(1998) 459 final of 14 July 1998, p. 8.

72 Lyotard, pt. 23.

73 Lyotard, p. 123.

74 Legrand, Pierre. "Siting Foreign Law: How Derrida can help." *Duke Journal of Comparative & International Law*, vol. 21, no. 3, Spring 2011, p. 598.

75 Lyotard, p. xi.

with. Of the two that best fit those requirements, I chose the French for its role as model in the civil law tradition. Even though I have tried to be as critical about them as possible in the aim of excluding that my experiences are not also the foundation for detrimental prejudice and have made honest efforts in this regard I have had to contend myself with rather approximative illustrations. I cannot claim that my examples are all exact to the pixels in regard of spatio-temporal commonality. To a certain extent I discovered that my experiences as sources of knowledge have aged – however not like a bottle of Bourgogne.

In Chapter 2 it was commented that both Lyotard and Derrida stress the responsibility of the judge – the judge being, in accordance with Lyotard's theory, the addressee of that which is to be judged and the addressor of the judgment. Both refute the possibility of a single, correct, objectivity as the subject is a necessary requirement for the just judgment. The collection of senses that the case is determined to be is in this thesis said to be one "that the judge can live with and that people accept as just."[76] This phrasing disregards the parties but does note the requisite that there is public acceptance of the judgment. Following both Derrida and Lyotard, the hearing of the party, as a recognition of singularity, is a minimum to avoid injustice.[77] Therefore, we find that the just judgment considers the parties as well as the person in the street. The approximately just judgment considers the interests of both and may therefore be torn between them.

In the traditional modern[78] understanding of the just judgment, the law prescribes rights which the parties can claim in court after having proven that the extra-legal circumstances are also legal. The circumstances qualify for those rights to take place, to paraphrase Motulsky.[79] There is a bipolar linking between the facts and the rights (if – then). A just judgment in this line of thinking is one which realizes the rights which one 'has.' This link is disturbed when the facts are impossible to establish. Therefore, the sense of justice that is suggested here must find another solution. And so, it also finds another tension. Perfection is not achievable. Justice is only ever approximate. But we carry on. Legal judgments regularly go against the perception of one of the parties for the benefit of that of the other and yet the haphazard of tyranny is not the common understanding of the daily practice of the courts. My suggestion is that what makes legal judgments from the court acceptable as 'just' is that they are possible to understand within the local spatio-temporal commonality, their sense is 'recovered.'[80] Even when

76 Chapter 4.

77 Chapter 3.

78 Gane, p. 95.

79 Motulsky, Henri. "Prolégomènes pour un futur Code de procédure civile: la consécration des principes directeurs du procès civil par le décret du 9 septembre 1971." *Écrits, études et notes de procédure civile*. Dalloz, 2010, p. 293.

80 Lyotard, pt. 78.

different human practices compete in determining the evidence and the case, I have argued that it is the spatio-temporal commonality which sorts the human practices, so that the extra-legal practice of expertise applicable is that which the spatio-temporal commonality determines to be the relevant human practice. This means that between the human practice of law and any other human practice, the spatio-temporal commonality must seep in for the judgment to be accepted as just.

Bibliography

Aït Ahmed, Lilia. Principe de cohérence et droit international privé de la famille européen. Université Panthéon-Sorbonne - Paris I, 2021. Français. NNT : 2021PA01D002.

Barron, Anne. "Lyotard and the Problem of Justice." *Judging Lyotard*, edited by Benjamin Andrew, Routledge, 1992.

Bell, Andrew S. *Forum Shopping and Venue in Transnational Litigation*. OUP, 2003.

Bjarup, Jes. "Scandinavian Legal Realism." *The Philosophy of Law: An Encyclopedia*, edited by Mark Tebbit, vol. 2, Routledge, 1999.

Bobek, Michal. "Why There Is No Principle of 'Procedural Autonomy' of the Member States." *The European Court of Justice and the Autonomy of the Member States*, edited by Hans-Wolfgang Micklitz and Bruno De Witte, Intersentia, 2012, pp. 305–324.

Bull, Thomas. "Rättighetsskyddet i Högsta förvaltningsdomstolen." *Svensk juristtidning*, 2017, pp. 216–244.

Cadiet, Loïc et al. *Approaches to Procedural Law: The Pluralism of Methods*. Nomos Verlag, 2017.

Carroll, David. "Rephrasing the Political with Kant and Lyotard: From Aesthetic to Political Judgments." *Diacritics*, vol. 14, no. 3, 1984, Special Issue on the Work of Jean-François Lyotard, pp. 74–88.

Cloots, Elke. *National Identity in EU Law*. OUP, 2015.

Cochran, Patricia. *Common Sense and Legal Judgment, Community Knowledge, Political Power, and Rhetorical Practice*. McGill-Queen's UP, 2017.

Crawford, James. *Brownlie's Principles of Public International Law*. 8th ed., OUP, 2012.

Ekelöf, P. O. *Processuella grundbegrepp och allmänna processprinciper: några problem inom den allmänna processrättsläran*. P.A. Norstedts & Söners Förlag, 1956.

Ekelöf, P. O. "Access to Justice." *Svensk juristtidning*, 1981, pp. 109–120.

Ekelöf, P. O. "Är den juridiska doktrinen en teknik eller en vetenskap?" *de lege*, edited by P. H. Lindblom, Iustus, 1991.

Everson, Michelle, and Christian Joerges. "Facticity as Validity: The Misplaced Revolutionary Praxis of European Law." *Research Handbook on Critical Legal Theory*, edited by Emilios Christodoulidis et al., Edward Elgar Publishing, 2019.

Gane, Nicholas. *Max Weber and Postmodern Theory: Rationalization Versus Re-enchantment*. Palgrave Macmillan, 2002.

Garnett, Richard Lyndon. *Substance and Procedure in Private International Law*. 1st ed. OUP, 2012.

Gearey, Adam. *Law and Aesthetics*. Bloomsbury Publishing Plc, 2001.

Geertz, Clifford. "Local Knowledge: Fact and Law in Comparative Perspective." *Local Knowledge: Further Essays in Interpretive Anthropology*. Basic Books, 1983.

Hazelhorst, Monique. *Free Movement of Civil Judgments in the European Union and the Right to a Fair Trial*. Springer, 2017.

Hill, Alfred. "State Procedural Law in Federal Nondiversity Litigation." *Harvard Law Review*, vol. 69, no. 1, Nov. 1955, pp. 66–117.
Ivainer, Théodore. *L'Interprétation des faits en droit.* L.G.D.J., 1988.
Janssens, Marie-Christine. "Belgium." *Intellectual Property and Private International Law: Comparative Perspectives*, edited by Toshiyuki Kono, Bloomsbury Publishing, 2012.
Joerges, Christian. "The Challenges of Europeanization in the Realm of Private Law: A Plea for a New Legal Discipline." *Duke Journal of Comparative & International Law,* vol. 14, no. 2, Summer 2004, p. 160.
Kakouris, C. M. "Do the Member States Possess Judicial Procedural 'Autonomy'." *Common Market Law Review*, vol. 34, no. 6, 1997, pp. 1389–1412.
Kant, Immanuel. *Kritik av omdömeskraften.* Translated by Sven-Olov Wallenstein, Thales, 2003 (Kant, Critique of Judgment).
Legrand, Pierre. "The Impossibility of 'Legal Transplants'." *Maastricht Journal of European and Comparative Law*, vol. 4, no. 2, Jun. 1997, pp. 111–124.
Legrand, Pierre. "What 'Legal Transplants'?" *Adapting Legal Cultures*, edited by David Nelken and Johannes Feest, Bloomsbury Publishing, 2001.
Legrand, Pierre. "Siting Foreign Law: How Derrida can help." *Duke Journal of Comparative & International Law,* vol. 21, no. 3, Spring 2011.
Lindell, Bengt. *Sakfrågor och rättsfrågor: en studie av gränser, skillnader och förhållanden mellan faktum och rätt.* Iustus, 1987.
Luhmann, Niklas. *Law As a Social System.* OUP, 2004.
Lyotard, Jean-François. *The Postmodern Condition: A Report on Knowledge.* Translated by Geoff Bennington and Brian Massumi. Manchester UP, 1984.
Lyotard, Jean-François. *The Differend – Phrases in Dispute.* Translated by Georges Van Den Abbeele, University of Minnesota Press, 1988.
Mayer, Pierre. *Droit international privé.* Montchrestien, 1977.
Motulsky, Henri. "Prolégomènes pour un futur Code de procédure civile: la consécration des principes directeurs du procès civil par le décret du 9 septembre 1971." *Écrits, études et notes de procédure civile.* Dalloz, 2010.
Ross, Alf. *On Law and Justice.* University of California Press, 1959.
Schlag, Pierre. "'Le Hors de texte, c'est moi' – The Politics of Form and the Domestication of Deconstruction." *Derrida and Law*, edited by Pierre Legrand, Ashgate, 2009.
Storskrubb, Eva. *Civil Procedure and EU Law, A Policy Area Uncovered.* OUP, 2008.
Storskrubb, Eva. "Mutual Trust and the Dark Horse of Civil Justice." *Cambridge Yearbook of European Legal Studies*, vol. 20, 2018, pp. 179–201.
Strang, Johan. "Two Generations of Scandinavian Legal Realism." *RETFÆRD*, årgång 32, no. 1/124, 2009.
Wallerman, Anna. *Om fakultativa regler: en studie av svensk och unionsrättslig reglering av skönsmässigt beslutsfattande i processrättsliga frågor.* Gothenburg. Iustus, 2015. Dissertation.
Wallerman, Anna. "Can Two Walk Together, Except They be Agreed? Preliminary References and (the Erosion of) National Procedural Autonomy in European Law Review." *European Law Review*, vol. 44, no. 2, 2019, pp. 159–177.
Ward, Ian. *Kantianism, Postmodernism and Critical Legal Thought. Law and Philosophy Library.* Vol. 31. Kluwer Academic, 1997.
Watson, Alan. *Legal Transplants: An Approach to Comparative Law.* University of Georgia Press, 1993.
Weller, Matthias. "Mutual Trust: In Search of the Future of European Union Private International Law." *Journal of Private International Law,* vol. 11, no. 1, 2015, pp. 64–102.

Works Cited

a) Treaties, Conventions and Other International Law Documents

Déclaration des Droits de l'Homme et du Citoyen de 1789.

Convention du 17 juillet 1905 relative à la procédure civile. (Hague Convention of 1905)

Explanations to the 1905 Hague Convention.

European Convention for the Protection of Human Rights and Fundamental Freedoms, as amended by Protocols Nos. 11 and 14, 4 November 1950, ETS 5.

Convention du 1 mars 1954 relative à la procédure civile. (Hague Convention of 1954)

Treaty Establishing the European Community, 25 March 1957. (Treaty of Rome)

Convention of 18 March 1970 on the Taking of Evidence Abroad in Civil or Commercial Matters. (Hague Convention of 1970)

UN Commission on Human Rights, Convention on the Rights of the Child, 7 March 1990, E/CN.4/RES/1990/74.

Treaty on European Union, OJ C 191, 29.7.1992, p. 1. (Maastricht)

Treaty of Amsterdam amending the Treaty on European Union, the Treaties establishing the European Communities and certain related acts, OJ C 340, 10.11.1997, p. 1.

Protocol no. 12 to the Convention for the Protection of Human Rights and Fundamental Freedoms, Rome, 4 December 2000, ETS 177.

Treaty of Lisbon amending the Treaty on European Union and the Treaty establishing the European Community, OJ C 306, 17.12.2007, p. 1.

Treaty on European Union, OJ C 202, 7.06.2016, p. 13. (Consolidated) (TEU)

Treaty on the Functioning of the European Union, OJ C 202, 7.6.2016, p. 47. (Consolidated) (TFEU)

Charter of Fundamental Rights of the European Union, OJ C 202, 7.6.2016, p. 389. (Consolidated) (CFR)

b) EU Legislation

Council Regulation (EC) No 1206/2001 of 28 May 2001 on cooperation between the courts of the Member States in the taking of evidence in civil or commercial matters, OJ L 174, 27.6.2001, p. 1.

Council Regulation (EC) No 2201/2003 of 27 November 2003 concerning jurisdiction and the recognition and enforcement of judgments in matrimonial matters and the matters of parental responsibility, repealing Regulation (EC) No 1347/2000, OJ L 338, 23.12.2003, p. 1. (Brussels II)

Regulation (EC) No 593/2008 of the European Parliament and of the Council of 17 June 2008 on the law applicable to contractual obligations, OJ L 177, 4.7.2008, p. 6. (Rome I)

Regulation (EU) No 650/2012 of the European Parliament and of the Council of 4 July 2012 on jurisdiction, applicable law, recognition and enforcement of decisions and acceptance and enforcement of authentic instruments in matters of succession and on the creation of a European Certificate of Succession, OJ L 201, 27.7.2012, p. 107. (Succession Regulation)

Regulation (EU) No 1215/2012 of the European Parliament and of the Council of 12 December 2012 on jurisdiction and the recognition and enforcement of judgments in civil and commercial matters (recast), OJ L 351, 20.12.2012, p. 1. (Brussels I)

Regulation (EU) No 1382/2013 of the European Parliament and of the Council of 17 December 2013 establishing a Justice Programme for the period 2014 to 2020, OJ L 354, 28.12.2013, p. 73.

Regulation (EU) 2020/1783 of the European Parliament and of the Council of 25 November 2020 on cooperation between the courts of the Member States in the taking of evidence in civil or commercial matters (taking of evidence) (recast), OJ L 405, 2.12.2020, p. 1. (Evidence Regulation)

Directive 2006/54/EC of the European Parliament and of the Council of 5 July 2006 on the implementation of the principle of equal opportunities and equal treatment of men and women in matters of employment and occupation (recast), OJ L 204, 26.7.2006, p. 23.

c) EU Preparatory Works and Other

Towards an Area of Freedom, Security and Justice, Brussels, COM(1998) 459 final of 14 July 1998.

European Union: Council of the European Union. *Presidency Conclusions, Tampere European Council, 15–16 October 1999*, 16 October 1999. (Tampere Conclusions)

Action Plan of the Council and the Commission on how best to implement the provisions of the Treaty of Amsterdam on an area of freedom, security and justice – Text adopted by the Justice and Home Affairs Council of 3 December 1998, OJ C 19, 23.01.1999, p. 1–15.

Initiative of the Federal Republic of Germany with a view to adopting a Council Regulation on cooperation between the courts of the Member States in the taking of evidence in civil and commercial matters, OJ 2000 C 314, 3.11.2000, p. 1.

Communication from the Commission to the Council and the European Parliament – Scoreboard to review progress on the creation of an area of "Freedom, security and justice" in the European Union, COM(2000) 167 final/2 of 13 April 2000.

Report on the initiative of the Federal Republic of Germany with a view to adopting a Council Regulation on cooperation between the courts of the Member States in the taking of evidence in civil or commercial matters, A5 73/2001, 27.2.2001 (not published in OJ).

Monthly summary of Council acts, of 4 July 2001, Document No 10571/01, statement 54/01.

Explanatory Report to the opinion of the EP A5 73/2001.

Explanation on Article 47 – Right to an effective remedy and to a fair trial, Explanations relating to the Charter of Fundamental Rights, OJ 2007 C 303, 14.12.2007, p. 17.

Report from the Commission to the Council, the European Parliament and the European Economic and Social Committee on the application of the Council Regulation (EC) 1206/2001 of 28 May 2001 on cooperation between the courts of the Member States in the taking of evidence in civil or commercial matters, COM(2007) 769 final, Brussels, 5.12.2007, p. 6.

The Stockholm Programme – An open and secure Europe serving and protecting citizens, OJ C 115, 4.5.2010, p. 1. (The Stockholm Programme)

EU Citizenship Report 2010 – Dismantling the obstacles to EU citizens' rights, Brussels, COM(2010) 603 final of 27 October 2010.

European Council, Conclusions 26–27 June 2014, EUCO 79/14, 27 June 2014.

Practice Guide for the application of the Regulation on the taking of evidence, drawn up by the Commission Services in consultation with the European Judicial Network in Civil and Commercial Matters. (Practice Guide)

Kadner Graziano, Thomas. *Cross-border traffic accidents in the EU – the potential impact of driverless cars*. Directorate-General for Internal Policies. PE 571.362, 2016, p. 18; http://www.europarl.europa.eu/RegData/etudes/STUD/2016/571362/IPOL_STU(2016)571362_EN.pdf (downloaded 6 May 2021). https://ec.europa.eu/eip/agriculture/en/news/growing-beyond-monoculture (visited 8 Dec. 2021).

d) European Caselaw

i) European Court of Human Rights (ECtHR)

Neumeister v Austria, 27 June 1968, Series A no. 8, ECHR:1968:0627JUD000193663

Dombo Beheer B.V. v the Netherlands, 27 October 1993, Series A no. 274, CE:ECHR:1993:1027JUD001444888
Pellegrini v France, 28541/95, ECHR 1999-VIII
Al-Adsani v the United Kingdom, 35763/97, ECHR 2001-XI
Reinhardt and Slimane-Kaïd v France, 23043/93, 22921/93, ECHR 1998-II, CE:ECHR:1998:0331JUD002304393

ii) Court of Justice of the European Union

Judgment of 5 February 1963, *Van Gend en Loos*, 26–62, EU:C:1963:1
Judgment of 15 July 1964, *Costa v ENEL*, 6–64, EU:C:1964:66
Judgment of 4 April 1968, *Lück*, 34–67, EU:C:1968:24
Judgment of 14 October 1976, *LTU v Eurocontrol*, 29–76, EU:C:1976:137
Judgment of 16 December 1976, *Rewe-Zentralfinanz*, 33–76, EU:C:1976:188
Judgment of 16 December 1980, *Netherlands v Rüffer*, 814/79, EU:C:1980:291
Judgment of 15 May 1986, *Marguerite Johnston v Chief Constable of the Royal Ulster Constabulary*, 222/84, EU:C:1986:206
Judgment of 15 October 1987, *Union nationale des entraîneurs et cadres techniques professionnels du football (Unectef) v Georges Heylens and others*, 222/86, EU:C:1987:442
Judgment of 14 February 1990, *French Republic v Commission of the European Communities*, Case C-301/87, EU:C:1990:67
Judgment of 19 November 1991, *Andrea Francovich and Others v Italian Republic*, joined Cases C-6/90 and C-9/90, EU:C:1991:428
Judgment of 3 December 1992, *Oleificio Borelli SpA v Commission of the European Communities*, C-97/91, EU:C:1992:491
Judgment of 14 November 2002, *Gemeente Steenbergen v Luc Baten*, C-271/00, EU:C:2002:656
Judgment of 28 April 2005, *St Paul Dairy*, C-104/03, EU:C:2005:255
Judgment of 5 October 2004, *Bernhard Pfeiffer and Others v Deutsches Rotes Kreuz, Kreisverband Waldshut eV*, Joined Cases C-397/01 to C-403/01, ECLI:EU:C:2004:584
Judgment of 22 December 2010, *Aguirre Zarraga*, C491/10, EU:C:2010:828
Judgment of 22 December 2010, *DEB Deutsche Energiehandels- und Beratungsgesellschaft mbH v Bundesrepublik Deutschland*, C279/09, EU:C:2010:811
Judgment of 17 February 2011, *Werynski*, C-283/09, EU:C:2011:85
Judgment of 28 July 2011, *Brahim Samba Diouf v Ministre du Travail, de l'Emploi et de l'Immigration*, C-69/10, EU:C:2011:524
Judgment of 15 September 2011, *Ministre du Budget, des Comptes publics et de la Fonction publique v Accor SA*, C-310/09, EU:C:2011:581
Judgment of 8 December 2011, *Chalkor AE Epexergasias Metallon v European Commission*, C-386/10 P, EU:C:2011:815
Judgment of 17 November 2011, *Homawoo*, C-412/10, EU:C:2011:747
Judgment of 6 September 2012, *Lippens*, C-170/11, EU:C:2012:540

Judgment of 6 November 2012, *Europese Gemeenschap v Otis NV and Others*, C199/11, EU:C:2012:684
Judgment of 22 November 2012, *M. M. v Minister for Justice, Equality and Law Reform, Ireland*, C-277/11, EU:C:2012:744
Judgment of 21 February 2013, *ProRail*, C-332/11, EU:C:2013:87
Judgment of 11 June 2015, *Fahrenbrock & Others*, C-226/13, EU:C:2015:383
Judgment of 14 September 2017, *The Trustees of the BT Pension Scheme v Commissioners for Her Majesty's Revenue and Customs*, C-628/15, EU:C:2017:687
Judgment of 19 October 2017, *Hansruedi Raimund v Michaela Aigner*, C-425/16, EU:C:2017:776
Judgment of the 5 June 2018, *Coman,* C673/16, EU:C:2018:385
Judgment of 11 September 2019, *Oana Mădălina Călin v Direcţia Regională a Finanţelor Publice Ploieşti – Administraţia Judeţeană a Finanţelor Publice Dâmboviţa and Others*, C-676/17, EU:C:2019:700

iii) Opinions of Advocate General

Opinion of 18 July 2007, *Tedesco*, C-175/06, EU:C:2007:451

iv) Order of the Court

Order of 27 September 2007, *Tedesco*, C-175/06, ECLI:EU:C:2007:552

e) Swedish Legislation

Lag (1915:218) om avtal och andra rättshandlingar på förmögenhetsrättens område (AvtL)
Rättegångsbalk (1942:740) (CJP)
Föräldrabalk (1949:381) (FB)
Ärvdabalk (1958:637) (ÄB)
Brottsbalk (1962:700) (BrB)
Jordabalk (1970:994) (JB)
Kungörelse (1974:152) om beslutad ny regeringsform (RF)
Lag (1974:371) om rättegången i arbetstvister (LRA)
Utsökningsbalk (1981:774) (UB)
Äktenskapsbalk (1987:230) (ÄktB)
Föräldraledighetslagen (SFS 1995:584)
Lag (SFS 1999:130) om åtgärder mot diskriminering i arbetslivet på grund av etnisk tillhörighet, religion eller annan trosuppfattning
Lag (2003:493) om EG:s förordning om bevisupptagning i mål och ärenden av civil eller kommersiell natur
Diskrimineringslagen (SFS 2008:567)
Offentlighets-och sekretesslag (2009:400)

Lag (2015:417) om arv i internationella situationer
Lag (2019:235) om ändring i äktenskapsbalken

f) Swedish Preparatory Works

Prop. 1942:5
Prop. 1986/87:89
Prop. 1990/91:194
Prop. 2004/05:131
Prop. 2004/05:137
Prop. 2005/06:99
Prop. 2018/19:50
SOU 1938:44
SOU 1986:26
SOU 2005:43

g) Swedish Cases

NJA 1969 s. 311
NJA 1975 s. 577
NJA 1981 s. 982
NJA 1982 s. 175 I and II
NJA 1982 s. 650
NJA 1982 s. 836
NJA 1985 s. 774
NJA 1986 s. 175
NJA 1986 s. 398
NJA 1986 s. 470
NJA 1987 s. 48
NJA 1987 s. 211
NJA 1987 s. 450
NJA 1987 s. 724
NJA 1987 s. 742
NJA 1987 s. 766
NJA 1988 s. 652
NJA 1989 s. 374
NJA 1990 s. 286
NJA 1990 s. 537
NJA 1990 s. 617
NJA 1991 s. 123
NJA 1991 s. 152
NJA 1991 s. 262
NJA 1991 s. 512
NJA 1992 s. 307

NJA 1993 s. 13
NJA 1993 s. 751
NJA 1994 s. 34
NJA 1994 s. 145
NJA 1995 s. 347
NJA 1997 s. 37
NJA 1997 s. 336
NJA 1997 s. 825
NJA 1998 s. 225
NJA 1998 s. 590
NJA 1998 s. 675
NJA 1998 s. 829
NJA 1999 s. 451
NJA 1999 s. 469
NJA 1999 s. 629
NJA 2000 s. 648
NJA 2000 s. 747
NJA 2001 s. 183
NJA 2001 s. 404
NJA 2001 s. 563
NJA 2001 s. 865
NJA 2002 s. 41
NJA 2003 s. 58
NJA 2003 s. 239
NJA 2003 s. 372
NJA 2004 s. 331
NJA 2004 s. 561
NJA 2004 s. 874
NJA 2005 s. 407
NJA 2006 s. 26
NJA 2006 s. 520
NJA 2007 s. 382
NJA 2007 s. 547
NJA 2007 s. 571
NJA 2007 s. 624
NJA 2007 s. 874
NJA 2007 s. 1032
NJA 2009 s. 64
NJA 2010 s. 122
NJA 2010 s. 151
NJA 2011 s. 241
NJA 2012 s. 269
NJA 2012 s. 289
NJA 2012 s. 628
NJA 2012 s. 804

NJA 2012 s. 1095
NJA 2013 s. 455
NJA 2014 s. 212
NJA 2014 s. 307
NJA 2014 s. 364
NJA 2014 s. 651
NJA 2015 s. 141
NJA 2015 s. 222
NJA 2015 s. 631
NJA 2015 s. 702
NJA 2016 s. 1195
NJA 2017 s. 210
NJA 2017 s. 1105
NJA 2018 s. 301
NJA 2018 s. 617
NJA 2018 s. 1062
NJA 2019 s. 327
MÖD 2017:24
AD 47/2008
AD 19/2014
AD 11/2018
RH 1994:11
RH 1994:48
RH 1994:67
RH 1995:38
RH 1995:145
RH 1997:109
RH 1998:98
RH 2000:39
RH 2005:38
RH 2009:50
RH 2009:68
RH 2011:5
RH 2015:60
RH 2016:1
RH 2019:27
RH 2021:4
RÅ 2000:58
RÅ 2001:67
Svea hovrätts dom av den 13 december 2016 i mål nr T 8932–15
Göta hovrätts dom den 27 december 2012 i mål nr B 3081–12
Decision of the Chancellor of Justice of 2013.01.18, Dnr 8473-12-32
Decision of the Chancellor of Justice of 2007.09.20, Dnr 6010-07-30, 6119-07-30, 6164-07-30, 6220-07-30 and 6339-07-30

h) French Legislation

Code civil (CC)
Code de procédure civile (CPC)
Code de procédure pénale
Code de commerce
Décret n° 2004–836 du 20 août 2004 portant modification de la procédure civile
Décret 2009–285 du 12 mars 2009 relatif aux enquêteurs sociaux et à la tarification des enquêtes sociales en matière civile, NOR: JUSC0819029D, JORF n°0062 du 14 mars 2009
Ordonnance n° 2016–131 du 10 février 2016 portant réforme du droit des contrats, du régime général et de la preuve des obligations, NOR: JUSC1522466R

i) French Cases

Cass. civ. 3e, 11 janv. 1978, 76–12.771, 76–12.772, *Bull. civ.* 3 N. 30 P. 22
Cass. civ. 2e, 8 mai 1980, 78–41.737, Bull. civ. 2 N. 101
Cass. civ. 3e, 20 nov. 1985, n° 84–13.353, *Bull civ.* III n° 153 p. 116
Cass. civ. 1e, 8 déc. 1987, n° 85–15.444, *Bull.* N° 337, p. 242
Cass. com., 7 mars 1989, n° 87–11.827, NP
Cass. civ. 1e, 25 avr. 1989, n° 87–19.253, *Bull. civ.* I N° 169, p. 111
Cass. civ. 1e, 15 nov. 1989, n° 88–13.548, NP
Cass. crim., 18 avr. 1991, n° 91–80.657, NP
Cass. civ. 1e, 10 mai 1995, n° 93–15.910, *Bull. civ.* I N° 200 p. 143
Cass. civ. 2e, 15 nov. 1995, n° 93–19.324, *Bull. civ.* II N° 281 p. 166
Cass. com., 9 déc. 1997, n° 95–16.777, NP
Cass. civ. 1e, 5 janv. 1999, N° 97–10.379, Non publié
Cass. civ. 1e, 28 mars 2000, n° 98–12.806, *Bull. civ.* I N° 103
Cass. civ. 1e, 24 sept. 2002, n° 00–22.466, *Bill. civ.* I N° 216 p. 167
Cass. civ. 1e, 2 mars 2004, n° 02–15.211, *Bull. civ.* I N° 70
Cass. civ. 3e, 10 févr. 2009, n° 07–21.134, NP
Cass. civ. 1e, 12 mai 2010, n° 09–11.133, Bulletin 2010, I, n° 111
Cass. civ. 2e, 10 mars 2011, n° 10–11.732, *Bill. civ.* II, n° 65
Cass. civ. 12, 16 juin 2011, n° 10–17.898, NP
Cass. soc., 23 nov. 2011, n° 10–20.933, NP
Cass. civ. 1e, 26 janv. 2012, n° 10–28.356, *Bull. civ.* I, n° 13
Cass. civ. 1e, 26 sept. 2012, n° 11–10.960, *Bull. civ.* I, N° 189
Cass. civ. 1e, 8 juil. 2015, 14–18.875, Bulletin 2016, n° 834, 1re Civ., n° 91, FR:CCASS:2015:C100811
Cass. soc., 30 sept. 2015, n° 14–25.736, NP, FR:CCASS:2015:SO01518
Cass. soc., 27 mars 2001, n° 98–44.666, Bull. 2001, V, n° 108
Cass. soc., 3 nov. 2010, n° 09–67.493, NP

Cass. soc., 5 déc. 2012, n° 11–21.113, *Bull. Civ.* V, n° 325, FR:CCASS:2012:SO02546
Cass. civ. 1e, 28 janv. 2015, N° 13–27.125, *Bull. Civ.* 2015, I, n° 21, FR:CCASS:2015:C100094
Cass. civ. 1e, 13 juil. 2017, 16–24.084, Publié au bulletin, FR:CCASS:2017:C101002
Cass. civ. 1e, 13 jan. 2021, n° 19–16.392, FR:CCASS:2021:C100043
Cass. civ. 1e, 10 mars 2021, N° 19–22.117, 19–22.656, Non publié, FR:CCASS:2021:C100216
CA. adm. de Marseille, 4e, 22 fév. 2011, n° 08MA00020, NP

j) Other Public Sources

Rapport de la Commission Spéciale, Ph. W. Amram, Actes et documents de la Onzième session, Conférence de la Haye, Tome IV, Obtention des preuves à l'étranger, 1968.
Rapport au Président de la République relatif à l'ordonnance n° 2016–131 du 10 février 2016 portant réforme du droit des contrats, du régime général et de la preuve des obligations, JORF n°0035 du 11 février 2016.
Accord portant sur l'égalité professionnelle entre les femmes et les hommes, 03/06/2019, T05119001312, Publication date on Légifrance: 23/07/2019.
Svensk/engelsk ordlista, Sveriges domstolar, AJ E-print AB, 2019.
OECD. *Preventing Harmful Alcohol Use*, OECD Health Policy Studies, OECD Publishing, 2021, https://doi.org/10.1787/6e4b4ffb-en. Accessed 5 Dec. 2024.
"Wine consumed in pure alcohol, litres per capita, age 15+." WHO Regional Office for Europe, Copenhagen, Denmark, https://gateway.euro.who.int/en/indicators/hfa_428-3052-wine-consumed-in-pure-alcohol-litres-per-capita-age-15plus/#id=20008&fullGraph=true. Accessed 5 Dec. 2024.

k) Bibliography

Abel, Olivier. *Paul Ricoeur, Jacques Ellul, Jean Carbonnier, Pierre Chaunu: Dialogues*. Labor et Fides, 2012.
Aït Ahmed, Lilia. Principe de cohérence et droit international privé de la famille européen. Université Panthéon-Sorbonne - Paris I, 2021. Français. NNT : 2021PA01D002.
Åhrén, Mattias. *Indigenous Peoples' Status in the International Legal System*. OUP, 2016. Oxford Scholarship Online. Accessed 23 Sep. 2021.
Anderson, Terence et al. *Analysis of Evidence*. 2nd ed. CUP, 2010. (Anderson et al.).
Andersson, Torbjörn. *Rättsskyddsprincipen*. Uppsala and Iustus, 1997. Dissertation. (Andersson).
Andersson, Torbjörn. *Harmonization and Mutual Recognition: How to Handle Mutual Distrust, Enforcement Agency Practice in Europe*. British Institute of International and Comparative Law, 2005.
Arendt, Hannah. *Lectures on Kant's Political Philosophy*. University of Chicago Press, 1989.
Augenstein, Daniel, editor. *'Integration Through Law' Revisited: The Making of the European Polity*. Ashgate Pub., 2012.

Austin, John. *How To Do Things With Words.* Clarendon Press, 1975.

Aynès, Augustin, and Xavier Vuitton. *Droit de la preuve, Principes et mise en œuvre processuelle.* 2nd ed., LexisNexis, 2017. (Aynès, Vuitton).

Balicco, Christian. "L'utilisation de la graphologie dans le recrutement de cadres au sein des cabinets conseils." *L'orientation scolaire et professionnelle*, vol. 31, no. 2, 2002. (Balicco).

Bamford, Kiff. "A Late Performance: Intimate Distance (Yingmei Duan)." *Rereading Jean-François Lyotard*, edited by Heidi Bickis and Rob Shields, Ashgate, 2013.

Barron, Anne. "Lyotard and the Problem of Justice." *Judging Lyotard*, edited by Benjamin Andrew, Routledge, 1992. (Barron).

Baxi, Upendra. "Towards a Climate Change Justice Theory." *Journal of Human Rights and the Environment*, vol. 7, no. 1, Mar. 2016, p. 7–31.

Bell, Andrew S. *Forum Shopping and Venue in Transnational Litigation.* OUP, 2003.

Bennington, Geoffrey. *Lyotard: Writing the Event.* Manchester UP and Columbia UP, 1988.

Bentham, Jeremy. *A Treatise on Judicial Evidence.* J.W. Paget, 1825.

Bentham, Jeremy. *Rationale of Judicial Evidence.* Edited by J. S. Mill, Vol. I, Hunt and Clarke, 1827.

Bentham, Jeremy. *Rationale of Judicial Evidence: Specially Applied to English Practice.* Vol. V, Hunt and Clarke, 1827. (Bentham, Vol. V).

Bentham, Jeremy. *The Works of Jeremy Bentham.* Vol. 7 (Rationale of Judicial Evidence Part 2). William Tait, 1843. Online Library of Liberty, https://oll.libertyfund.org/titles/bowring-the-works-of-jeremy-bentham-vol-7-rationale-of-judicial-evidence-part-2. Accessed 3 Dec. 2024.

Bjarup, Jes. "Scandinavian Legal Realism." *The Philosophy of Law: An Encyclopedia*, edited by Mark Tebbit, vol. 2, Routledge, 1999. (Bjarup).

Blanc, Emmanuel. *La Preuve judiciaire. Commentaire du Décret du 17 décembre 1973.* Librairie du Journal des notaires et des avocats, 1974. (Blanc).

Bobek, Michal. "Why There is No Principle of 'Procedural Autonomy' of the Member States." *The European Court of Justice and the Autonomy of the Member States*, edited by Hans-Wolfgang Micklitz and Bruno De Witte, Intersentia, 2012, pp. 305–324.

Bogdan, Michael. "The Brussels/Lugano lis pendens rule and the 'Italian torpedo'." *Scandinavian Studies in Law,* vol. 51, 2007, pp. 89–98.

Bolard, Georges. "La Matière du procès et le principe du dispositif." *Droit et pratique de la procédure civile – Droit interne et européen*, edited by Serge Guinchard, 9th ed., (2017/2018). Dalloz, 2016. (Bolard).

Bolding, P. O. *Går det att bevisa?: Perspektiv på domstolsprocessen.* Norstedts, 1989.

Boman, Robert. *Om åberopande och åberopsbörda i dispositiva tvistemål.* P.A. Norstedt & Söners Förlag, 1964. (Boman).

Boman, Robert. "Om mellandom och omröstningar om omständigheter." *Festskrift till Welamson*, edited by Olle Höglund and Lars Welamson, Norstedts, 1987.

Brush, Stephen B., and Doreen Stabinsky. *Valuing Local Knowledge: Indigenous People and Intellectual Property Rights.* Island Press, 1996.

Bull, Thomas. "Rättighetsskyddet i Högsta förvaltningsdomstolen." *Svensk juristtidning*, 2017, pp. 216–244.

Bylander, Eric. "Part närstående vittne – Handtag, famntag, klapp eller kyss?" *Juridisk Tidskrift,* no. 3, 2007/08, pp. 660–667.

Bylund, Torleif. *Repetitionskompendium i processrätt.* Iustus, 2010. (Bylund).

Cadiet, Loïc, and Emmanuel Jeuland. *Droit judiciaire privé.* 10th ed., LexisNexis, 2017. (Cadiet, Jeuland).

Cadiet, Loïc et al. *Approaches to Procedural Law: The Pluralism of Methods.* Nomos Verlag, 2017.

Cadiet, Loïc et al. *Théorie générale du procès*. 3rd ed., PUF, 2020.
Caire, Anne-Blandine. *Relecture du droit des présomptions à la lumière du droit européen des droits de l'homme*. l'Université de Limoges, 2010. Thèse.
Cappelletti, Mauro et al., editors. *Integration Through Law: Europe and the American Federal Experience*. de Gruyter, 1985. (Cappelletti, Mauro et al., Integration through Law).
Carbonnier, Jean. *Droit civil*. Vol. I, 1st ed., 2004, Quadrige PUF. (Carbonnier).
Carroll, David. "Rephrasing the Political with Kant and Lyotard: From Aesthetic to Political Judgments." *Diacritics*, vol. 14, no. 3, 1984, Special Issue on the Work of Jean-François Lyotard, pp. 74–88. (Carroll).
Cegrell Karlander, Isa. *Officialprincipen i migrationsprocessen: Domstolens utredningsansvar*. Uppsala, 2021. Dissertation. (Cegrell Karlander).
Chung, Kyung-Sook. *Space in Tense: The Interaction of Tense, Aspect, Evidentiality and Speech Acts in Korean*. John Benjamins Publishing, 2012.
Cisney, Vernon, W. *Deleuze and Derrida. Difference and the Power of the Negative*. Edinburgh UP, 2018. (Cisney).
Clark, Timothy. "Derrida: a Pragmatics of Singularity." *The Poetics of Singularity: The Counter-Culturalist Turn in Heidegger, Derrida, Blanchot and the Later Gadamer*. Edinburgh UP, 2005. (Clark).
Cloots, Elke. *National Identity in EU Law*. OUP, 2015.
Cochran, Patricia. *Common Sense and Legal Judgment, Community Knowledge, Political Power, and Rhetorical Practice*. McGill-Queen's UP, 2017. (Cochran).
Cohen, L. Jonathan. *The Probable and the Provable*. Clarendon, 1977.
Cornell, Drucilla. *The Philosophy of the Limit*. Routledge, 1992. (Cornell).
Cornu, Gérard. *Vocabularie juridique*, 9th ed. Quadrige PUF, 2011.
Crawford, James. *Brownlie's Principles of Public International Law*. 8th ed., OUP, 2012.
Croze, Hervé. *Procédure civile. Technique procédurale civile*. 6th ed., LexisNexis, 2017.
de Man, Paul. "The Epistemology of Metaphor." *Critical Inquiry*, vol. 5, no. 1, 1978, pp. 13–30.
de Montesquieu, Charles de Secondat baron. *De l'esprit des lois*, Vol. 1, Livre XI, Chap. VI, Lebigre frères, 1831.
Derrida, Jacques. "Force de loi: le Fondement mystique de l'autorité." *Cardozo Law Review*, vol. 11, nos. 5–6, Jul/Aug. 1990, pp. 949–1046. (Derrida)
Derrida, Jacques. "Politics of Friendship." *American Imago*, FALL 1993, Vol. 50, No. 3, LOVE (FALL 1993), pp. 378–380. (Derrida, Politics of Friendship).
Derrida, Jacques. *L'Autre Cap*. Minuit, 1997.
Derrida, Jacques. *Marx Spöken: Skuldstaten, sorgearbetet och Den nya internationalen*. Translated by Jonas Magnusson, Daidalos, 2003. (Derrida, Specters of Marx).
Derrida, Jacques. *Sovereignties in Question: The Poetics of Paul Celan*. Fordham UP, 2005.
Derrida, Jacques. "In Human Language, Fraternity." *Politics of Friendship*, Verso, 2005. (Derrida, In human language).
Diesen, Christian. *Utevarohandläggning och bevisprövning i brottmål*. Juristförlaget, 1993. Dissertation.
Diesen, Christian. *Bevisprövning i brottmål*. Juristförlaget, 1994.
Diesen, Christian, and Magne Strandberg. *Bevisprövning i tvistemål: Teori och praktik*. Norstedts Juridik, 2012. (Diesen, Bevisprövning i tvistemål).
Douzinas, Costas. "The Metaphysics of Jurisdiction." *Jurisprudence of Jurisdiction*, edited by Shaun McVeigh, Routledge, 2016.
Douzinas, Costas, and Adam Gearey. *Critical Jurisprudence: the Political Philosophy of Justice*. Hart Publishing, 2005. (Douzinas, Gearey).

Douzinas, Costas, and Ronnie Warrington. "'A Well-Founded Fear of Justice': Law and Ethics in Postmodernity." *Law and Critique*, vol. II, no. 2, 1991, pp. 115–147. (Douzinas, Warrington).

Dunn, Allen. "A Tyranny of Justice: The Ethics of Lyotard's Differend." *Boundary 2*, vol. 20, no. 1, (Duke UP), 1993, pp. 192–220.

Dwyer, Déirdre. *The Judicial Assessment of Expert Evidence*. Cambridge UP, 2008.

Edelstam, Henrik. *Sakkunnigbeviset*. Uppsala, 1991. Dissertation. (Edelstam).

Egelund, Tine. *Beskyttelse af barndommen: Socialforvaltningers risikovurdering og indgreb*. Lund, 1997. Dissertation.

Ekelöf, P. O. *Processuella grundbegrepp och allmänna processprinciper: några problem inom den allmänna processrättsläran*. P.A. Norstedts & Söners Förlag, 1956. (Ekelöf, Processuella grundbegrepp).

Ekelöf, P. O. "Free Evaluation of Evidence." *Scandinavian Studies in Law*, vol. 8, 1964, pp. 45–66.

Ekelöf, P. O. "Access to Justice." *Svensk juristtidning*, 1981, pp. 109–120.

Ekelöf, P. O. "My Thoughts on Evidentiary Value." *Evidentiary Value: Philosophical, Judicial, and Psychological Aspects of a Theory*, edited by Peter Gärdenfors et al., Gleerups, 1983.

Ekelöf, P. O. "Review of Sakfrågor och rättsfrågor. Akademisk avhandling. Bengt Lindell. Uppsala 1987." *Svensk juristtidning*, 1988, p. 23–39.

Ekelöf, P. O. "Bevisvärdemodellen kontra bevistemamodellen." *Svensk juristtidning*, 1989, pp. 26–38.

Ekelöf, P. O. "Om rätt och moral." *Process och exekution, Vänbok till Robert Boman*, edited by Per Henrik Lindblom, Iustus, 1990, pp. 71–83.

Ekelöf, P. O. "Är den juridiska doktrinen en teknik eller en vetenskap?" *de lege*, edited by P. H. Lindblom, Iustus, 1991.

Ekelöf, P. O. *Rättegång II*. 8th ed., Norstedts Juridik, 2010. (Ekelöf, II).

Ekelöf, P. O. et al. *Rättegång IV*. 7th ed., Norstedts Juridik, 2009. (Ekelöf, IV).

Ekelöf, P. O. et al. *Rättegång V*. 7th ed., Norstedts Juridik, 2010. (Ekelöf, V).

Ekelöf, P. O. et al. *Rättegång I*. 9th ed., Norstedts Juridik, 2016. (Ekelöf, I).

European Law Institute, European Law. & UNIDROIT. *ELI-Unidroit Model European Rules of Civil Procedure: From Transnational Principles to European Rules of Civil Procedure*. OUP, 2021.

Euvrard, Jean-Louis. "Aristote." *Dictionnaire de la Justice*, edited by Loïc Cadiet, PUF, 2004.

Everson, Michelle. "A Citizenship in Movement." *German Law Journal*, vol. 15, no. 5, Aug. 2014, pp. 965–984.

Everson, Michelle, and Christian Joerges. "Reconfiguring the Politics-Law Relationship in the Integration Project through Conflicts-Law Constitutionalism." *European Law Journal*, vol. 18, no. 5, Sep. 2012, pp. 644–666.

Everson, Michelle, and Christian Joerges. "Facticity as Validity: The Misplaced Revolutionary Praxis of European Law." *Research Handbook on Critical Legal Theory*, edited by Christodoulidis, Emilios et al., Edward Elgar Publishing, 2019.

Fartunova-Michel, Maria. *La preuve dans le droit de l'Union européenne*. Bruylant, 2013.

Fischer-Lescano, Andreas, and Gunther Teubner. "Regime-Collisions: The Vain Search for Legal Unity in the Fragmentation of Global Law." *Michigan Journal of International Law*, vol. 25, no. 4, Summer 2004, pp. 999–1046.

Fish, Stanley. "Fish v. Fiss." *Stanford Law Review*, vol. 36, no. 6, Jul. 1984, pp. 1325–1348.

Fish, Stanley. "Force." *Doing What Comes Naturally: Change, Rhetoric, and the Practice of Theory in Literary and Legal Studies*. Duke UP, 1989.

Fitger et al. "Rättegångsbalken." *Kommentaren till 38 kap*. JUNO, 2020. Accessed 01 Oct. 2020.

Fitger et al. "Rättegångsbalken." *Kommentaren till 36:5*. JUNO, 2020. Accessed 01 Oct. 2020.

Font I Segura, Albert. "A EC Reading of the Principle Lex Fori Regit Processum." *Anuario Espanol de Derecho Internacional Privado*, vol. 1, 2001, pp. 283–313.

Forner Delaygua, Joaquín J. "The Impact of the Enforcement Directive on the Brussels I Regime." *International Litigation in Intellectual Property and Information Technology*, edited by Arnaud Nuyts, Kluwer Law International, 2008.

Frege, Gottlob. "On Sense and Nominatum." *The Philosophy of Language*, edited by A. P. Martinich, translated by Herbert Feigl, 2nd ed., OUP, 1990 (Frege, On Sense and Nominatum).

Fricero, Natalie. "Garanties de nature procédureale: équité, publicité, célérité et laïcité." *Droit et pratique de la procédure civile – Droit interne et européen*, edited by Serge Guinchard, 9th ed., (2017/2018). Dalloz, 2016.

Fridström Montoya. *Therése. Homo iuridicus: Den kapabla människan i rätten*. Iustus, 2017.

Fritzman, J. M. "Overcoming Capitalism." *Lyotard, Just Education*, edited by Pradeep Ajit Dhillon and Stanley Paul, Routledge, 2000.

Frödén, Sara and Moira von Wright. "The Waldorf Kindergarten." *International Handbook of Early Childhood Education*, edited by M. Fleer and B. van Oers, Springer International Handbooks of Education and Springer Science+Business Media B.V., 2018, pp. 1401–1420.

Gane, Nicholas. *Max Weber and Postmodern Theory: Rationalization Versus Re-enchantment*. Palgrave Macmillan, 2002. (Gane).

Garnett, Richard Lyndon. *Substance and Procedure in Private International Law*. 1st ed., OUP, 2012. (Garnett).

Gasché, Rodolphe. *Inventions of Difference: on Jacques Derrida*. Harvard UP, 1994.

Gearey, Adam. *Law and Aesthetics*. Bloomsbury Publishing Plc, 2001. (Gearey).

Gearey, Adam. "Tell All the Truth, But Tell It Slant: A Poetics of Truth and Reconciliation." *Journal of Law and Society*, vol. 31, no. 1, Mar. 2004, pp. 38–59. (Gearey, Tell All the Truth)

Geertz, Clifford. "Local Knowledge: Fact and Law in Comparative Perspective." *Local Knowledge: Further Essays in Interpretive Anthropology*, Basic Books, 1983.

Geertz, Clifford. "Common Sense as a Cultural System." *The Antioch Review*, vol. 67, no. 4, Geertz at Antioch Fall 2009, pp. 770–790.

Gehring, Petra. "The Jurisprudence of the 'Force of Law'." *Derrida and Law*, edited by Pierre Legrand, Ashgate, 2009. (Gehring).

Goodwin, Jean. "Wigmore's Chart Method." *Informal Logic*, vol. 20, no. 3, 2000, pp. 223–243. (Goodwin).

Goyal, Reena. "Serving Justice through Authorship: A Phenomenological Approach to the Authority of Law." *University of Toronto Faculty of Law Review*, vol. 62, no. 1, 2004.

Grahn-Farley, Maria. *Barnkonventionen: en kommentar*. Studentlitteratur, 2019.

Gualandi, Alberto. *Lyotard*. 2nd ed., Les Belles Lettres, 2004. (Gualandi).

Günther, Gotthard. "Life as Polycontexturality." *Wirklichkeit und Reflexion*, edited by H. Fahrenbach, Festschrift für Walter Schulz, 1973, pp. 187–210, http://vordenker.de/ggphilosophy/gg_life_as_polycontexturality.pdf, 2014, p. 4. (Gotthard, Life as Polycontexturality)

Halperin, Jean-Louis. "La preuve judiciaire et la liberté du juge." *Communications*, vol. 84, no. 1, 2009, pp. 21–32.

Hamson, C.-J. "La procédure civile en Angleterre et en France." *Revue internationale de droit comparé*, vol. 2, no. 1, 1950, p. 77–83.

Hart, H. L. A. "Positivism and the Separation of Law and Morals." *Harvard Law Review*, vol. 71, no. 4, (*The Harvard Law Review Association*), 1958, pp. 593–629.

Hassler, Åke. *Svensk civilprocessrätt*. Nord. bokh., 1963. (Hassler).

Hazelhorst, Monique. *Free Movement of Civil Judgments in the European Union and the Right to a Fair Trial*. Springer, 2017. (Hazelhorst).

Herzog, Peter E., and Martha Weser. *Civil Procedure in France*. Springer, 2014.

Hess, Burkhard. "Preservation and Taking of Evidence in Cross-Border Proceedings – Comparative Remarks in the Context of IP Litigation." *International Litigation in Intellectual Property and Information Technology*, edited by Arnaud Nuyts, Kluwer Law International, 2008.

Heuman, Lars. *Bevisbörda och beviskrav i tvistemål*. 1st ed., Norstedts Juridik, 2005. (Heuman, Bevisbörda).

Hill, Alfred. "State Procedural Law in Federal Nondiversity Litigation." *Harvard Law Review*, vol. 69, no. 1, Nov. 1955, p. 66–117.

Hilt, Patrice, and Frédérique Granet-Lambrechts. *Droit de la Famille*, 6th ed., Ebook Pdf and PUG, 2018.

Ingram, David. "The Kantianism of Arendt and Lyotard." *Judging Lyotard*, edited by Benjamin Andrew, Routledge, 1992. (Ingram).

Ivainer, Théodore. *L'Interprétation des faits en droit*. L.G.D.J., 1988.

Janssens, Marie-Christine. "Belgium." *Intellectual Property and Private International Law: Comparative Perspectives*, edited by Toshiyuki Kono, Bloomsbury Publishing, 2012.

Jeuland, Emmanuel. "Expertise." *Dictionnaire de la Justice*, edited by Loïc Cadiet, PUF, 2004.

Joerges, Christian. "The Challenges of Europeanization in the Realm of Private Law: A Plea for a New Legal Discipline." *Duke Journal of Comparative & International Law*, vol. 14, no. 2, Summer 2004, p. 149–196.

Joerges, Christian. "How is a Closer Union Conceivable under Conditions of Ever More Socio-Economic and Political Diversity Constitutionalising Europe's Unitas in Pluralitate." *EurLJ*, 24, 2018, pp. 257–267.

Joerges, Christian, and Michelle Everson. "Law, Economics and Politics in the Constitutionalization of Europe." *Developing a Constitution for Europe*, edited by Erik O. Eriksen et al., Routledge, 2004.

Kahneman, Daniel. *Thinking Fast and Slow*. MacMillan Publishers, 2015.

Kahneman, Daniel et al. *Noise*. Harper Collins, 2021.

Kakouris, C. M. "Do the Member States Possess Judicial Procedural 'autonomy'." *Common Market Law Review*, vol. 34, no. 6, 1997, pp. 1389–1412.

Kaldal, Anna. *Parallella processer: en rättsvetenskaplig studie av riskbedömningar i vårdnads- och LVU-mål*. Stockholm, Jure, 2010. Dissertation. (Kaldal).

Kallenberg, Ernst. *Svensk civilprocess*. Bd 2.1, Gleerup, 1927.

Kant, Immanuel. *Kritik av omdömeskraften*. Translated by Sven-Olov Wallenstein, Thales, 2003. (Kant, Critique of Judgment).

Kant, Immanuel. *Kritik av det rena förnuftet*. Translated by Jeanette Emt, Thales, 2004. (Kant, Pure Reason).

Kennedy, Duncan. *A Critique of Adjudication: Fin de Siècle*. Harvard UP, 1997.

Kenny, David, and Rosemary Hennigan. "Choice-of-Court Agreements, the Italian Torpedo, and the Recast of the Brussels I Regulation." *International and Comparative Law Quarterly*, vol. 64, no. 1, Jan. 2015, pp. 197–210.

Key, Ellen. *Folkbildningsarbetet särskilt med hänsyn till skönhetssinnets odling*. K. W. Appelbergs boktryckeri, 1906, http://runeberg.org/folkbildn/0027.html. Accessed 18 Sep. 2021.

King, Michael, and Chris Thornhill. *Niklas Luhmann's Theory of Politics and Law.* Springer, 2003.
Kingsbury, Benedict. "Sovereignty and Inequality." *European Journal of International Law,* vol. 9, no. 4, 1998, pp. 599–625.
Kolflaath, Eivind. "Bevisbedømmelse: sannsynlighet eller fortellinger?" *Jussens Venner,* vol. 39, no. 5–6, Mars 2005, pp. 279–304.
Kramer, Xandra E. "The Structure of Civil Proceedings and Why It Matters: Exploratory Observations on Future ELI-UNIDROIT European Rules of Civil Procedure." *Uniform Law Review*, vol. 19, no. 2, Jun. 2014.
Krans, Bart, and Anna Nylund, editors. *Procedural Autonomy Across Europe.* Intersentia, 2020.
Lacroix-Andrivet, Jean-Paul. "Preuves à conserver." *Droit et pratique de la procédure civile – Droit interne et européen*, edited by Serge Guinchard, 9th ed., (2017/2018). Dalloz, 2016. (Lacroix-Andrivet, Preuves à conserver).
Lacroix-Andrivet, Jean-Paul. "Mesures d'instruction – droit interne." *Droit et pratique de la procédure civile – Droit interne et européen*, edited by Serge Guinchard, 9th ed., (2017/2018). Dalloz, 2016. (Lacroix-Andrivet, Mesures d'instruction).
Lagarde, Xavier. *Réflexion critique sur le droit de la preuve.* L.G.D.J., 1994. (Lagarde).
Lebeau, Daniel, and Marie-Laure Niboyet. "Regards croisés du processualiste et de l'internationaliste sur le règlement CE du 28 mai 2001 relatif à l'obtention des preuves civiles à l'étranger." *Gaz. Pal.*, vol. 6, 2003.
Leclerc, Olivier. *Le Juge et l'expert: Contribution à l'étude des rapports entre le droit et la science.* L.G.D.J., 2005. (Leclerc).
Legrand, Pierre. "Sens et Non-Sens d'un Code Civil Européen." *Revue Internationale de Droit Comparé*, vol. 48, no. 4, Jan. 1996, pp. 779–812.
Legrand, Pierre. "European Legal Systems Are Not Converging." *International and Comparative Law Quarterly,* vol. 45, no. 1, Jan. 1996, pp. 52–81.
Legrand, Pierre. "Against a European Civil Code." *Modern Law Review,* vol. 60, no. 1, Jan. 1997, pp. 44–63.
Legrand, Pierre. "The Impossibility of 'Legal Transplants'." *Maastricht Journal of European and Comparative Law*, vol. 4, no. 2, Jun. 1997, pp. 111–124.
Legrand, Pierre. "What 'Legal Transplants'?" *Adapting Legal Cultures*, edited by David Nelken and Johannes Feest, Bloomsbury Publishing, 2001.
Legrand, Pierre. "Paradoxically, Derrida: For a Comparative Legal Studies." *Cardozo Law Review*, vol. 27, no. 2, Nov. 2005, pp. 631–718.
Legrand, Pierre. "On the Singularity of Law." *Harvard International Law Journal,* vol. 47, no. 2, Summer 2006, pp. 517–530.
Legrand, Pierre. "Siting Foreign Law: How Derrida can help." *Duke Journal of Comparative & International Law,* vol. 21, no. 3, Spring 2011, pp. 595–630.
Léonard, Sarah, and Christian Kaunert. "Beyond Stockholm: In Search of a Strategy for the European Union's Area of Freedom, Security, and Justice." *European Politics and Society*, vol. 17, no. 2, 2016, pp. 143–149.
Lévy, Jean-Philippe. *La Preuve.* Deuxième partie, Recueils de la société Jean Bodin pour l'histoire comparative des institutions and Éditions de la Librairie encyclopédique, 1965.
Lévy-Bruhl, Henri. *La Preuve judiciaire.* Essai de sociologie juridique, Marcel Rivière, 1963.
Lim, Boo Yeun. "The Magic of the Brush and the Power of Color. Integrating Theory into Practice of Painting in Early Childhood Settings." *Early Childhood Education Journal*, vol. 32, 2004, pp. 113–119.
Lind, Göran, and Gösta Walin. *Ärvdabalken Del I, En kommentar Del I (1–17 kap.) Arv och testamente*, 7th ed., electronic version, JUNO, 2021. Accessed 25 Aug. 2021.

Lindell, Bengt. *Sakfrågor och rättsfrågor: en studie av gränser, skillnader och förhållanden mellan faktum och rätt.* Iustus, 1987. (Lindell, Sakfrågor).
Lindell, Bengt. *Notorietet och kontradiktion.* Iustus, 2007. (Lindell, Notorietet).
Lindell, Bengt. *Civilprocessen*, 3rd ed., Iustus, 2012. (Lindell, Civilprocessen).
Lindblom, P. H. "The Role of the Supreme Courts in Scandinavia." *Scandinavian Studies in Law*, vol. 39, 2000, pp. 325–366. (Lindblom, The Role of the Supreme Courts).
Lindblom, P. H. "Processens arkitektur." *Vänbok till Torleif Bylund*, edited by Torbjörn Andersson and Bengt Lindell, Iustus, 2003, pp. 171–260. (Lindblom, Processens arkitektur).
Lindblom, P. H. "The Growing Role of the Courts and the New Functions of Judicial Process – Fact or Flummery?" *Scandinavian Studies in Law*, vol. 51, 2007, pp. 281–310.
Luhmann, Niklas. "Law As a Social System." *Northwestern University Law Review*, vol. 83, no. 1 & 2, 1988–1989, pp. 136–150.
Luhmann, Niklas. "Operational Closure and Structural Coupling: The Differentiation of the Legal System." *Cardozo Law Review*, vol. 13, no. 5, Mar. 1992, pp. 1419–1442.
Luhmann, Niklas. "Legal Argumentation: An Analysis of its Form." *Modern Law Review*, vol. 58, no. 3, May 1995, pp. 285–298.
Luhmann, Niklas. *Law As a Social System*. OUP, 2004. (Luhmann).
Lyotard, Jean-François. *Le Différend*. Editions de minuit, 1983. (Lyotard).
Lyotard, Jean-François. *The Postmodern Condition: A Report on Knowledge*. Translated by Geoff Bennington and Brian Massumi, Manchester UP, 1984. (Lyotard, The Postmodern Condition).
Lyotard, Jean-François. *Driftworks*. Semiotexte, 1984.
Lyotard, Jean-François. "Judicieux dans le différend." *La Faculté de juger*, Derrida, Jacques et al., Minuit, 1985, pp. 195–236.
Lyotard, Jean-François. *The Differend – Phrases in Dispute*. Translated by Georges Van Den Abbeele, University of Minnesota Press, 1988. (Lyotard).
Lyotard, Jean-François. "Sensus communis." *Judging Lyotard*, edited by Andrew Benjamin, Routledge, 1992, p. 1.
Lyotard, Jean-François. "The Affect-Phrase." *The Lyotard Reader and Guide*, edited by Keith Crome and James Williams, Edinburgh UP, 2006, pp. 104–110. Supplement to The Differend, 2000.
Lyotard, Jean-François. *Discourse, figure*. Translated by Antony Hudek, and Mary Lydon, University of Minnesota Press, 2011.
Marchal, Emmanuelle. "Graphologie et entreprises: histoire et controverses." *Sociologies pratiques*, vol. 10, no. 1, 2005, pp. 57–76.
May, Todd. *The Political Philosophy of Poststructuralist Anarchism*. Penn State UP, 1994.
Malpas, Simon. *Jean-François Lyotard*. Routledge, 2003. (Malpas).
Mindus, Patricia. *A Real Mind: The Life and Work of Axel Hägerström*. Springer Science & Business Media, 2009. (Mindus).
Mayer, Pierre. *Droit international privé*. Montchrestien, 1977.
Motulsky, Henri. *Principes d'une réalisation méthodique du droit privé. La théorie des éléments générateurs des droits subjectifs*. préf. Paul Roubier, Sirey, 1948; Dalloz, 1991.
Motulsky, Henri, "La cause de la demande dans la délimitation de l'office du juge." *Écrits, études et notes de procédure civile*. Dalloz, 2010.
Motulsky, Henri. "La Réforme du Code de procédure civile par le Décret du 13 octobre 1965 et les principes directeurs du procès." *Écrits, études et notes de procédure civile*. Dalloz, 2010.

Motulsky, Henri. "Le droit naturel dans la pratique jurisprudentielle: le respect des droits de la défense en procédure civile." *Écrits, études et notes de procédure civile.* Dalloz, 2010.

Motulsky, Henri. "Prolégomènes pour un futur Code de procédure civile: la consécration des principes directeurs du procès civil par le décret du 9 septembre 1971." *Écrits, études et notes de procédure civile.* Dalloz, 2010. (Motulsky, Prolégomènes).

Nobel, Agnes. *Educating Through Art.* Floris Books, 1996.

Nordh, Robert. "35:5 rättegångsbalken. En rättsfråga om vad?" *Svensk juristtidning*, 1994, pp. 81–93.

Nordh, Robert. *Bevisrätt A: allmänna bevisfrågor: om ansvaret för bevisning, vittne, syn, sakkunnig m.m.* Iustus, 2009.

Nordh, Robert. *Bevisrätt C, Bevisvärdering.* Iustus, 2013.

Nordh, Robert. *Processens ram i tvistemål: om yrkande och grunder*, ändring av talan m.m. 4th ed., Iustus, 2019.

Normand, Jacques. *Le juge et le litige.* L.G.D.J., 1965.

Normand, Jacques. "Procédure civile." *JCl., Fasc 152, n° 13, as indicated in Aynès, A., Vuitton, X. Droit de la preuve, Principes et mise en œuvre processuelle*, 2nd ed., LexisNexis, 2017.

Nylund, Anna, and Magne Strandberg, editors. *Civil Procedure and Harmonisation of Law: The Dynamics of EU and International Treaties.* Intersentia, 2019.

Olivecrona, Karl. "Frågeförbud beträffande försvarare." *Svensk juristtidning*, 1947, pp. 357–359.

Olivecrona, Karl. "The Legal Theories of Axel Hägerström and Vilhelm Lundstedt." *Scandinavian Studies in Law,* vol. 3, 1959, pp. 125–150.

Oppenheimer, Sharifa. *Heaven on Earth: A Handbook for Parents of Young Children.* SteinerBooks, 2006.

Pattaro, Enrico. "From Hägerström to Ross and Hart." *Ratio Juris*, vol. 22, no. 4, Dec. 2009, pp. 532–548.

Payne, Kim John. *Being at Your Best When Your Kids Are at Their Worst: Practical Compassion in Parenting.* Shambhala Publications, 2019.

Peers, Steve. *EU Justice and Home Affairs Law.* OUP, 2012. KVAR?.

Perelman, Chaïm. *Justice et raison.* Editions de l'Université de Bruxelles, 1972. (Perelman).

Peterson, Keith. "Derrida's Responsibility." *Journal of the British Society for Phenomenology*, vol. 28, no. 3, Oct. 1997, pp. 287–303, doi: 10.1080/00071773.1997.11007206. (Peterson).

Piché, Claude. "The Philosopher-Artist: A Note on Lyotard's Reading of Kant." *Research in Phenomenology*, vol. 22, 1992, pp. 152–60. (Piché).

Plonowska Ziarek, Ewa. *An Ethics of Dissensus, Postmodernity, Feminism, and the Politics of Radical Democracy.* Stanford UP, 2001.

Poché, Fred. *Penser avec Derrida: Comprendre la déconstruction.* Chronique sociale, 2007. (Poché)

Quétand-Finet, Claire. *Les Présomptions en droit privé.* IRJS, 2013.

Rawls, John. *A Theory of Justice.* Original Ed., Belknap and Harvard UP, 2005.

Rainey, Bernadette et al. *The European Convention on Human Rights.* 7th ed., Oxford UP, 2017.

Ramshaw, Sara. "Jamming the Law: Improvisational Theatre and the 'Spontaneity' of Judgment." *Law Text Culture,* vol. 14, no. 1, 2010, pp. 133–159.

Rasch, William. "In Search of the Lyotard Archipelago, or: How to Live with Paradox and Learn to like It." *New German Critique*, no. 61, 1994, pp. 55–75.

Reiertsen, Michael. *Effective Domestic Remedies and the European Court of Human Rights: Applications of the European Convention on Human Rights Article 13.* Cambridge UP, 2022.

Ricœur, Paul. *Le Discours de l'action*. Edited by Catherine Goldenstein et Jean-Claude Monod. Fonds Ricœur, 2015.

Ricœur, Paul, and Jean-Pierre Changeux. *La Nature et la règle: Ce qui nous fait penser*. Odile Jacob, 1998.

Ross, Alf. *On Law and Justice*. University of California Press, 1959.

Russell, Bertrand. "On Denoting." *The Philosophy of Language*, edited by A. P. Martinich, 2nd ed., OUP, 1990.

Samuelsson, Joel. *Tolkning och utfyllning*. Iustus, 2008.

Samuelsson, Joel. *Tolkningslärans gåta*. Iustus, 2011.

Sawyer, Dylan. *Lyotard, Literature and the Trauma of the Differend*. Palgrave Macmillan, 2014. (Sawyer).

Schiller, Friedrich. "Über die ästhetische Erziehung des Menschen, in einer Reihe von Briefen, Fünfzehnter Brief." *Schillers Sämmtliche Werke, vierter Band,* J. G. Cotta'sche Buchhandlung, 1879, https://www.projekt-gutenberg.org/schiller/aesterz/aesterz3.html. Accessed 8 Dec. 2021.

Schlag, Pierre. "'Le Hors de texte, c'est moi' – The Politics of Form and the Domestication of Deconstruction." *Derrida and Law*, edited by Pierre Legrand, Ashgate, 2009.

Schlag, Pierre, and Amy J. Griffin. *How to Do Things with Legal Doctrine*. University of Chicago Press, 2020.

Schmid, Christoph. "Vertical and Diagonal Conflicts in the Europeanisation Process" *Private governance, democratic constitutionalism and supranationalism*, edited by Christian Joerges and Olivier Gerstenberg, European Commission, 1998.

Schum, David. "Inference Networks and their Many Subtle Properties." *Information and Decision Technologies*, vol. 16, 1990, pp. 69–98 as quoted in Goodwin. (Schum).

Schum, David. "A Science of Evidence: Contributions from Law and Probability." *Law, Probability and Risk*, vol. 8, 2009, pp. 197–231. (Schum, A Science of Evidence).

Searle, John, P. "What Is a Speech Act?" *Perspectives in the Philosophy of Language: A Concise Anthology,* edited by Robert J. Stainton, Broadview Press, 2000 (1965).

Settem, Ola Johan. *Applications of the 'Fair Hearing' Norm in ECHR Article 6(1) to Civil Proceedings: With Special Emphasis on the Balance Between Procedural Safeguards and Efficiency*. Springer, 2015.

Silfverberg, Christer. "Arvs- och gåvoskatt." *Skattenytt*, 2002, pp. 319–322.

Spiro, Erwin. "Forum Regit Processum (Procedure Is Governed by the Lex Fori)." *The International and Comparative Law Quarterly*, vol. 18, no. 4, Oct. 1969.

Storskrubb, Eva. *Civil Procedure and EU Law, A Policy Area Uncovered*. OUP, 2008. (Storskrubb, Civil Procedure).

Storskrubb, Eva. "Mutual Trust and the Dark Horse of Civil Justice." *Cambridge Yearbook of European Legal Studies*, vol. 20, 2018, pp. 179–201.

Strang, Johan. "Two Generations of Scandinavian Legal Realism." *RETFÆRD*, årgång 32, no. 1/124, 2009.

Stürner, Rolf. "Principles of European Civil Procedure or a European Model Code? Some Considerations on the Joint ELI-UNIDROIT Project." *Uniform Law Review*, vol. 19, no. 2, June 2014.

Svenungsson, Jayne. "Justice in the Prophetic Tradition." *Eco-Ethica,* vol. 6, 2017, pp. 135–149.

Swedberg, Richard, and Ola Agevall. "Justice." *The Max Weber Dictionary: Key Words and Central Concepts*. 2nd ed., Stanford Social Sciences, 2016.

Taruffo, Michele. "Notes for a Theory of Justice." *Justice, Morality and Society, A Tribute to Alexander Peczenik*, edited by Aulis Aarnio, Juristförlaget i Lund, 1997.
Tarski, Alfred. "The Semantic Conception of Truth and the Foundations of Semantics." *The Philosophy of Language*, edited by A. P. Martinich, 2nd ed., OUP, 1990.
Terré, François. *Droit civil, Les Obligations*. Dalloz, Paris, 2005. (Terré).
Teubner, Günther. "Self-Subversive Justice: Contingency or Transcendence Formula of Law?" *The Modern Law Review*, vol. 72, no. 1, 2009, pp. 1–23. (Teubner).
Torres, Gerald. "Environmental Burdens and Democratic Justice." *Fordham Urban Law Journal*, vol. 21, no. 3, Spring 1994, pp. 431–460.
Tournier, Clara. *L'intime conviction du juge de jugement*. ANRT, 2003. Lille thèses.
Twining, William. *Theories of Evidence: Bentham and Wigmore*. Weidenfeld & Nicolson, 1984.
Twining, William. *Rethinking Evidence: Exploratory Essays*. 2nd ed., Cambridge University Press, 2006. (Twining, Rethinking Evidence).
Villaverde, Marcelino Agís. *Knowledge and Practical Reason: Paul Ricoeur's Way of Thinking*. LIT Verlag Münster, 2012.
Villenave. *Des Jurés et de la conviction intime*. Malassis, 1796.
von Hein, Jan. "Drawing the Line between Brussels I and the Evidence Regulation." *European Legal Forum*, no. 1, 2008, pp. 1–35.
Wagenaar, Willem A. et al. *Anchored Narratives: the Psychology of Criminal Evidence*. Harvester Wheatsheaf, 1993.
Wahlberg, Lena. *Legal Questions and Scientific Answers: Ontological Differences and Epistemic Gaps in the Assessment of Causal Relations*. Lund University, 2010. Dissertation.
Wallerman, Anna. *Om fakultativa regler: en studie av svensk och unionsrättslig reglering av skönsmässigt beslutsfattande i processrättsliga frågor*. Gothenburg, Iustus, 2015. Dissertation.
Wallerman, Anna. "Can Two Walk Together, Except They be Agreed? Preliminary References and (the Erosion of) National Procedural Autonomy in European Law Review." *European Law Review*, vol. 44, no. 2, 2019, pp. 159–177.
Walter, Bruno. "Bruckner and Mahler." *Chord and Discord*, vol. 2, no. 9, 1948, p. 41, https://www.uv.es/~calaforr/walter.html. Accessed 31 Mar. 2022.
Ward, Ian. *Kantianism, Postmodernism and Critical Legal Thought. Law and Philosophy Library*. Vol. 31, Kluwer Academic, 1997.
Watson, Alan. *Legal Transplants: An Approach to Comparative Law*. University of Georgia Press, 1993.
Watt, Horatia Muir. "Private International Law beyond the Schism." *Transnational Legal Theory*, vol. 2, no. 3, 2011, pp. 347–428.
Weber, Max. *From Max Weber: Essays in Sociology*. Edited and translated by H. H. Gerth and C. Wright Mills, Routledge, 2014. (Weber, From Max Weber).
Welamson, Lars. "Civil-och straffprocessrätt 1980–1987." *Svensk juristtidning*, 1989, pp. 497–652.
Weller, Matthias. "Mutual Trust: In Search of the Future of European Union Private International Law." *Journal of Private International Law*, vol. 11, no. 1, 2015, pp. 64–102.
Wennergren, Bertil. "Om vittnesplikten." *Svensk juristtidning*, 1998, pp. 40–83.
Westberg, Peter. "Processtaktik och bevisbörda i dispositiva tvistemål." *Festskrift till Per Henrik Lindblom*, edited by Torbjörn Andersson and Bengt Lindell, Iustus, 2004.
Westberg, Peter. *Anskaffning av bevisning i dispositiva tvistemål*. Norstedts Juridik, 2010.

Westen, Peter. *Speaking of Equality: An Analysis of the Rhetorical Force of 'Equality' in Moral and Legal Discourse*. Princeton UP, 2014.
Wigmore, John H. *Treatise on the System of Evidence in Trials at Common Law: Including the Statutes and Judicial Decisions of All Jurisdictions of the United States*. Little, Brown, and Co., 1904.
Wigmore, John H. *The Principles of Judicial Proof*. Little, Brown, and Co., 1913.
Wigmore, John H. "Problem of Proof." *Illinois Law Review,* vol. 8, no. 2, 1913–1914, pp. 77–103. (Wigmore, Problem of Proof).
Wittgenstein, Ludwig. *Filosofiska undersökningar*. Translated by Anders Wedberg, Thales, 2012 (Philosophical Investigations).
Woodward, Ashley. "Testimony and the Affect-Phrase." *Rereading Jean-François Lyotard,* edited by Heidi Bickis and Rob Shields, Ashgate, 2013 (Woodward, Testimony and the Affect-Phrase).
Zajonc, Arthur. *Meditation as Contemplative Inquiry: When Knowing Becomes Love*. Lindisfarne Books, 2009.
Zehr, Howard. *The Little Book of Restorative Justice*. Good Books, 2015.

l) Digital Encyclopedias

https://www.etymonline.com. Accessed 26 Aug. 2024.
Merriam-Webster.com Dictionary, Merriam-Webster, https://www.merriam-webster.com/dictionary/evidence.
Wikipedia contributors. "Wet-on-wet." *Wikipedia, The Free Encyclopedia*. 2021, https://en.wikipedia.org/w/index.php?title=Wet-on-wet&oldid=1241702572. Accessed 22 Aug. 2024.
Woodward, Ashley. "Jean-François Lyotard (1924–1998)." *Internet Encyclopedia of Philosophy*, http://www.iep.utm.edu/lyotard/. Accessed 02 Sep. 2021.

m) Mass-Media Sources and Other

i) Signed

Dalén, Karl. *Dagens Nyheter,* 22 Nov. 2012, http://www.dn.se/dnbok/forlaget-det-ar-sa-otroligt-sorgligt/.
Eklund, Bernt. *Expressen*, 20 Sep. 2012, http://www.expressen.se/noje/recensioner/film/liten-skar-och-alla-sma-brokiga/.
Eklund, Bernt. 26 Sep. 2012, http://allavibarn.blogspot.se/2012/09/stina-wirsen-och-lilla-hjartat.html.
Helmersson, Erik. *Svenska Dagbladet*, 23 Sep. 2012, http://www.dn.se/ledare/signerat/filmdebatt-den-mest-krankta-har-inte-alltid-ratt/.
Janson, Malena. *Helsingfors Dagblad*, 21 Sep. 2012, http://hd.se/kultur/film/2012/09/21/oemotstandligt/?from=rss.
Jonsson, Sherlot. *Dagens Nyheter*, 12 Nov. 2012, http://www.dn.se/kultur-noje/kulturdebatt/vagra-se-varlden-vit-och-svart/.
Juggas, Bodil. *Arbetarbladet*, 28 Sep. 2012, http://www.arbetarbladet.se/noje/film/fantastisk-film-for-de-allra-minsta.

Karlsson, Elise. *Svenska Dagbladet*, 15 Sep. 2012, http://www.svd.se/kultur/gulligt-kan-ocksa-vara-stereotypt_7500338.svd.
Polite, Oivvio. *Expressen*, 15 Oct. 2012, http://www.expressen.se/kultur/det-ar-ju-ratt-ruttet/.
Polite, Oivvio. *Expressen*, 26 Oct. 2012, http://www.expressen.se/kultur/brokiga-ar-business/.
Pousette Blomé, Lisa. 4 Sep. 2012, http://kulturbloggen.com/?p=59937.
Sigroth-Lambe, Susanne. *Uppsala Nya Tidning*, 21 Sep. 2012, http://www.unt.se/kultur/film/film-liten-skar-och-alla-sma-brokiga-1863697.aspx.
Söderling, Fredrik. *Dagens Nyheter*, 22 Nov. 2012, http://www.dn.se/dnbok/lilla-hjartat-uppenbart-rasistisk-enligt-forskare/.
Sörenson, Margareta. *Expressen,* 22 Oct. 2012, http://www.expressen.se/kultur/fargade-historier/.
Stiernstedt, Jenny. *Svenska Dagbladet*, 22 Oct. 2013, https://www.svd.se/alhem-dom-om-smygfilmning-i-gota-hovratt-konservativ.
Wirsén, Stina. *Dagens Nyheter*, 23 Oct. 2012, http://www.dn.se/kultur-noje/kulturdebatt/mina-kritiker-har-begransad-utblick/.

ii) Unsigned

Svenska Dagbladet, 25 Jul. 2013, http://www.svd.se/kultur/wirsen-talar-ut-om-lilla-hjartat_8373942.svd.
Sveriges Radio, 7 Sep. 2012, http://sverigesradio.se/sida/artikel.aspx?programid=1646&artikel=5262162.
Sveriges Radio, 22 Nov. 2012, http://sverigesradio.se/sida/artikel.aspx?programid=478&artikel=5354382.
Sveriges Television, 11 Sep. 2012 (originally published 10 September 2012), http://www.svt.se/kultur/film/barnfilm-anklagas-for-rasistisk-stereotyp.

Index

For Product Safety Concerns and Information please contact our EU representative GPSR@taylorandfrancis.com
Taylor & Francis Verlag GmbH, Kaufingerstraße 24, 80331 München, Germany

www.ingramcontent.com/pod-product-compliance
Lightning Source LLC
LaVergne TN
LVHW021128300926
849160LV00010B/908